IRONCLAD

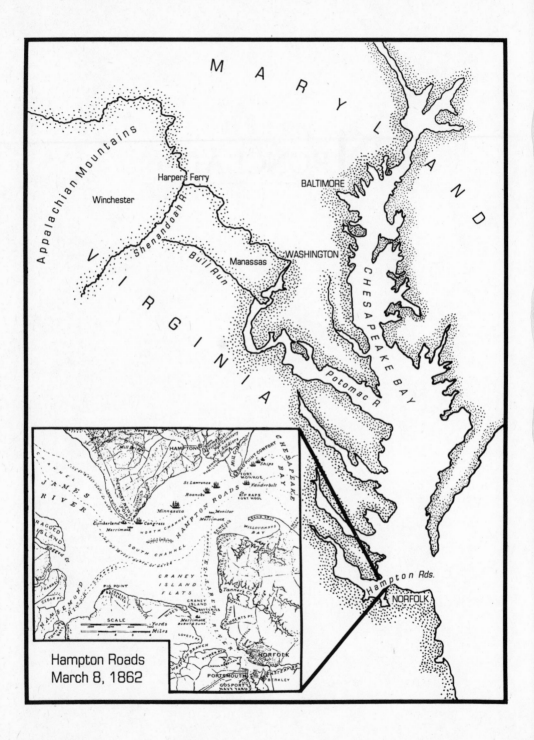

Hampton Roads
March 8, 1862

Published by Presidio Press
31 Pamaron Way, Novato CA 94949

Library of Congress Cataloging-in-Publication Data

Mokin, Arthur, 1923-
    Ironclad : the Monitor and the Merrimack / Arthur Mokin.
      p.   cm.
    Includes bibliographical references.
    ISBN 0-89141-405-3
    1. Monitor (Ironclad) 2. United States—History—Civil War, 1861-1865—Naval operations. I. Title.
    E595 . M7M65 1991   90-22031
    973.7'57—dc20   CIP

Typography by ProImage

Printed in the United States of America

IRONCLAD

The *Monitor* and the *Merrimack*

Arthur Mokin

PRESIDIO

for   G
     B
   NYPL

I acknowledge with gratitude my debt to Tom Lask and Hugh Van Dusen, two professionals who gave me encouragement when I needed it most.

The major personalities, events, and circumstances depicted herein are taken from history and are as accurately portrayed as prime sources and research allow.

I have taken the liberty of creating scenes along with dialogue and interior monologue by way of explicating motive, feeling, and a sense of the time. In every instance said creations have their roots in and are a natural outgrowth of the documented events. In no instance are they frivolous invention, fabricated in contradiction of established fact.

Conversely, in the interests of a less labored narrative, I have chosen to omit certain details, omissions which I hope will not offend the serious reader. I refer, for example, to the fact that although the Confederacy renamed the *Merrimack* "Virginia," I employ only her original name, as did the vast majority of Americans, North and South.

Arthur Mokin

CHAPTER

I

THE SIXTH OF APRIL

It is said that animals sense certain natural disasters, particularly earthquakes, hours and, according to some reports, even days before the actual occurrence. Horses, cattle, and dogs are known to become restive and show distinct signs of anxiety in anticipation of impending natural catastrophes. Happily or unhappily, as the case may be, there is no evidence to show that man can similarly anticipate disasters of either the natural or the man-made variety.

Such were the somber thoughts of Gideon Welles as he swung around the corner at Pennsylvania Avenue and with quick, short strides made his way down 17th Street. During his walk of several blocks from the hotel he had seen nothing out of the ordinary, had read nothing in the faces along the avenue that would suggest the possibility of great and tragic events in the offing. Traffic on the avenue was a bit heavier than usual, and there was perhaps a heightened sense of expectancy, but that was normal for this city during the first few weeks of a new administration.

Perhaps, he reflected, the people he passed on the street were more accurate seers than he, and there was indeed no cause for concern. A devoutly religious man, Welles prayed to God that it was so.

The sonorous, reassuring chimes of St. Paul's in stately cascade flooded the spring morning. It was half past the hour. In the middle of the street an empty horsecar drawn by a single horse plodded slowly toward the avenue. A blue-clad conductor strolled the length of the car counting his ticket stubs. The tableau of silent horsecar and echoing chimes combined to make Welles feel somewhat more sanguine.

Walking briskly past the building that housed the War Department, he came to that structure's twin—the modest, three-story, red-brick building that housed the Department of the Navy. At the portal the sentry, in round, visorless seaman's cap, presented arms smartly and barked, "Mornin', sir!" As he strode past him, Welles brought up his arm in a gesture that could have been either a wave of greeting or a salute. In a letter to Mary Jane, he had written that as the civilian chief of a military agency, he felt neither fish nor fowl. He wasn't sure how to acknowledge the sentry's greeting.

Quickly climbing the flight of stairs to his office, Welles noted with a pang of displeasure that no one was about; not a single officer or clerk was to be seen. True, it was not yet eight, and the official day didn't begin until nine, but given the times, one expected more zeal on the part of those responsible for the defense of the nation. Well, his recent order requiring make-up work at night for those who fell behind should go a long way toward correcting some of the tardiness and slovenly work habits he had seen around the department.

In his office he hung his frock coat and soft, wide-brimmed gray hat on a coat tree and settled his short, stocky body behind the massive, flat-topped desk, its surface completely covered with untidy stacks of paper.

Welles surveyed the hundreds of documents, every one of which he had read several times, with the air of one eyeing an adversary he couldn't quite fathom. Reaching out he picked up one from the top of a pile, scanned it, and, satisfied that he was familiar with its contents, put it back in place. He repeated the procedure several times. He was, he reflected, somewhat like a solitaire player whose game was stuck. Reshuffling the cards and picking them up in random order didn't help.

Leaning back in his swivel chair, he tossed his pencil onto the cluttered desk and slowly shook his head in reluctant resignation. A truth that he had uneasily sensed rather than acknowledged, facts that had been lurking at the corners of his consciousness and that he had tried to dismiss as figments of his natural pessimism, were emerging to take shape with unrelenting clarity.

The morning sun, still low, breached the partially shuttered windows in refracted shafts of light that cast the room into uneven patches of light and shadow. The office, furnished in the spartan manner peculiar to government agencies, held several glass-enclosed bookcases, a worn refectory table laden with departmental literature, several battered oak file cabinets, a coat tree, and an odd chair at the side of his desk. Hanging on the walls were a half dozen steel engravings depicting sloops and frigates of war from revolutionary war days to the present.

Lit by a ray of sunlight at the far edge of his desk was the one interesting ornament in the room, a scale model of Noah's ark. Somehow it had survived the depredations of a constantly changing guard. It was there when he took over and, of course, it would be there when he left. Doubtless it belonged to the department, but no one seemed to know where it came from. Fox had told him it was of authentic construction, built according to the specifications set forth in the sixth chapter of Genesis.

With an uneasy sense that he was allowing himself to be diverted from the task at hand, he reached over the stacks of paper to retrieve the ark. Turning it in his hand, he speculated. How many administrations had it seen come and go? How many crises had it witnessed? How many of his predecessors had been diverted by it, maybe even found some comfort in it? Nothing like a biblical artifact to give one a sense of perspective.

The papers on his desk came back into focus. There was no denying them or the story they told. The message was clear and unequivocal. To be sure, not every document was to be trusted. A letter here, a memo there were obvious attempts to mislead. But in the aggregate the great bulk of the material was consistent. It spoke with the dispassionate eloquence of information accumulated from many independent sources. The conclusion was inescapable. And now, God help him, where was he to begin?

The most optimistic estimate the documents permitted was that at the moment the United States Navy consisted of ninety vessels of all classes, fifty of which were useless—disabled beyond repair. Of the remaining forty, only twenty-four were steam powered. Of these, thirteen were at distant foreign stations. Of the remaining eleven, seven were either assigned to the supplementary expedition en route to reinforce Fort Pickens or were part of the squadron being staged for the possible provisioning of Fort Sumter.

The cold fact was that theoretically he had exactly four ships mounting twenty-five guns at his disposal. Theoretically because he didn't dare order the four available ships to duty that would take them away from Washington City. In unsettled times such as these, one didn't strip the capital of all naval vessels. The message then, strewn across the top of his desk in those untidy stacks of paper, was that he was the secretary of a navy with no ships.

Welles felt the long gray knife of panic wedging into his vitals. The feeling was reminiscent of the recurring nightmare he had been suffering of late, wherein he was pursued by a nameless terror. Rowing desperately in a small skiff, he tried to escape. Just as the pursuer was about to overtake him, he would wake up, his bedclothes and nightshirt soaked with perspiration, his body twitching and jerking to the irregular rhythms of a pounding heart.

Welles sighed and restored the ark to its accustomed place. Reaching deep into the middle drawer on the right side of the desk, he fished out a long-stem clay pipe. He filled it with tobacco from a delft jar that was decorated with a blue line drawing of an Indian sitting cross-legged and smoking a long-stem clay pipe. The fragrance of the drawer saturated with the odor of good Virginia tobacco comforted him, as did the jar and the pipe, old friends. The act of lighting up invariably took him back to the old days, to the long New England winter nights, to the good talk with old friends before a glowing charcoal fire, platters of hot oysters at hand. That was when he was "Gid" Welles, editor of the *Hartford Times,* and his and Mary Jane's only concerns were their rapidly growing family and the newspaper.

With an effort he wrenched his thoughts back to the present. About the lack of ships he could at the moment do nothing. He sure as Satan could not manufacture more out of thin air. Clearly, his first priority then, was to conserve those he had, keep them from falling into the hands of the secessionists. God help us, he thought, if war comes it should be obvious even to the dullest that our primary weapon has to be blockade. If the South were able to import the materiel to feed a war machine, there would be no way to subdue her. It would mean the death of the Union.

But how in the name of God can one mount a blockade from the Potomac to the Rio Grande—more than thirty-five hundred miles of shoreline—with four blessed frigates? As secretary of the Navy, he was faced with precisely that problem. At least in concept the question was not complex. He had at last brought it out into the open, where he could begin to get a handle on it.

Reaching into his vest pocket, Welles took out his watch. Its round, gold heft was familiar in his hand. A gift from his Connecticut constituents. Probably never should have left Hartford. At least he would be with Mary Jane and the children now. Lord, how he missed them. The forsythia would be budding. Bright yellow sprigs. Wonderful how they cheered up the yard, eclipsing the winter mud and the trampled grass. If he didn't find a house in Washington pretty soon, he'd go berserk.

He pressed the button on the winding stem of the watch, and the thin, slightly convex cover flipped open. The black filigree hands and precise Roman numerals on the immaculate white face told him it was six minutes before nine. Snapping the cover shut, he quickly got to his feet, jammed a single sheet of paper containing a summary of his findings into his inside breast pocket, and walked out.

It was exactly nine o'clock when, puffing slightly from the two-block walk through the President's Park and the climb up the flight of stairs to the executive office, he said to John Hay, "Is he alone?"

Hay nodded and, preceding Welles to the executive chamber, opened the door and announced, "Mr. Welles, sir, for his nine o'clock appointment."

The president was writing at the small, round table near the window at the far end of the room. Silhouetted against the light in his black suit, he seemed even leaner and more gaunt than usual. His boots were under his chair. He continued to write for a moment, the steel nib scratching the heavy linen paper. Finished writing, he turned the document on its face and pressed it on the desk blotter. He rose to his feet and with a gesture invited Welles to take a chair at the long, rectangular conference table. Taking a seat directly opposite, the president said with a warm smile, "Well, sir, how are you and the fleet this fine morning?"

Always, thought Welles, the up note, the sense that it's been too long since he's seen you, and that no matter what news you bring, he's glad you're here. There he sits in his stockinged feet, looking more worn every day. He's been in the office since before seven and he'll be here long after everyone else has gone.

"Mr. President, I've asked for this time with you because of the situation at the Norfolk Navy Yard." As he anticipated, the president nodded slowly, deliberately—as if to say, Worthy subject for discussion; glad you've brought it up. But Welles knew that he promised nothing except an attentive and perceptive ear.

"I've been acquainting myself with our inventory—ships, personnel, ammunition, shore installations, everything—and I've come to the conclusion that there is an alarming concentration of floating stock and materiel at the Norfolk yard. How or why this is so, I'm not certain. But that's a question for another time."

The barest hint of a smile played about the president's gray eyes. "You detect the fine hand of Stephen Mallory?" Welles refused to be drawn in, refused to confirm or deny the suggestion. He suspected that the president and probably the whole cabinet felt he was going dotty on the subject of the machinations—real or imagined—of his Southern counterpart, the secretary of the Confederate Navy.

"In any case," continued Welles, "according to my calculations, there are no less than nine men-o'-war in various stages of repair at Norfolk. None of them is quite ready for sea. By some peculiar coincidence [Mallory again?] they all lack the condensers used in the conversion of seawater." Welles paused to give the president an opportunity to comment. But he remained silent and expressionless, chin in hand, half-closed eyes fixed unwaveringly on him. Rarely interrupts, thought Welles. Good listener. Successful lawyer. Made his money defending the Illinois Central. But he'll always look like the poor boy from the wrong side of the tracks.

"The nine ships by themselves would constitute a most serious loss. But along with the yard itself—it's by far the best equipped naval facility in the country—and the one ship that is probably the equal of the other eight, loss of the Norfolk yard would be a devastating blow. I'm not sure we would ever recover from it."

"What's the one ship that is so valuable?"

"The *Merrimack*."

The president questioned with his eyes.

"She's a full-rigged war frigate of thirty-two hundred tons. Unlike the others, which are exclusively sail, she has auxiliary steam power.

She was completed in '56—only five years old—and mounts forty guns. She's the sister ship to the *Minnesota* and the *Roanoke*. You will recall that they are the first of the new generation; they mark the transition from sail to steam. In short, Mr. President, *Merrimack* is one of our three most advanced warships, and, according to Mr. Fox, the most valuable in the fleet. We can ill afford to lose her."

Welles decided that he had said enough. It was time to listen. The president took his chin from his hand and with the tips of his fingers massaged his brow over both eyes. "Why," he said, "do you assume that we are going to lose the yard at Norfolk?"

Of course, thought Welles, he assumes nothing. Is he debating with me or does he really think Virginia will not secede? "I believe, sir, that Virginia will follow Texas and the others into secession. Everything points to it. And when she goes, her first act will be to seize all federal property that isn't vigorously defended, just as the Confederates did with the arsenals in Charleston, Savannah, Baton Rouge, Chattahoochee, Pensacola, and others I can't recall at the moment.

"That Norfolk yard," continued Welles, "has a new granite dry dock, shops full of the latest machine tools, and acres of guns and ammunition. It could provide Mallory with the nucleus of a navy." Welles hesitated for a moment. He had not intended to allude to Mallory again. Then with the air of one willing to accept responsibility for his convictions, he added, "And yes, I believe it is no coincidence that there are nine ships there now, including the *Merrimack*. I see a calculated conspiracy."

The president apparently chose to ignore the treasonous implications. Leaning back in his chair he clasped his hands behind his head and reflected for a moment. "My information from Richmond," he said in a tone that was not one of rebuttal but rather of speculation, "is that the convention meeting on the secession question is evenly divided. Indeed, I am told that if there is an edge, it is with the pro-Union forces."

"That may be, Mr. President, but Virginia is too committed to a slave economy to remain in the Union. She derives more capital from traffic in slaves than from any other resource—including tobacco. She must inevitably secede. Her business community believes that she can survive in no other way. I believe too that to formulate policy on the assumption that she will remain in the Union is to . . . to . . ." He couldn't summon the right phrase. He wanted to emphasize the gravity of the situation without underlining the president's personal culpability. ". . . is to invite disaster," he finished.

Before responding, the president walked to his desk, reached into a drawer, and pulled out an apple. With a curved, ivory-handled pocketknife he cut it in two and offered half to Welles, who declined with thanks. "What do you propose?"

"I think we should send at least a company, perhaps two, of infantry to the Norfolk yard to prevent its capture when Virginia secedes. At the same time, we should immediately take vigorous steps to remove as many of the ships as possible."

"Have you approached General Scott?"

"Yes, sir."

"What was his reaction?"

Welles hesitated. Good God! What would you expect of General-in-Chief Winfield Scott? That poor old six-foot-five, three-hundred-pound monument to his former glory. That massive, epauletted, stuffed uniform who needs an aide to keep him awake lest he sleep the day away. That seventy-five-year-old toothless tiger who can no longer sit a horse or even work at a desk. What, sir, would you expect his reaction to be? In fact Welles had applied to Scott and expressed his concern about the ships and the Norfolk yard, pleading that he send a force to forestall their capture. The general, his blood-suffused complexion glowing in the light of the gas lamp, his gouty leg extended straight before him on a much-pillowed footstool, regarded him through rheumy eyes. Drumming sausage fingers on his desk, he portentously raked a chain of phlegm from his enormous crop . . . and refused. He had no troops to spare. His priorities were to guard the capital and Harper's Ferry (only fifty miles from Washington City) and to garrison Fortress Monroe at the mouth of Hampton Roads, all of which were in jeopardy should Virginia secede.

But Welles's only response to the president was, "The general has other priorities."

The president nodded, "Yup, I reckon Scott's spread pretty thin." He sliced a crescent of apple, which he popped into his mouth. Munching, he regarded Welles thoughtfully. "Have I ever told you how it was when I was a young lawyer riding the circuit with other young lawyers in the wilds of Illinois?"

"No, sir."

The president settled back in the practiced attitude of a storyteller. "Once, a long spell of pouring rain flooded the whole state, making small creeks into rivers. Ahead of us was the Fox River, larger than all the rest, and we couldn't help saying to each other, 'If these small streams give us so much trouble, how shall we get over the Fox River?'

"Darkness fell and we stopped at a log tavern, had our horses put up, and resolved to spend the night. Here, we were right glad to fall in with the Methodist presiding elder of the circuit, who rode it in all weather, knew all its ways, and could tell us all about the Fox River.

"So we gathered round him and asked if he knew about the crossing of the Fox River. 'O yes,' he replied, 'I have crossed it often and understand it well. But I have one fixed rule with regard to the Fox River: I never cross it till I reach it!' " The president's homely face creased into a broad grin and he popped another slice of apple into his mouth.

Welles smiled weakly. "I understand, Mr. President, but the sit—"

"Now what's the use of stirring up the good folks of Virginia, sending troops down there, when they're in the middle of a decision that just might solve the whole problem? And I don't believe I'd remove any ships from the yard, just yet. Don't you think that would show a lack of confidence?"

"Yes, sir." There was no point in even trying to persuade him to change his mind. The president took as long as any man he knew to come to a decision. He stewed, and fretted, and meditated, and asked endless questions of everyone from the elderly Negro at the White House door to his secretary of state. But once his mind was made up, he was a rock.

"Welles, have you had any word from Fort Pickens or Pensacola?"

"No, sir."

"Not even a rumor?"

"Nothing, Mr. President."

"What was the date of General Scott's order to Captain Adams?"

"March 12."

"It's been almost a month."

"Yes, sir."

"Well, I'm sure you'll advise me of any developments, no matter what time of day or night. I'm mighty curious to know how our secessionist friends react to the reinforcement of Pickens."

"Yes, sir." And Welles departed, walking slowly back through the President's Park to Navy.

The April air was cool and laced with the scent of conifers, a promise of the warmth to come evident in the pools of sunshine that lit the tree trunks and bathed the rich, layered soil of the park. It was the kind of spring day that was all too rare in the capital, where an abrupt change from the chill blasts of winter to the steamy, airless clutch of summer was the general rule.

A jay, in gaudy flashes of blue and white, streaked squawking across Welles's path and disappeared into a thicket of trees. A pair of sparrows locked in a swooping, stunning pas de deux, fussing, bickering, chittering, slammed into a patch of sand, which they scattered with frantic wings.

Welles saw nothing of jay and sparrows and was unaware of the fresh, fragrant air. He was lost in his interview with the president, which he saw as a complete failure. He had not accomplished his mission. There was no man he loved and revered more, but bless his sweet soul, Lincoln could be infuriating. With all his wisdom and political cunning, he was, withal, an innocent. His unflagging optimism, his naive refusal to see anything but elevated motives in the people around him, could be downright dangerous—scandalous on the part of a chief executive and commander in chief. Yes, an innocent, and ultimately quite defenseless. But that was why he loved him. It dated back to that frigid March night when Lincoln, alone, campaigning through New England, showed up on a windswept Hartford railroad platform, his suit rumpled, his shirt soot-begrimed, carrying a worn carpetbag valise. From that moment, Welles was his man.

Virginia was going to secede. Of that there was no doubt. Unlike the president, he harbored few illusions about that "Mother of States," that "Mother of Presidents." Yes, there was Jamestown, where it all began; there was George Washington, and Patrick Henry, and Thomas Jefferson, and James Madison, and James Monroe. But the fact was that Virginia counted slaves and the slave trade as her largest single economic asset. In the final analysis, the "Aristocrat of the South" would go the way of her pocketbook. The arsenal at Harper's Ferry, and the navy yard and the *Merrimack* at Norfolk would become part of the Confederate war machine.

When Welles arrived at his office, an aide advised that a messenger was waiting. He claimed to have a dispatch "for the eyes of the secretary of the Navy only." Welles nodded, and a young lieutenant of medium but muscular build, with pleasant features and thinning straw-colored hair, was admitted.

The young man saluted, "Lieutenant Washington Gwathmey, sir. I bear a message from Captain Henry Adams, senior officer in command of the squadron lying off Fort Pickens at Pensacola, Florida."

Gesturing toward the chair at the side of his desk, the secretary invited the lieutenant to sit. But he remained standing. Opening his dust-covered blue tunic, he unbuttoned the white shirt beneath and pulled out a leather belt that had been strapped around his middle. From a pocket in the belt he withdrew a sealed envelope, which he handed to Welles.

While Welles read the message, Gwathmey stood at ease, cap tucked under his arm, eyes curious and searching, as he surveyed the office, including worn furniture, engravings, and model of the ark. His eyes then came to rest on the secretary himself. Gwathmey saw a massive head topped by a carefully marcelled brown wig that spilled two fat curls onto the broad brow. Flowing from side beards and lower lip, obscuring the black bow tie, was a voluminous white Santa Claus beard. The total effect, however, of wig, beard, and generous torso was neither jolly nor avuncular. It was apparent from the eyes and the set of the secretary's small mouth that he was an *homme sérieux*.

In the month Welles had been in office, the scuttlebutt that circulated through the officer corps was that the new administration's secretary of the Navy was energetic if inexperienced; was a political appointee, and no saltwater sailor; tended to be remote and aloof; tolerated nothing less than all-out effort on the part of his staff; and, unlike at least one other member of the cabinet, was incorruptible and almost slavishly loyal to the president. He was a former newspaper publisher from Hartford, and a state politician. A renegade Democrat, he was an ardent supporter of states' rights but only insofar as they did not threaten the Union. He helped the president win the Republican nomination at the Chicago convention.

Welles, emitting periodic grunts that sounded to Gwathmey like expressions of mingled surprise and frustration, read the message a second time to be certain he understood. Shouting for an aide, he asked for a copy of General Scott's March 12 order to Captain Adams. He laid the documents side by side and carefully examined both. "Did Captain Adams personally hand this message to you?"

"Yes, sir," said the lieutenant.

Welles got to his feet, a surprisingly short, thickset figure on stumpy legs. "Come along, Lieutenant, the president will want to see this."

Taking Gwathmey by the arm, he led him down a flight of stairs to a backdoor on the east side of the building, which opened to the President's Park, a preserve the lieutenant found to be an agreeable, heavily wooded campus planted with a variety of trees native to the thirty-four states. Anchoring the corners of the park were the four

Departments of State, Treasury, War, and Navy. As they made their way along a path lined with evergreens, Gwathmey saw, at a distance he estimated at a hundred and fifty yards, the executive mansion rising from the center of the park, equidistant from the four departments.

As they walked single file because of the narrowness of the path, Welles, in the lead, asked over his shoulder, "What is the situation at Pensacola?"

"Things have been rather tense, sir, since January."

"I expect. What has been the posture of the squadron?"

Gwathmey, stumbling and trotting by turns in an effort to keep up with Welles, replied, "It's been a waiting game, sir, each side waiting for the other to make the first move."

"Have you noted any rebel activity?"

"Yes, sir. They're digging in all around the bay."

"The squadron is not in the bay?"

"It lies just outside the bay on the gulf side of Pickens."

Unchallenged, they let themselves in at a side door of the White House. The din that descended on them as they opened the door, echoing throughout the building like the roar of a crowd at a sporting event, overwhelmed and astonished the lieutenant, who glanced at Welles to see his reaction. The secretary's expression remained constant, indicating to Gwathmey that the din was not unusual. How in the name of everything holy, he wondered, does anyone get anything done with this noise?

They squeezed their way up a flight of stairs between slowly ascending and descending lines of men who had a rough-hewn, out-of-town look, presumably Western. In the second floor corridor, which led directly to the president's office, dozens were gathered, milling, shouting, chewing, spitting.

Here was the new wave, Gwathmey observed, Republicans, abolitionists, antislave, pro-Union opportunists of every stripe. It was their hour. Their man was in the White House, and they were the new broom bent on sweeping out the old Whigs and Democrats. Nothing like a fat job wrapped in the righteous cover of ideology to stir a man's passions. Each had his urgent claim to a favor—a contract; a commission in the military; a job as postmaster, port collector, marshal, paymaster, clerk, commissioner, or agent. And each claimed a crucial role in getting the president elected.

In shifting groups of three and four, each man kept one eye on his group and the other on the president's door, awaiting the moment when he, usually unattended, would come forth.

The clamor subsided to a curious hush as Welles and the lieutenant threaded their way through the crowd to the president's door, and rapped. The throng eyed the newcomers. Who were they? What was their business? Were they competition or were they members of the government? Someone said, "Oh, it's the secretary of the Navy," and the babble resumed. Then a voice within said, "Come in."

Trained by vocation and avocation to be observant, Gwathmey fixed the scene with his artist's eye.

The executive office was long and rectangular with two high, draped windows at the far end, facing south. In the center of the room stood a long, rectangular blond-oak table ringed with a dozen straight-backed matching chairs. On the right wall was a marble fireplace in which a log fire blazed against the early spring chill. Over the mantel was a faded portrait of Andrew Jackson. Along the opposite wall hung three large military maps of Virginia, Kentucky, and Charleston harbor; beneath the maps were a green sofa and two stuffed chairs. The lieutenant found the ambience neither luxurious nor elegant. It was, in fact, shabby.

The president was sitting at a small, round table near the window on the right. At his back, standing against an apparently unused door, was a large, high desk with numerous pigeonholes in which, it was rumored, he filed assassination threats. "Good morning," and Abraham Lincoln, the man whose election had thrown the South into turmoil, had caused seven states to secede, and who at that moment was the subject of black banner headlines from Maryland to Texas, rose and came toward the lieutenant with outstretched hand. The president's grasp was firm, his handshake warm and vigorous but at the same time curiously stiff and awkward.

To Welles, he said, "'Tis a rare pleasure, sir, to see you twice in one day, let alone in one morning." The secretary grinned. Mr. Lincoln knew he would appreciate the implication. Welles was not one to seek the company of the president without good reason.

Towering over Welles, Mr. Lincoln was, Gwathmey judged, about six feet four. His black frock coat accentuated his slenderness and minimized the powerful arms and shoulders of an ex-farmer and master axman. His clothes were neither well fitted nor well pressed. The trousers bagged at the knee and were, the lieutenant noted to his own embarrassment, quite short. On his feet were a pair of well-worn, beaded moccasin slippers. The voice that issued from the tall, strong frame was surprisingly high pitched. But figure, clothes, and voice faded to insignificance before the president's long, lean face.

The complexion was sallow and dark, the lines deeply etched. His black hair was unkempt and spiky; the beard short and dark, touched lightly with gray. Nose and mouth were prodigious almost to coarseness. It was a face that lent itself to cruel caricature. Gwathmey realized that it was the eyes, eyes gray and luminous, that softened and redeemed; eyes that spoke of a gentle, thoughtful soul. About the whole there was an inexpressible weariness that transcended fatigue, a weariness that spoke of eternity.

"The lieutenant," said Welles, "brings a message from Pensacola."

"Well, you've had a long and, I expect, not too comfortable ride."

"Five days, sir. I left on the first of the month."

"What do you have for us, Lieutenant?"

"I have it," said Welles, producing the dispatch. "Please read it." Welles looked at the president with a question and then shifted his gaze to Gwathmey. Lincoln nodded, and Welles asked Gwathmey to wait outside. "Mr. President," said Welles when the door closed, "Captain Adams, commander of the squadron at Pensacola, has replied to General Scott's March 12 order directing him to land troops for the reinforcement of Fort Pickens."

"I didn't think a written response was called for."

"Adams's message is lengthy—it runs to several pages—but I think I can fairly summarize it." Lincoln nodded. "The captain says he feels bound by the truce that was negotiated by the previous administration whereby President Buchanan agreed not to reinforce Pickens as long as the secessionists did not attack it. Adams has therefore refused to supply the boats for landing the troops. Moreover, as a naval officer he says that he does not feel bound by an order from General Scott. I quote the last few lines: 'While I cannot take on myself under such insufficient authority as General Scott's order the fearful responsibility of an act which seems to render civil war inevitable, I am ready at all times to carry out whatever orders I may receive from the honorable, the secretary of the Navy.' "

Lincoln ran nervous fingers through his already disheveled hair. Another day, another crisis. Each of the past thirty-three days since the inauguration had brought at least one. He hated hasty and precipitate action. And it seemed that all he had been doing since he had become president was making on-the-spot decisions. He had never had the time to settle in, to calmly and unhurriedly assess the situation. Even in the days before the inauguration, he had been confronted with the need to make critical decisions regarding the government's response to the seceded states.

Bemused, he strolled back to the window and gazed out over the south lot. The first thing that had struck him about Adams's message was his resistance to taking orders from Scott, who was general in chief. Apparently, interservice cooperation was not something one could presume. Beyond the lot and across the canal, his eye came to rest on the truncated stone shaft that was the abandoned monument to George Washington. Had he faced the problem? What was the Navy's role in the Revolution? He shook his head. That was not the question. The question was whether to confirm Scott's order to Adams. And that had to be decided immediately. Interesting. Adams's recalcitrance was giving him a second chance, an opportunity to change his mind about reinforcing Pickens. Was this Providence's way of suggesting that he back off— maybe choose a less aggressive course? Was he being sent a sign?

Adams was surely right about one thing—this could be the torch to the powder keg. In a way he could sympathize with the captain for backing away from Scott's order. Adams wanted confirmation from Welles, or more likely from the president himself. What could be worse than being responsible for starting a war that would pit American against American, brother against brother, father against son. He happened to know that Adams had three sons in the Confederate service, and was reported to have said, "God knows when I open my broadside but that I may be killing my own children."

But what was the alternative? Not to reinforce Pickens was to give it up. He turned to Welles. "The military are unanimous in their opinion that Pickens is essential, are they not?"

"Yes, sir. With Forts McRae and Barrancas occupied by the Florida militia, Pickens becomes absolutely essential to us."

Shameful episode, thought Lincoln. Two days after Florida seceded in January, her militia seized the federal navy yard on Pensacola Bay while Buchanan's commodore stood by. Then, to compound the disgrace, Buchanan's people abandoned the nearby forts of McRae and Barrancas because they deemed them untenable. "What is the status of the supplementary expeditionary force ordered for Pickens?" asked Lincoln.

"It should be leaving from Brooklyn tonight or first thing in the morning," said Welles, laboring under the weight of a huge and somewhat dilapidated old atlas, which he was lugging from a shelf at the north end of the room to the table near the window.

"Then there's still time to call it off?"

Oh, no, not after all that agonizing. "Yes, Mr. President, there's still time, but our military feels that Pickens can be reinforced and defended much more easily than McRae or Barrancas. Situated as it is on Santa Rosa Island, Pickens can be provisioned and reinforced from the gulf side. A look at this map tells the story."

Welles carefully folded out the heavily creased page that contained the state of Florida. They both bent over it. There at the extreme western corner of the state was the irregular circle of Pensacola Bay, barely separated from the Gulf of Mexico by the forty-mile curving saber of sand that was Santa Rosa Island. Fort Pickens lay on the western point of the saber, accessible from both bay and gulf.

"We presently have a force of two steamers, *Brooklyn* and *Wyandotte*; and three sailing ships, *Sabine*, *Macedonia*, and *St. Louis*, lying off Pickens, in the gulf," said Welles. "I believe the troops are aboard the *Brooklyn*. Adams, squadron commander, is aboard *Sabine*."

Lincoln smiled inwardly. Uncle Gideon had done his homework. He turned back to the window. Yes. Pickens must be held. But it wasn't because of its strategic importance, or because it could be easily defended. That was almost irrelevant. He wouldn't risk the life of a single soldier for the sake of strategy. The real issue cut deeper, went beyond Pickens.

On March 4, on the steps of the Capitol, his hand on the Bible, he had sworn before all the world to preserve, protect, and defend the Union. And in his inaugural address he had declared that that oath obliged him to "hold, occupy, and possess the property and places belonging to the government." That was the core of it. That was the irreducible proposition. And Fort Pickens was unquestionably the property of the U.S. government. Hold, occupy, and possess the property and places belonging to the government. How could he turn his back on that oath?

"Mr. President, have you been advised that the Confederates are fortifying the entire Pensacola Bay area, and that they are ringing Pickens itself with batteries?"

"Yes, Scott has so advised."

"And are you aware that the Army has intercepted a message from the Confederate secretary of war to their commandant, General Bragg at Pensacola, asking when he will be ready to attack Pickens?"

"Yes, I have a memorandum to that effect." Father Neptune knows I know about the batteries and the intercepted message. It's his way of applying pressure. He needn't bother. It's quite clear that if we don't move first, they'll take it. No, he couldn't let Pickens go. It would be the equivalent of saying to the South—and to the world—that we have neither the strength nor the resolve to protect and defend our government. If he didn't keep his word and stand by his oath of office, nothing thereafter would matter. The government would dissolve into chaos. In a choice of evils, war may not always be the worst. Pickens would be reinforced and it had to be done quickly, before the South became aware of the intent.

"Why," the president asked, "has it taken Adams almost a month to respond?"

"We felt we couldn't rely on the security of the telegraph, and decided to send Scott's order by ship. It was delayed by a storm and took almost three weeks to reach Adams."

"Would you agree that the proper course now is to get another order to Adams as quickly as possible, affirming that he is indeed to land troops?"

"Yes, sir!" There was a discernible note of relief in Welles's response. "I'll send the lieutenant back immediately."

Accompanied by Gwathmey, Welles returned to his office and directed the lieutenant to refresh himself, have some breakfast, and report back in an hour. He then drafted a dispatch to Adams, indicating that the department regretted that he had not complied with the order of General-in-Chief Scott, and that he was to afford every available facility for the immediate landing of troops to reinforce Fort Pickens.

Gwathmey walked rapidly from the Navy Department down Pennsylvania Avenue. Five days of a jolting, dust-choked, and virtually sleepless journey had left him bone tired and famished. Southern trains had no dining cars and he had eaten nothing but quick, cold snacks. But foremost on his mind was not food; it was a hot, hot bath.

At 14th Street he stopped in front of Willard's Hotel, and hesitated. It was pandemonium. The crowd spilling out of the lobby onto the sidewalk was loud and shrill, resembling the one at the White House.

Gesticulating, eager, ardent, they were quiet only, it seemed to Gwathmey, when they paused to pick the remains of breakfast from their teeth or to squirt tobacco juice from practiced lips.

He decided it was worth the extra time to continue east to 6th Street and the National Hotel. The National was a stronghold of the Southern leadership, a quiet, shaded refuge of thick Oriental carpets, gleaming brass, and immaculate white-vested houseboys who moved through the softly lit and richly draped parlors at a pace congenial to Southern sensibilities.

As Gwathmey lay soaking out five days of accumulated soot and grime, and reflecting that one of life's true blessings is a tub of hot water, a houseboy steamed and brushed out his uniform. Lulled to drowsiness by the combination of fatigue and hot bath, while at the same time stimulated by his unexpected meeting with the president, it was only by dint of extreme effort that he was able to concentrate on the decision at hand.

It was a decision he knew he had to face the moment a tortured and distraught Adams summoned him to his cabin and confided to him the substance of the order from Scott. There, with the *Sabine* riding easily at anchor, her timbered decks and masts softly creaking and groaning to the caressing crosscurrents of bay and gulf, the white sands of Santa Rosa transformed to blinding snow in the noonday glare, the two officers regarded each other mutely as each tried to understand how that brief dispatch was going to change their lives. Gwathmey understood that whatever his choice, it would reach deep into his life and color his days forever after. It was one of those fateful, blind forks in the road that come perhaps once or twice in a man's life.

Reaching from the tub to the kettle on the hob for more hot water, he speculated that the president had two probable alternatives: Either he'll confirm Scott's order and direct Adams to land reinforcing troops at once, or he'll wait to see if the Confederacy fires the first shot. If the former, I have no choice. But if he waits, I'll wait. The problem is, how will I know what he decides? The noisy pendulum clock over the mantel told him he had less than a quarter of an hour to report back to Secretary Welles. Reluctantly, the lieutenant wrenched himself out of the tub.

On the way back to the department, considerably refreshed but without having eaten, he bought an apple from a street vendor. If Benjamin

Franklin could eat a roll on the streets of Philadelphia, he could munch an apple on Pennsylvania Avenue.

Upon returning to the secretary's office, he was ordered, as he had anticipated, to return to Pensacola posthaste with a message for Adams. And Gwathmey did not have to speculate as to its contents. Welles read the text aloud and advised him to commit it to memory and destroy it after he was certain he would be able to recite it for Adams. Welles placed the dispatch in an envelope, which he handed to the lieutenant.

To the secretary's evident surprise, Gwathmey refused to accept it. Standing stiffly at attention and staring at a point directly over the seated Welles's head, Gwathmey declared in an obviously rehearsed statement: "Sir, as I do not think it honorable to hold the commission of a government who deems itself bound to execute acts in which I cannot conscientiously assist, I have no alternative but to offer to the department my resignation as a lieutenant in the United States Navy."

For a moment after Gwathmey concluded his declaration, Welles's only response was to flush through his beard. No words came. Then the corners of his small mouth twisted to a snarl. Ripping his spectacles from his face with one hand in the manner of someone preparing for physical assault, he cried, "You shall not resign, sir! Your resignation is not accepted! You are hereby dismissed forthwith as an officer of the United States Navy!" Gwathmey saluted, about-faced, and walked out of the office.

Trembling with anger, Welles closed his eyes and breathed deeply in an effort to stem his fury and collect himself. His heart was pounding in that infernal irregular rhythm. He knew that if he were to pick up his pen at that moment and try to write, his hand would not obey the command; twitching uncontrollably it would leave a wake of chicken scratches. Forty confounded naval officers had resigned to "go south"— their euphemism for desertion—in just the last two weeks of March. And he had no doubt that this was just the beginning.

Damn Gwathmey and his ilk! He was fed to the teeth with their sanctimonious reasoning, which was nothing more than an excuse for traitorous, treasonous behavior. They deserved jail and worse. They were no better than deserters.

He was as humane and progressive as the next man. Hadn't he fathered the bill in the Connecticut legislature to end imprisonment for debt? Hadn't he been instrumental in abolishing property and religious requirements for voting? Hadn't he provided for the freedom and integrity of a Negro family by purchasing their freedom and, at their request, employing them all in his household? But when it came to traitorous military officers, he was inclined to be neither liberal nor generous. His instincts were to prosecute them to the limit of the law. At the very least they should be clapped into jail and tried for treason—with hanging in the offing.

The gall of Gwathmey and his kind! Having learned everything they knew of their profession at the expense of the United States, they were now resigning to put their expertise (and God knows what information of a sensitive nature) at the service of a government that might well become a wartime enemy.

With an unsteady hand Welles poured a glass of water from a ceramic pitcher on his desk. Sipping it slowly in an effort to settle his nerves, he resolved to turn his thoughts away from Gwathmey and what he represented. He could ill afford the time to ponder the treachery of Southern-born officers who placed allegiance to state above loyalty to country. Disloyalty in all areas of government was becoming commonplace. Gwathmey was simply further confirmation of his long-held conviction about employees of the federal government, especially in the upper echelons. The cabinet was a good example, stocked with power-hungry, self-serving men, loyal only to the gratification of their own ambitions. He trusted none of them, with one exception. Happily, that was the president.

He himself was essentially an outsider, in Washington only to serve at the pleasure of Mr. Lincoln. He had not sought the job, didn't even know what the president had in mind when he summoned him. That chill and bleak March morning, three days before the inauguration, when at the invitation of Abe Lincoln he had made his way down from Hartford and through the milling throng of office seekers to plush Parlor Six, the presidential suite at Willard's, he was quite unprepared for the offer of a place in the cabinet. From a president-elect besieged and stunned by the avalanche of people seeking jobs and favors and commissions, he accepted the post at Navy. But he was not then and was not now part of Lincoln's inner circle. They still thought of him as a renegade Democrat. Yes, he was that. Never denied it. Proud to be a supporter of states' rights—until it became madness and treason—and unashamed that his conversion to Republican was a matter of conscience. Unashamed too that the matter of conscience was slavery—

that evil, doomed, and dooming institution. Not that he was an abolitionist; no, he was far from that. As he had expressed it many times during those late-night debates with friends in Hartford, "Until I can be persuaded to admit Negroes to be companions and associates, I shall not be likely to advocate their emancipation." Like the president, he wanted to confine slavery to regions where it already existed and to prevent its spread to the territories.

It was only recently, just a few days ago, that he had learned Mr. Lincoln's reasons for appointing him. Fox reported that a friend of a friend heard the president say he doubted that Welles (actually, he referred to him as "Father Neptune") knew stem from stern. But he was as honest as they came; as for the rest, he could learn it. Obviously his reputation as state comptroller had preceded him. In Hartford his passion for honesty and economy made him—depending upon whose ox—the most respected or the most feared civil servant in the state capital.

As soon as the president's term was over, he would be on the first train back to Connecticut, where he belonged. His true vocation was journalist. Secondarily he was a state politician. But if it ever came to a conflict between state and Union, it would be no contest. One owed allegiance to one's country, not to Alabama or Mississippi or Connecticut.

With feelings of guilt at having spent so much time pondering the subject he had resolved to dismiss, but with his nerves somewhat settled, Welles walked out of his office and down the corridor to a door marked "G. Fox, Assistant Secretary." He rapped and entered.

"Fox, I need your help." Captain Gustavus Vasa Fox, USN, a tall, rangy man, was seated at his desk. He looked up and smiled a greeting. Clean shaven from lower lip up, with a pate hairless as an egg, Fox's thick raven black beard seemed to be compensation for the absence of hair on the rest of his face and head. The color of his eyes matched his beard, and from deep wells in his sharp-featured face they glinted with a certain vivacity. Though twenty years Welles's junior, Fox moved with much more deliberation than his superior and, at least outwardly, at a much slower pace.

"An officer I was counting on to bear a message to the squadron at Pensacola turned out to be a rebel. Do you know anyone who's trustworthy and immediately available?"

Fox considered for a moment. Leaning back in his chair he stroked his beard. "I may have just the man." Pawing through a pile of personnel folders on his desk, he said, "He's supposed to report to me today for work on that discipline and efficiency project, but he's requesting transfer to sea duty." Fox fished out a folder and handed it to Welles, who immediately began to leaf through the service jacket of Lt. John Lorimer Worden.

The lieutenant was forty-three and a veteran of twenty-seven years in the Navy. He had attended the naval school in Philadelphia before the establishment of the academy at Annapolis, and had seen service in the Brazil and Pacific squadrons, the naval observatory, the Mexican War, and the Mediterranean and home squadrons. There seemed to be nothing negative in his record. Service was continuous and his health excellent; some years ago he had contracted a tropical fever, but he had evidently fully recovered. Born in Ossining, New York, he was raised on a farm near Fishkill, a Hudson River community, whence he was appointed midshipman. Married and the father of four, he was frequently accompanied by his family when he was on shore duty. Otherwise, they lived in the village of Pawling in Dutchess County, not far from his childhood home. As far as anyone in the department knew, he was "untainted by treason."

Welles found the most striking aspects of his record to be his length of service and his apparent ability to inspire the loyalty and respect of his subordinates. "Interesting," observed Welles, "that after twenty-seven years in the service, he's still a first lieutenant. His rise through the ranks has been less than meteoric."

"A bit on the slow side of normal," agreed Fox. "He's had four promotions—passed midshipman to master, to lieutenant, and then first."

"True." Welles hadn't been certain of the progression.

"But," said Fox, "he is probably one of the most senior lieutenants in grade."

"How do you account for that when, at least according to his efficiency reports, he shows outstanding leadership ability?"

"Sounds like an advanced case of no friends in high places," drawled Fox.

"Do you know him?"

"I know of him. I don't think anyone, except maybe one or two old friends from navy school, really knows him. Bit of a loner. Devout . . . bookish . . . abstemious. Not your 'have another drink' kind of sailor."

"That would be an impediment to advancement right there, in a navy that runs on alcohol."

"Well, Mr. Secretary, we have our traditions, you know."

Welles tried to repress a smile. Fox ran true to form. A naval officer never apologized for the Navy, not to a civilian at any rate. "Please ask Worden to report to me immediately."

"Aye, sir."

Welles rose to leave, but Fox stayed him. "I was about to knock on your door when you came in. I have some interesting news, and I want to ask you about your meeting with Uncle Abe. How did it go? Will he let us go down and get the *Merrimack*?"

Welles shook his head, his expression indicating his frustration and disappointment. Settling back in his chair, he fished his pipe from his pocket. "No. He still believes that Virginia will remain in the Union. And I, for one, cannot persuade him otherwise."

"Well, cheer up. I have some good news. I was at the White House a few minutes ago. The president gave me the order to take command of the provisioning force for Sumter. I leave shortly to join the squadron."

"So," breathed Welles, exhaling a stream of pungent smoke, "he's made the move. How do your orders read?"

"They're oral. The written orders are to come from Simon Cameron. But as I understand it, the plan is essentially the one you and I worked out." Fox was being modest. The plan was in fact his alone, formulated by him, and presented by him to the president. Welles had simply initialed his approval, thereby making the ships and personnel available.

"The ships are coming from New York, Washington, and Boston. I am to act as victualler and will have command of the provisioning boats. The supplies are to be transported by my ship, the *Baltic*, an unarmed steamer. At the rendezvous we shall transship to the three tugs, also unarmed. They'll cross the bar and do the actual landing; they're of light draft—less than seven feet. Captain Mercer will be lying outside the bar with the four armed steamers. If I run into resistance, I am to call on him. He will then force entry for me."

"Sounds reasonable."

Welles and Fox had fallen into a working arrangement that divided their responsibilities along the lines of their respective strengths. Welles concerned himself with departmental policy, administration, and legislative affairs, whereas Fox, with twenty years of experience in the Navy, oversaw operations. In official Washington they had already achieved a reputation as a strong team. With Fox—tall, slender, and bald—towering over his bewigged colleague, they made a striking if incongruous pair. It was inevitable that the president would be heard to refer to his navy chiefs as "the long and the short of it."

"Like most plans," Fox said, "it depends on execution, and luck. Lots of luck. Planning is the easiest part. The hard part is getting all the ships together at the appointed time and place. And the weather has to cooperate. Weather is always critical in an operation of this kind."

"Where and when do you plan to rendezvous?"

"Ten miles off the Charleston bar on the morning of April 11."

Welles rose and offered Fox his hand in silent expression of Godspeed. "By the way, I've changed my mind about Worden. Alert him immediately, but ask him not to come to my office until eleven this evening." Welles labored under no illusion that Worden's visit would go unreported to Confederate authorities. They knew everything of significance that transpired in the President's Park, including cabinet resolutions, within forty-eight hours. But he believed in security and discretion as matters of principle, and therefore preferred that Worden come to his office under cover of darkness.

At the same moment, at the other end of the President's Park, another cabinet member was acting with little regard for discretion and less for security. Gesturing toward the executive mansion with his long, custom-made Havana cigar, the silver-haired secretary of state was saying to a visitor, ". . . he fiddles and diddles and when he does make a move it's invariably misguided because he has no overall concept, no vision. How can we expect anything else from an Illinois backwoods lawyer?" The rhetorical question was edged with bitterness.

William H. Seward, hawk nosed, in a high, stiff collar bound by a flowing silk blue and white scarf loosely knotted at the throat, dragged deeply on his cigar. "Sumter is a lost cause. That fort is in the mouth—the very jaws—of Charleston harbor, ringed with shore batteries. It doesn't stand a chance. You don't have to be a tactical genius to see that. Why then does he choose to make Sumter a symbol of federal authority? Against the advice of his secretary of state *and* his military advisers, Mr. President Lincoln has decided to provision Fort Sumter come what may, and you know what that means." His visitor nodded.

"Now Fort Pickens down at Pensacola," continued Seward, "is another matter. It's defensible and should be held. That's where we should make a stand. But Sumter? Madness! Charleston is teeming with slavers—reckless brutes—secessionists, militia, all spoiling for a fight."

The secretary's visitor, as became a newly appointed minister to the Department of State, listened attentively to his superior and chief officer. James Harvey was not about to interrupt and he certainly wouldn't dream of contradicting the secretary of state.

But Harvey was confused. Seward enjoyed a reputation for guarding his tongue and choosing his words. After all, one doesn't rise to be governor of New York, then go on to the United States Senate, become head of the Republican party, and be appointed secretary of state by indulging in reckless and indiscreet talk. Yet here he was confiding secrets of state to a very junior minister, one he hardly knew. Though somewhat flattered by the implied confidence, Harvey was nonetheless puzzled.

The fact was, Seward was not confiding completely in Harvey. He had understandably chosen to omit from his tirade a singular detail, the very detail that was at the bottom of his ire. Had Seward chosen to tell the whole story, he might well have begun with the three men who were at that moment seated a mere two blocks away in a suite at Willard's, earnestly debating their next move. The three were charged with a most delicate diplomatic mission.

Having been appointed as a commission by Jefferson Davis in February, several days after he had been elected president of the Confederacy, the three were to go to Washington City and there negotiate a two-part agreement on behalf of the Confederate States of America (CSA). Neither Davis nor the three commissioners had any doubt but that on the success or failure of their mission hinged nothing less than war or peace.

Although the mission was delicate and the means complex, the two principal objectives were neither subtle nor devious. They went, as Davis said in his farewell meeting with the three men, to the heart of the matter. The commission's first charge was to negotiate diplomatic recognition of the Confederacy by the United States, a bold initiative that would in one stroke peacefully solve the problems attending secession and give the CSA everything it sought by way of achieving nationhood and sovereignty. The commission's second objective was to negotiate the immediate removal of federal troops from their bastion at Fort Sumter in Charleston harbor.

Though Jefferson Davis, a perceptive and intelligent statesman, had been well aware of the odds against a completely successful mission, he had reason to hope for a not entirely unsuccessful outcome. His hopes reposed in the person of one William H. Seward, secretary of state of the United States.

The two men had known each other as members of the U.S. Senate, Davis of Mississippi and Seward of New York, for more than a decade. But it was during the past winter that their friendship had blossomed. That winter when Davis lay bedridden and pain wracked, gradually losing sight in a frightfully inflamed right eye, it was the senator from New York who cheered him. For one hour every afternoon until the January day that Davis resigned his seat, Seward brought the news of the senate floor and the gossip of the cloakroom to a grateful colleague.

Davis knew as well as anyone Seward's ambitions. He had witnessed Seward's disappointment when he was defeated for the presidential nomination by that Illinois lawyer, and he agreed with his friend and colleague from New York that of all the men in the administration, he, by virtue of experience and ability, was best qualified to govern. Moreover, Davis believed that Seward was sincerely devoted to the cause of peace and was ready to go to extraordinary lengths to achieve it. Little wonder, then, that the three Southern commissioners were instructed by their government to deal with Seward.

But Lincoln had refused to permit his secretary of state to meet with the three Confederate commissioners, for to do so would have been tantamount to granting the commission its first objective—recognition of the CSA as a sovereign and independent power. For the resourceful Seward, however, the president's embargo was but a minor impediment. Seward had promptly invited the dignified and respected Supreme Court Justice John A. Campbell to act as intermediary between himself and the Southern commissioners. Justice Campbell, who thought slavery an abomination but nonetheless made no secret of his allegiance to the South, was like Seward, sincerely devoted to peace. He accepted the secretary's invitation with alacrity and with pleasure.

Since recognition of the CSA was, for the moment, patently out of the question, the first topic for negotiation became Fort Sumter. Seward had no doubt that the correct course was to abandon the fort. Not only would the move ease tension and thus make war less probable, it would extricate the federal government from a militarily untenable position and thereby avoid certain and embarrassing defeat. At the time that Seward invited Campbell to his office, he was convinced that the president would heed the advice of his councillors and withdraw from Sumter.

When the courtly Justice Campbell, who believed in thorough and clear-cut understandings, came to Seward's office for instructions, he advised the secretary that not only was he going to transmit his information to the three commissioners, but he was also going to write directly to Jefferson Davis. "And what exactly," inquired Campbell, "shall I say to him on the subject of Fort Sumter?"

"You may say to him," replied Seward, pausing for a moment to knock the fine gray ash from his cigar, "that before your letter reaches him—how far is it to Montgomery?"

"Three days."

"You may say to him that before your letter reaches him, the telegraph will have informed him that Sumter has been evacuated."

That very day, an elated President Davis received Seward's pronouncement via telegram from the commission. Naturally, Davis assumed that Seward was speaking for Lincoln. Great good news. In the contest of wills between himself and that Illinois imposter, he had prevailed. Davis saw the possibility of a bloodless birth for the Confederacy. And in a few weeks, with the addition of Virginia, Arkansas, and North Carolina, the Confederate States of America would become a formidable force and a nation of substance. Thereafter, anything was possible.

Unhappily, Seward had reckoned without a true understanding of his man. It was a fact that when Lincoln learned that the secessionists had imposed an embargo on Fort Sumter, preventing supplies of any kind from reaching the garrison, he consulted with his war council on the advisability of sending an expeditionary force with provisions. And it was a fact that a majority of the cabinet had been opposed. His military advisers, seeing a tactically hopeless situation, had also been opposed.

Lincoln agonized for twenty-four days. At dawn of a gray March morning, having sat up all night on the sofa in his office, wrapped in his long, wool "thinking shawl," he came to the conclusion that he couldn't rely on cabinet secretaries and generals to make up his mind for him. He directed Welles to assemble a supply fleet for Sumter.

Now Seward was compounding his indiscretion. To his young visitor, Harvey, he insisted, "The president is out of his depth. He isn't equal to the situation and he isn't managing the crisis." Rising from an upholstered Chippendale armchair, he walked to a beautifully polished mahogany sideboard, furnishings that had come from Seward's own residences. "Drink?" With raised hand Harvey mutely signaled a grateful no thanks. From a silver-latticed decanter, Seward poured himself a generous tot of Portuguese brandy.

"No worse calamity could befall this country than a civil war. It would solve nothing and would leave us so enervated that we would be easy prey for the European powers. I tell you, this hick lawyer is going to explode the negotiations I've been laboring over for weeks in an effort to avoid civil war."

Swirling the brandy in his glass and absently savoring the aroma, Seward was silent for a moment in apparent contemplation of the president's folly. "And the consequence is that we're going to blunder into war." Picking up a recent copy of the *New York Times*, he pointed to an editorial and placed it in front of Harvey. "Wanted," declared the bold headline, "A Policy." The administration, asserted the *Times*, was dangerously adrift and had shown no evidence that it was equal to an "active, resolute, and determined enemy."

"The pity of it," said Seward, leaning forward to emphasize the point, "is that there is a solution far less painful than civil war; there is a strategy equal to the problem. There's England, France, and Spain eager to fish in troubled waters, openly sympathetic to the South, and not even bothering to conceal their designs on Mexico, which are in clear violation of the Monroe Doctrine. The United States should demand an immediate explanation of their posture. And if no satisfactory answers are forthcoming . . . declare war.

"That," said Seward with a jab of his cigar, "would for damn sure unify this country." And he left no doubt that if Lincoln wasn't equal to the task of governing in perilous times, he was willing and able to assume the responsibility. Indeed, he had so advised the president in a memorandum.

Throughout Seward's philippic, his visitor had said little. From time to time he had nodded sympathetically or murmured softly to indicate appreciation for his chief's position. James E. Harvey, South Carolina born, had moved north as a young man, achieved success as a journalist and politician, and had just been appointed the new administration's minister to Portugal. He was paying a courtesy call on the secretary before assuming his post.

"Well," said Seward without conviction, "let's hope that we can muddle through and that the consequences won't be too severe." Rising to his feet, a slender figure in an impeccably tailored pearl gray suit, he indicated that the meeting was at an end by expressing his hope that Harvey enjoy a successful tour in Lisbon. There was a warm exchange of farewells.

Harvey left the office and walked the several blocks from State, down Pennsylvania Avenue to the telegraph office on the street floor of the National Hotel. There he sent the following wire to an old friend and classmate in Charleston: "Government positively determined not to withdraw. Supplies go immediately supported by naval force." It was signed, "A Friend."

At the executive mansion, the president was in conference with a short, slight man with thinning, sand-colored hair and a wispy mustache. Though his age was indeterminate, it had been established that he had been laboring in the bowels of the State Department longer than any of his peers; no one could, in fact, recall when Robert Chew had arrived, nor could any recall a time when he hadn't been there. It was clear that he had survived administration after administration, not by virtue of having rendered outstanding service but rather by having developed the essential survival skill of the civil service—benign inconspicuousness. In any case, it was Chew who was plucked from the ranks when Mr. Lincoln sent for a messenger who was proven reliable and whose loyalty was not in question.

To Chew the president gave careful instructions, both written and oral, impressing upon him the need for following his directions precisely and to the letter. There must be no possibility for misinterpretation of the message he was to bear to Francis Pickens, governor of South Carolina.

Chew was to proceed directly to Charleston, and if on his arrival the flag of the United States was flying over Fort Sumter and it was not under attack, he was to procure an interview with the governor and advise him that the federal government was planning to supply the fort with provisions only. And if such attempt was not resisted, the government would make no effort to throw in men, arms, or ammunition unless and until further notice had been given. If, on the other hand, the fort was under attack or had already surrendered, Chew was to seek no interview and was to return to Washington immediately.

Chew said that he understood. To his credit, unused as he was to being summoned to the councils of the mighty, he seemed neither awed nor flustered, and was quite in command of himself during the interview. At six that evening he left the capital in the company of a U.S. Army captain who had been assigned as his aide.

Some five hours after Chew's departure for Charleston, Gideon Welles sat awaiting the arrival of John L. Worden. He could not help but speculate as to the person and personality of the lieutenant. He decided that, because of the leadership ability indicated in his dossier, Worden would be a young-looking forty-three, possessed of a virile, commanding presence. And because of his farm rearing and abstemious habits, he would be physically robust.

At precisely eleven o'clock, there was a soft rap at his door, and an officer wearing the blue uniform of a lieutenant in the United States Navy entered. Welles was disappointed on all three counts.

Except for his color, which was ruddy and healthy, bespeaking years on an open deck, the lieutenant, tall, slender, and small boned, was almost delicate in appearance. The full, square-cut, light brown beard that hung almost to his chest served to emphasize his forty-three years. The reading glass he wore on a ribbon suspended from a button on his tunic, along with a quiet, thoughtful manner, lent him the retiring, almost professorial air of an academician. His features, regular and finely chiseled, were not unpleasant.

The hour was late and Welles was tired; he came right to the point. Worden was needed to perform a "secret, responsible, and somewhat dangerous duty." Dispatch was essential. He was to leave as soon as possible and say nothing to anybody, not even his wife. Presenting him with the message for Captain Adams, the secretary said, "I suggest that you commit the text to memory, burn this message, and when you arrive in Pensacola make a certified copy as you remember it." He paused to note Worden's reaction and to give him a chance to respond. But the lieutenant, keeping his eyes steadily on Welles, remained silent. "I don't foresee any difficulty in reaching Adams, since the Confederates are allowing federal forces free communication with the squadron."

Worden said that he understood. Noting that there were no more trains south that evening, he said he would make an early start the following morning. Welles concurred. The lieutenant saluted and departed.

Around midnight, as Welles walked wearily from his office to the hotel, he reflected that the day had been eventful and, he trusted— aside from the president's refusal to let him mount a rescue mission for the *Merrimack*—fruitful. The supplementary relief expedition ordered by the president for Fort Pickens was probably getting under way from the Brooklyn Navy Yard. A similar expedition for Sumter, part of which was being fitted out at the same yard, each unaware of the other for security reasons, would sail in a couple of days under Fox's command.

Before retiring for the night, Welles wrote in his journal: "... although but brief time had been permitted to us to fit out the expedition, I congratulated myself when I went to my room at Willard's on the evening of the sixth of April, that it had been accomplished within the time given us . . ." He drifted off to sleep with the sense that irretrievable forces had been set in motion, and they were now quite out of his hands.

CHAPTER

II

When Gwathmey, stripped of his commission in the U.S. Navy, left Welles's office, he turned once again down Pennsylvania Avenue. He walked at a deliberate pace and observed his surroundings, much like a tourist in the capital for the first time. It seemed to his searching and familiar eye that Washington City was, aside from a slightly heavier stream of traffic, unchanged of a normal Saturday afternoon.

The narrow sidewalk was jammed with businessmen and clerks hurrying back to offices after the noonday break. Negroes, free and slave, went about their chores. The middle of the street, bisected by iron tracks, was alive with horsecars, carriages, and equestrians of every class and vocation. The metallic clang of iron wheels on iron track and the ringing of conductors' warning gongs were punctuated by the hollow clip-clop of horses' hooves on cobblestone.

Along the gutter an occasional pig rooted in the mud and garbage. In front of the two- and three-story frame and brick buildings that lined the avenue, vendors hawked oysters, roasted chestnuts, fruits, and pastries, their raucous huckster cries adding to the commotion.

At 1st Street the lieutenant circled around the Capitol, which was, as it had been ever since he could remember, bristling with scaffolds and hoists, and ringing with the hammer blows of construction workers as they labored to finish the new house and senate wings. The central structure, which was being remodeled for a larger dome, resembled nothing so much as a wedding cake with its top tier rudely lopped off. A skeletal iron crane poked out of the aperture to the cloud-scattered afternoon sky.

On the east lawn the massive but temporarily deposed bronze figure of Freedom with feathered helmet and olive branch rose abruptly from the clutter. Eyeless, she surveyed the jungle of iron plates and marble blocks strewn at her feet while she waited to be elevated to her new and higher eminence atop the unfinished dome.

Teams of stonemasons cut and chiseled and polished. Trains of twelve-horse and -mule teams drawing long, flatbed wagons arrived and departed, chains thick as a man's arm looped beneath, cradling columns and slabs of marble. The cries and curses of mule skinners and teamsters pierced the echoing, clanging roar.

Gwathmey, stimulated despite his fatigue by the energy and industry, reflected that were these other times, he might well be here with easel and paint recording the moment. Looping south, he skirted the Washington Navy Yard and turned west for the Long Bridge to Virginia. In Alexandria he caught an evening train on the Orange and Alexandria Railroad for the connection to Richmond, his home.

After a night of fitful catnaps, Gwathmey walked up the narrow stone path to his parents' home in time to meet them leaving for church on Sunday morning, April 7. They were not expecting their only son, whom they had not seen for the better part of a year. The surprise compounded their delight.

Against the lieutenant's objections, they insisted on abandoning their plans for devotions in order to remain at home and give him a proper welcome, his father happily maintaining that since Easter Sunday was last week, this week's service was bound to be an anticlimax. And when his mother learned that her son hadn't eaten a hot meal for a week, nothing could keep her from fleeing to the kitchen, where she laid on Sunday dinner a bit earlier than planned.

Along with news and family gossip (discreetly saving their questions for another time), they plied him with baked ham, yams, greens, corn bread, fruit, and cheese, along with a bottle of imported Burgundy they'd been saving for just such a happy occasion. Sated at last, Gwathmey staggered off to his room with his parents' promise to let no one, including a loving sister and other well-meaning relatives and friends, interrupt his rest.

Gwathmey slept through until the following forenoon, when he arose much refreshed and relaxed. He spent the day leisurely piecing together from his wardrobe a presentable suit of civilian clothes, since he had decided to quit his uniform.

Early in the morning of Tuesday, April 9, after a long and emotional farewell, he boarded a Richmond and Danville train for the first leg of the seven-hundred-mile journey southwest to Montgomery, Alabama. After six changes of train and traveling through Lynchburg, Bristol, Knoxville, and Dalton, he arrived in the Confederate capital on the afternoon of Thursday, April 11. Although the man with whom he sought an interview was occupied, he did send word through an aide that he would be available that evening, after dinner.

It was shortly after ten in the evening when Gwathmey knocked on the door of the converted town house that held the offices of the Department of the Navy, Confederate States of America; and it was close to eleven when he was ushered into the presence of the secretary of the Navy.

"How may I help you?" asked Stephen Russell Mallory.

"Thank you, sir," replied Gwathmey. "Perhaps I may be of service to you."

"Please sit."

Gwathmey took the proffered chair. Seated opposite the secretary, he could not resist the impulse to compare him with his counterpart in Washington City. In frame, the two men were quite similar, both being short and rather heavy. But there the resemblance ended. In contrast to Welles's craggy, stern New England aspect, Mallory tended to the pudgy and rotund. There were no sharp corners. He wore a loop of whiskers that ran from ear to ear under his chin, thus emphasizing the broad features of his otherwise clean-shaven, round face. In manner and in mien both men seemed to reflect their respective places of birth.

Mallory, radiating cheer, patience, and the easy manner one associates with sunny climes, had, in fact, been born on an island in the southern Caribbean. His eyes shone with good humor, and a smile came readily to his lips. After a few minutes of conversation, however, Gwathmey decided that to see in his air of easygoing affability a lack of industry and intelligence would be a perilous mistake.

"A note tells me that you are late a lieutenant of the United States Navy."

"That is correct, sir."

"Where was your last service?"

"With the squadron lying off Fort Pickens, at Pensacola, Florida."

"My home state," smiled Mallory, obviously pleased by the coincidence.

Gwathmey nodded. Anyone remotely connected with the U.S. Navy was acquainted with the saga of Stephen Russell Mallory. Born in Trinidad to an engineer from Connecticut and an Irish mother, he was orphaned at the age of six. Determined to find his "grandpa in Connecticut," this man-child emigrated to the United States, where he got as far as Key West. The citizens there made him a ward of the county, and boarded him with a farm family. Without the benefit of formal schooling, he, like Abraham Lincoln of Kentucky, went on to become a lawyer of distinction. From 1851 to 1861 he represented Florida in the U.S. Senate, where he served as chairman of the Committee on Naval Affairs.

"What brings you here, Lieutenant?"

Gwathmey related the details of his last mission for the U.S. Navy, including his resignation, and concluded with, "Sir, I believe a messenger is at this moment en route to the squadron with an order to land troops for the reinforcement of Fort Pickens."

"Why are you telling me this?"

"I am a Virginian."

"Virginia is not a member of the Confederacy."

"She soon will be."

Mallory's eyes, alert and good-humored, had never left Gwathmey's face. Now they became reflective. Then, having apparently made up his mind, he picked up a pen and said, "Please excuse me for a moment." Scrawling a note, he gave it to an aide just outside his office door, and returned to resume the conversation. "Can you tell me a bit more about your years of service?"

Gwathmey obliged by reciting the date he became a midshipman, the dates of his various promotions, and the names of some of the ships on which he had served. When he mentioned the USS *Minnesota,* Mallory interrupted, "One of the new steam-assisted ships of the line?"

"Yes, sir."

"Are you acquainted with one of her sister ships, *Merrimack*?"

"Ah, I believe she's currently undergoing repairs at the Norfolk yard."

"Yes," confirmed Mallory. "Can you tell me anything else about her?"

"It's my understanding that her engines leave something to be desired, but withal, she's a formidable, full-rigged war frigate. Mounts forty guns." Mallory nodded and smiled, pleased either by Gwathmey's knowledge or by the information, or perhaps both.

"What are your thoughts about ironclad men-of-war?"

Surely, thought Gwathmey, he is testing me. He knows more about the subject than anybody. It was he who headed the inquiry into the feasibility of ironclads and it was his committee that investigated the Stevens battery. Gwathmey said, "Don't know too much about them, sir. I do recall that the Congress refused to support the Stevens experiment—wasn't he that Hoboken engineer? And I understand that England and France are experimenting with iron-belted ships."

"Yes," said Mallory. "Poor Stevens. Every time he came up with a new armored hull, another gun came along that was able to pierce it. John Ericsson's twelve-inch smoothbore gun broke through Stevens's four-inch wrought-iron hull as though it were beech bark." The handsome brass carriage clock on the secretary's desk chimed the half hour. "My goodness," said Mallory, plucking his watch from a vest pocket, "the hour is late, half past eleven. I've found our conversation so interesting that time has plumb gotten away." And he chuckled as though forgetting the hour was cause for a small, private joke. "Before you go, I would appreciate your estimate of the federal government's readiness for war, should it come. What is their attitude and their expectation?"

Gwathmey reflected for a moment, and then said slowly, choosing his words with care, "I can only judge by what I've seen. I was not, of course, privy to the thinking of the administration. On my last walk through Washington City, less than a week ago, I saw neither troops nor batteries, nor a single gun emplacement or indeed preparation for such. In the president's office I noted three maps; they were of Virginia, Kentucky, and Charleston harbor."

The interview was at an end except for one additional bit of business. Gwathmey was pleased to accept the offer of a commission as first lieutenant in the Navy of the Confederate States of America.

The note that Mallory had written containing Gwathmey's information regarding Fort Pickens was addressed to Gen. Leroy Pope Walker, secretary of war for the CSA. Walker had been locked in conference with Jefferson Davis most of the night of Thursday, April 11, and thus did not act immediately on the intelligence. He was diverted again the following day by events that occurred in Charleston harbor early in the morning of April 12.

CHAPTER

III

"No questions, Jack. But are there any answers?"

"No answers, darling. You know I would if I could. I can tell you that I should be home in a couple of weeks." Worden kissed her good-bye, and she remained in the room while he went downstairs to bid farewell to their hosts and good friends, Lt. and Mrs. Henry Wise.

Worden hailed a hack for the ride to the railroad station at North Capitol and C. There he caught the Washington and Alexandria for the five-mile trip across the Potomac to Alexandria, where he boarded a connecting train for Richmond.

Settling in for the ride through Virginia, Worden felt quite at ease. He tended to dismiss rumors that Richmond was seething with strong anti-Union and secessionist feeling. It had not been in evidence at Alexandria, nor did it seem to be on his train, where the passengers were, as always, quietly civil. The conductor who collected his ticket asked politely how far he was going. "All the way to Pensacola," replied Worden.

"Well," smiled the conductor, "we'll take you as far as Lynchburg."

Worden enjoyed a sense of well-being in this state where he had traveled often, and where he found a degree of gentility and hospitality that was most agreeable. It was his conviction that the people of Virginia would not opt to secede. Her ties to the Union were too strong. Too many of her sons had fought and died for the Constitution and its principles.

Relaxed, he surrendered to the charm of April in Virginia, where spring came early and with the multicolored splendor of rhododendron and dogwood, magnolia and apple blossom. The fields rolling gently by his window were showing tender flecks of green. The three-tiered fences sparkled with fresh white paint, and the horses were beautiful, grazing or galloping with the sweet madness of spring and the joy of a sunlit morning. His car rocked gently, and the click of the wheels was lulling rather than harsh.

Olivia, he mused, was on her train by now, probably nearing Baltimore. She was traveling in exactly the opposite direction, north and east, back to the children.

Marvelous woman. This past week with her and without the children had been like newlywed days. She was lovely this morning. No silly questions. No useless expressions of concern. Yet she must have guessed he was going south, else why the need for secrecy. She was full of plans for his spring leave. They would do just what he liked. A month of staying home and playing paterfamilias. Maybe a little fishing with Johnny and Dan. The girls could come if they liked. They'd go to Green Mountain Lake, an easy walk from the house. He might even get to help with the spring planting. That garden fence needed raising and repair. Olivia said she saw a deer clear it from a standing start—seven feet. What the deer didn't get, the 'coons did. But that never seemed to bother her. Someone or something was eating, she said, and that was what really mattered.

It was years since he'd worked in the garden. There were few things he enjoyed more. Strange avocation for a sailor. But then he probably was a bit odd . . . odd enough to be one of the most senior lieutenants in the Navy. He didn't know anyone except old Henry Wise, his classmate who had been in grade as long. But he had no complaints. The Navy didn't owe him a thing. It had already given him more than he could possibly repay. Serious little man that Secretary Welles. Direct. No nonsense. Probably just as well. Serious things were afoot. But rumor had it that he was quite inexperienced in naval affairs. Well, there was Fox. Good man, if Welles chose to use him.

The repercussions of the message he was bearing to Adams could be serious. As far as he knew, the government had not reinforced any federal installations in the seceded states. The rebels' reaction will be interesting. Would they see it as cause for war? What happens if he is in the Confederacy and hostilities begin? What would be his status? Traditionally, envoys of warring powers were allowed egress. After delivering the message, should he remain with the squadron or try to return to Washington by train? Welles had not been specific on that score. He decided to leave the decision to Adams, although his preference was for returning to Washington for a sea duty assignment. No point, though, in looking too far ahead. After twenty-seven years in the Navy he had learned that decisions usually took care of themselves. He returned to his book, an anthology of Shakespeare's plays and sonnets. But he found that he couldn't concentrate, and he put the book back in his duffel.

Since no one was in the seat next to him, he pulled Welles's message out of his pocket and read it several times. Although he felt he had it memorized, he decided not to destroy it until he reached Confederate territory.

Arriving in Richmond early that evening, Worden learned that his connecting train was due in about an hour. He elected to remain at the terminal rather than walk downtown. He enjoyed train stations, especially the high-domed, large, busy ones where dozens of private dramas in greetings and good-byes were enacted every few feet. The Richmond station was crowded and festive that evening, with people wearing their Sunday best, mothers and daughters in gaily beribboned, colorful spring frocks. Many families, he suspected, were returning to the capital, having spent the Easter holiday at home on the farm. For those departing there was a certain added poignance in the farewells, inevitable in the presence of military uniforms. The Virginia militia was rather more in evidence than usual.

Finding himself at a bootblack stand, Worden took a seat in a row of old, cracked leather-backed chairs and slipped his boots onto the worn, brass footrests. Two well-turned-out men, sleek in richly tailored suits and immaculate white shirts, holding cigars and the Sunday paper, sat next to him.

"Were you at the auction yesterday mornin'?"

"No, couldn't get down there. How'd it go?"

"Ah saw a splendid buck, in his prime, y'know, knocked down for nine hundred."

"That's a shame. That's dirt cheap. Ah think we should be gettin' well over a thousand. Problem is those damn traders still runnin' 'em in from Africa. They're ruinin' the market."

"I know it. If they would jus' leave it to the breedin' states—Virginia and Kentucky—why, we'd keep the market sane. There's enough bein' born here. We don't have to reach to Africa anymore . . ."

Worden felt a gentle tap under his toes. "Dat be five cents, massa."

At Lynchburg he caught a night train on the Virginia & Tennessee, which took him to Bristol on the state line. Dreary border town; didn't seem to belong to either state. Nothing to do but wait in the station for his connection. He sat on one of the long oak benches and tried to read, but the combination of gas from the lamp and the flickering light gave him a headache. The room smelled of stale tobacco and unemptied spittoons. It was better outside on the platform. Dawn was bringing a fresh breeze and the promise of a gentle, sunlit morning.

After several more changes, one for track gauge, the East Tennessee & Georgia carried him over the border to Dalton. Having traveled two days and two nights, he was now in the Confederate States of America, wearing the uniform of a lieutenant in the United States Navy.

The change was abrupt and palpable; no more the soft, cultivated Virginia tones. Voices were shrill and strident. Rebellion was in the air. Georgians took no pains to conceal their feelings. The most frequent target of their ire was Lincoln, with the abolitionists running a close second. If that Illinois ape wanted war, he would get more than he bargained for.

As far as Worden knew, the seceded states had not yet adopted their own military uniforms. It was rumored that they planned to issue a regulation calling for naval officers and enlisted men to wear a uniform that substituted cadet gray for the traditional navy blue. But thus far, he was confident, the Union officers who had gone south were wearing the same uniforms they had worn as officers of the U.S. Navy. Nevertheless, he felt conspicuous and vulnerable. He rarely closed his eyes for more than a few minutes at a time.

South of Atlanta the train filled with a company of green troops who, with the swagger of young men on an outing, emboldened by some good ole home brew, grew louder and more boisterous as the train progressed south. Amid rebel yells and recruit bravado they made it known that they were on their way to Pensacola, where they were going to drive Mistah Lincoln's niggah-lovin' Yankees into the Gulf of Mexico.

One beefy lad with straw-colored hair, from the Georgia backwoods, waved a canteen, from which he took frequent pulls, and declaimed to all in earshot on the differences between the men of the South and the back-alley refuse of the North: "How they goin' field an army against us'n? Just tell me that!" The very idea seemed to inflame him. "Just tell me that . . . them white-livered, two-assed tailors—never sit a hoss. Doan know one end of a rahfle from anothuh. We uns allus inna saddle, shootin', huntin'. . . scummy-assed bastards doan belong in the same war . . ."

Worden assumed they thought he was an officer who had gone south. He made sure not to speak lest his accent stir curiosity.

On the station platform at Montgomery, he noticed stores of fieldpieces and rifles and ammunition being readied for shipment. According to the markings on the wooden crates, their destination was Pensacola.

When the train left the station he made his way to the water closet, where he carefully reread Welles's dispatch several times. When he was satisfied that he would be able to reproduce it, he tore it to shreds, which he let trickle slowly into the toilet, thus scattering the message along several miles of track south of Montgomery.

Worden arrived at Pensacola on the howling, rain-drenched midnight of April 10. While looking for the boat that was to ferry him to the squadron, he was accosted by a man in civilian dress. Shouting to make himself heard above the deafening wind, he identified himself as a Confederate officer and politely advised Worden that he was obliged to report to Gen. Braxton Bragg, commanding officer of the Confederate forces in the bay area, before communicating with the squadron. He suggested that Worden get some rest in a nearby hotel, and report at eight in the morning.

The only available room was in a two-story frame hotel that was listing to port in the gale. Its name had been weathered into illegibility, but the bedclothes were, the officer assured Worden, bedbug-free. The night clerk, sleepy, unshaven, tobacco juice seeping down the corners of his mouth, stared at him through slitted eyes and without a word handed him the pen for registering. Worden lay down for a few hours of fitful sleep.

A few minutes before eight, unrefreshed and breakfastless, bending into the shrieking wind, he made his way along the harbor road. The dazzling white beaches were now desolate strands of rain-pocked brown mud that curved into the mist-shrouded bay.

General Bragg made his headquarters in a nearby naval hospital that had been a fifty-bed dispensary of the U.S. Navy. The general had converted several rooms of the long, low white frame building for his use. Had the day been fine, Fort Pickens, across the bay, would have been easily visible from its windows. As it was, the driving rain and mist limited visibility to a few yards.

The general's office, bare save for a cabinet and a battered table at which he sat, was lit by virtue of a small window, which admitted the bleak light of the storm-darkened morning. The rain drummed on the roof and pelted the glass. A rivulet collected on the sill and dripped off the corner, making a circle of dampness on the floor. The place still smelled of ether and an assortment of clinical odors, which Worden, on an empty stomach, found decidedly unpleasant.

Dressed in the uniform of a Union general, Braxton Bragg, one of Jefferson Davis's most trusted officers, was a man of angular, not unpleasant features that were more often than not twisted into a scowl of impatience. He was clearly unhappy in his present surroundings, an office that stank of illness and its successor, mortality. He belonged elsewhere, in sunlit fields with men and horses and clanking sabers and regimental flags. A notorious martinet in command, dyspeptic and irascible, he regarded Worden with unmistakable ill humor. "Whence do you come, Lieutenant?"

"Washington City, sir."

"Do you carry dispatches?"

"None written. I do have a message for Captain Adams aboard the frigate *Sabine*." There was a pause as both men pondered the question that could not be asked. This renegade army officer, thought Worden, could be my executioner. Wingless angel of death with side beards, and stars on his collar.

With the air of one acting against his better judgment, the general scrawled an authorizing pass.

The boldest way is the safest. "Sir, I plan to return north via Pensacola. Will I be permitted to land?"

"You shall, providing you and Captain Adams do nothing to violate the agreement that exists between us."

"I'm sorry, sir, I know of no such agreement."

"Then Captain Adams will apprise you of same."

Worden hastened to the navy yard, where he sought out the gunboat USS *Wyandotte,* which was permitted to lie in the harbor under a flag of truce. She was, by prearrangement, to ferry him to the squadron.

Drenched to the skin, he finally found her. To his dismay, her captain refused to cross the bar into the gulf where the *Sabine* and the rest of the squadron lay, because of the strong wind and heavy sea. He did, however, take the lieutenant aboard, invite him to dinner, and put him up for the night.

At daybreak, an unhappy Worden awoke to the sounds of keening wind and crashing breakers, clear signals that passage into the gulf was still impossible.

Later in the morning a senior officer from Fort Pickens came aboard to invite him to tour the fort. Bored and frustrated by the storm, he gratefully accepted, and the *Wyandotte* put them ashore at the tip of Santa Rosa Island.

While walking the ramparts, his fears and impatience were sharpened. With the aid of a glass, and the help of the accompanying officer, an artilleryman who pointed out the aggressive nature of Confederate preparations, Worden was satisfied that a rebel assault on Pickens was forthcoming in a matter of days if not hours.

At about ten o'clock, the wind subsided enough for the *Wyandotte* to sail out to the *Sabine*. It was noon on April 12 when Worden boarded the frigate. He reported to the captain on the quarterdeck and Adams immediately invited him to the privacy of his cabin. There, with pen and paper, the lieutenant carefully transcribed the text of Welles's message.

After reading it, Adams was silent. As Worden waited for his response, the sound of the wind whistling through the rigging and the groaning protest of timber in a running sea seemed to grow louder. Adams replied at last. "If we are not already at war," he said slowly, "we shall be when I execute this order." He was clearly saddened at the prospect.

Worden related what Bragg had said with respect to the agreement between the two sides, and asked Adams how he should proceed. Adams responded by writing out an order directing Worden to return to Washington as a "special messenger"; he advised Worden to waste no time, adding that it was not necessary that he stop at Bragg's office. The lieutenant was tempted to ask when Adams planned to land the troops, but decided on second thought that such a question on the part of a junior officer would be presumptuous.

After a lunch of fresh amberjack caught by the crew, Worden embarked for the mainland, where he arrived late in the afternoon. Since there were no northbound trains until nine in the evening, and the storm had considerably abated, Worden used the enforced leisure to stroll about the piers.

Pensacola, part naval base and part resort, did not want for establishments that catered to idle hours. Bars, restaurants, and gaudily appointed billiard parlors abounded in the bay area. Worden was not a teetotaler, but neither was he a bar drinker. And though a game of billiards seemed appropriate enough, he didn't have the stomach for it. He was anxious. He told himself he would feel better when he was on the train heading north.

Worden continued to stroll until six o'clock, when he bought several newspapers whose contents, he noted, were dated by a day or two. He then sought out a restaurant that boasted fish, caught that very day. Seated near a window that faced the bay, and grateful for the wood fire that burned off the evening dampness, he read the papers and made a leisurely dinner of prawns and mackerel. Punctually at nine he boarded a Florida & Alabama train for the first leg of the journey north.

As Worden was settling in for the long ride, Gen. Leroy Pope Walker, secretary of war for the CSA, in Montgomery, acting at last on Stephen Mallory's note written almost twenty-four hours earlier, got off a wire to Bragg:

Lieutenant Worden of U.S. Navy has gone to Pensacola with dispatches. Intercept them.

Before midnight Walker had his response:

Mr. Worden had communicated with the fleet before your dispatch received. Alarm guns have just been fired at Fort Pickens. I fear the news is received and it will be reinforced before morning. It cannot be prevented. Mr. Worden got off in cars before I knew of his landing. Major Chambers is in the cars. He will watch Mr. Worden's movements. If you deem it advisable, Mr. Worden can be stopped in Montgomery.
                                        Braxton Bragg
                                        Brigadier-General

A few minutes later another telegram followed:

                                        Pensacola, April 13, 1861

Reenforcements thrown into Fort Pickens last night by small boats from the outside. The movement could not even be seen from our side, but was discovered by a small reconnoitering boat.
                                        Braxton Bragg
                                        Brigadier-General

*   *   *

Worden, sitting toward the front of his car rattling north, speculated on Adams's response to Welles's order. He had no doubt that this time the captain would execute the order. It was a question of when, and whether by that time he would be over the Georgia line into Tennessee. Perhaps he should have insisted on remaining with the squadron. That would have been the safer way. Well, no point worrying; only make a long ride longer. Determined to pass the time constructively, he pulled his book out of the duffel, loosened his collar and his tunic, and began to read.

In back of him, toward the rear of the otherwise empty car, sat a large man in a light gray suit, wearing a bowler and reading a newspaper.

CHAPTER
IV

Toward the end of March and in the early days of April, the eyes of the Western world were drawn to a tiny hatbox of a man-made island lying within the long, archipelagic coastline of South Carolina.

When South Carolina seceded in December of 1860, her governor, Francis Pickens, an imperious man, demanded that Maj. Robert Anderson, commander of the U.S. garrison in Charleston, surrender the several federal properties under his command.

Anderson refused. Instead, toward midnight of a moonless January night he assembled his entire force, which was garrisoned throughout mainland Charleston and the offshore islands, at Fort Moultrie on Sullivan's Island. There in the darkness of the small hours he ordered all guns knocked from their trunnions and spiked. Everything of possible use to the rebels was piled on the parade ground. Before evacuating the fort, the mound of guns, gear, and miscellaneous supplies was torched. Anderson and his men then embarked in rowboats. Oars muffled, officers whispering commands, the contingent, barely shadows in the windswept pitch-black bay, withdrew to the least exposed and best protected position in the Charleston area.

When dawn broke and the citizens of Charleston awoke, they saw the column of smoke spiraling up from Moultrie. And when they saw the rays of the rising sun strike the Stars and Stripes rippling high in the harbor breeze, they realized that Anderson had consolidated his force at the entrance to Charleston harbor on the diminutive island known as Fort Sumter.

From Anderson's standpoint, Sumter had two obvious virtues. Although far from impregnable, it was the most remote and therefore the least vulnerable of the Union positions. It was also reinforceable from the sea. The fort itself was a pentagon of fifty-foot-high brick walls that varied in thickness from twelve feet at the base to eight and a half feet at the top. Though pierced for one hundred forty guns, only forty-eight were operational.

For the citizens of South Carolina, first of the states to secede, font of secessionist doctrine, and home of the late John C. Calhoun, hallowed voice of states' rights, the Stars and Stripes flying over Sumter was an insult, a bone in the civic throat.

No sooner had Anderson made his move than Governor Pickens cut off the flow of all provisions and materiel to the island. Mail alone was permitted. It was apparent that it was only a question of weeks before the garrison was starved out.

Anderson's move and the governor's response galvanized the radical anti-Union forces in the state. The streets of Charleston rang with belligerent and abusive anti-Lincoln ("that baboon"), anti-Union speech. Town squares and undeveloped lots throughout the city echoed to the clatter of muskets and the sharp commands of close order drill. Carolinians were raising their voices in unequivocal demand. They wanted war and they wanted it now. The immediate object of their wrath was in plain sight, lying just three miles across the bay from Charleston, flaunting the hated Yankee Stars and Stripes.

In Montgomery, Jefferson Davis, newly elected president of the Confederate States of America, heard the cry for war. This Jefferson Davis, now half blind and wracked with the pain of neuralgia; this war hero who with a smashed foot and a bootful of blood led his Mississippi Rifles to victory at Buena Vista in the Mexican War; this tenderest of men who knew the pain of watching his beloved bride of three months die before his eyes; this slave holder who educated and encouraged his slaves to form a self-governing community; this intellectual in a planter aristocracy; this West Point graduate who disdained a military career but became secretary of war in the Franklin Pierce administration; this complex man who accepted the mandate to lead the South with tears of reluctance and foreboding: This was the tortured and conflicted soul who answered the war cry of the Carolinians in a predictably ambivalent manner.

He dispatched his three commissioners to negotiate with Secretary Seward for the evacuation of the federal garrison from Sumter. But at the same time he opted for a more direct military solution. He ordered Gen. Pierre Gustave Toutant Beauregard to Charleston, where the general was to prepare for the capture of the fort.

Beauregard, the extravagance of his name notwithstanding, was a capable and determined officer. Of swarthy complexion, brooding Gallic eyes, hair brushed forward at the temples—Napoleonic in aspect and ambition—the general acted quickly and decisively. He impressed a small army of laborers who immediately began erecting fortifications on the three islands surrounding the fort.

Tactically, Sumter's position was ultimately hopeless. Ringed by three armed islands, all within easy range, it was caught in a steel triangle. Having been designed to protect against incursion from the sea, Sumter had no mortars with which it could lob missiles over barriers onto the rebel batteries. It could respond only with horizontal fire directed at gun positions that the rebels had entrenched in heavy sandbanks or in shelters overlaid with railroad iron.

Sumter's garrison consisted of nine officers, sixty-eight enlisted men, eight musicians, and forty-three noncombatant laborers. It was, however, the garrison's fifty-six-year-old commander who was the focus of national attention.

Major Robert Anderson, of erect military bearing and with clean-shaven aquiline features and a shock of iron-gray hair, had become a metaphor for the nation's agony. Gradually but inexorably he was being drawn into a fight for which he had no stomach but which as a professional soldier and man of honor he could not avoid. A devout churchman and West Pointer, he was born and raised in the border state of Kentucky, married a Georgia girl, and owned a plantation in Georgia but had sold the slaves. Unswervingly loyal to the United States, he nevertheless confided to a brother officer that if Kentucky should secede, his preference would be to go to Europe.

As commander at Sumter, Anderson had a twofold task: to maintain the morale and integrity of his slowly starving garrison, and at the same time keep a cool head in the face of mounting insult and provocation. Letters and messages poured into Sumter from all over the country congratulating him on his forbearance and dignity in an impossible situation. Newspapers east and west paid tribute to him. Even the Charleston *Mercury,* a rabid secessionist sheet, conceded that he was a gentleman whose word was his bond.

Beauregard was tightening the noose. Having interdicted the flow of all supplies and provisions, he posted pickets with orders to deny all visitors (including family of the garrison) access to the fort unless they could produce a pass from Governor Pickens—a clear challenge to the majesty of the United States. On April 7, the general advised Major Anderson, his former artillery instructor at West Point, that although the embargo on provisions was to remain in force, the major might continue to look forward to an uninterrupted flow of mail. The Confederate command hoped that Anderson's mail might contain instructions from Washington to abandon the fort.

On that same day, Sunday, April 7, Anderson and his supply officer made formal inspection of the fort. Priority was the stock of food stores. Anderson instructed the officer to make an independent assessment. Later on they compared notes, and found that each had come to the same conclusion. Food would be exhausted in less than a week.

On the following morning, Lincoln's messenger, Robert Chew, along with his military aide, arrived in Charleston. They proceeded at once to the harbor, where they saw the Stars and Stripes flying over a Sumter that was not under visible attack. They made their way immediately to the capitol and sought an interview with the governor. Pickens took great care to establish their bona fides, demanding identification papers from both Chew and the captain, and questioning them closely as to the circumstances of their commission from Lincoln. Apparently satisfied, he accepted the letter.

As soon as the two emissaries left his office, Pickens summoned Beauregard and acquainted him with Lincoln's message. The text was then telegraphed to Montgomery. It was received by Jefferson Davis in his office on the second floor of the State House, a red-brick architectural hodgepodge that overlooked a downtown corner of the city. An aide rapped on the door, on which was pasted a piece of yellow foolscap paper with "The President" handwritten across it, and handed Davis the message pencil-written as it came from the telegrapher.

As Davis read, his left eyelid began to flutter as it did when the pain began to mount to his private red zone. The entire left side of his head was lost to the throbbing ache that focused in the eye. Most alarming was that now his right eye too was showing strange and frightening symptoms. It was as if there were holes in the field of vision, the middle and the lower right side being absent, like a wall with clusters of brick missing, leaving irregular blanks. The pain, as always, was followed by the thought that he should have died with her. They had both caught the fever at the same time. Confined to separate rooms, each too sick to be told about the other, he managed, crawling, to make it to her room in time to see her die. They had been married not quite three months. The sickness had never left him.

Now Mr. Lincoln was telling him that "an attempt will be made to supply Fort Sumter with provisions only." The rage began to mount with the ache. They fed off each other. That Yankee president must think him stupid or a dupe. Three messages from Washington, each one telling a different story.

Davis convened his Council of War, his hawk face eroded to the bone, left eye veiled with the film of his illness and slitted with pain, lending him an even more determined if not maniacal look. "Is there no end to the duplicity of the Lincoln government? On the one hand we have the assurance of his secretary of state that Sumter will be evacuated. On the other is the wire from our 'friend' in Washington asserting that the fort is to be supplied by force. And now, to complete the cycle, there is the president's emissary in Charleston with a new message contradicting the first two." He paused, needing the rest, letting his words and his ire take hold of the others.

"Gentlemen, I am for no more attempts at good-faith negotiation with a government that responds with fraud and prevarication. I am prepared, and intend, to take Fort Sumter." It was no ringing declaration. It was said quietly, in soft, Southern tones. An experienced military commander stating his intention.

There was no immediate response. Neither Memminger (Treasury), nor Mallory (Navy), nor Benjamin (Justice), nor Walker (War), nor Vice President Stephens had anything to say. They had been pondering the question for weeks.

"Mr. President, I beg to differ." It was Toombs, shaggy, square faced, jowly Robert Toombs of Georgia, secretary of state. When he made his farewell address on the floor of the U.S. Senate, he had concluded with a grand oratorical flourish, "The Union, sir, is dissolved!" And he warned those in the North who might propose to maintain it by force: "Come and do it! Georgia is on the warpath! Treason? Bah!" With that he stalked out of the senate chamber to the treasury building, where he demanded his salary to date plus mileage back to Georgia.

But here in cabinet council he was inclined to caution. "Firing on Sumter will inaugurate a civil war greater than any the world has yet seen. Mr. President, at this time it would be both suicide and murder, and you will lose us every friend in the North. It is unnecessary; it puts us in the wrong. It is fatal."

Davis was in no mood to listen to counsels of restraint. The criticism brought a flush of color to his face, a daub of red in a winter landscape. "To wait for the sake of having them fire the first gun, Mr. Toombs, is as unwise as it would be to hesitate to strike down an assailant with a deadly weapon leveled at one's breast, until he actually fires. I am obliged to remind you, sir, that he who makes war is not necessarily he who strikes the first blow." The president adjourned the meeting.

Stewing and fretting, he waited for two days before taking action, convinced that Union forces were using the interval to strengthen their positions by land and sea.

On the evening of Wednesday, April 10, Davis ordered Walker to telegraph Beauregard in Charleston: "If you have no doubt of the authorized character of the agent who communicated to you the intention of the Washington government to supply Fort Sumter by force, you will at once demand its evacuation, and, if this is refused, proceed in such a manner as you may determine, to reduce it."

Beauregard promptly complied. The following morning he sent two men in a small boat to Anderson with a note demanding evacuation of the fort. He assured the major that all "proper facilities" would be afforded for the removal of himself and his command, and that the flag that he had upheld with so much fortitude might be saluted on taking it down.

Anderson replied with thanks for the courteous terms. His sense of honor, however, and obligation to his government prevented, albeit regretfully, his compliance.

As soon as Beauregard's messengers quit the fort, the major ordered an assembly of all personnel. He ordered the entire garrison to take up quarters in the casemates, which afforded the best protection. Water pipes and faucets were to be secured for fire-fighting purposes. The six remaining sewing needles were to be employed to make powder bags from unessential clothing and blankets. At dinner the last of the provisions, with the exception of a bit of salt pork, were consumed.

During the previous weeks Anderson had taken steps to strengthen the fort's defensive capabilities. A stone shield was erected over the main gate against shelling from Cummings Point. Masons had cut openings through the walls of the officers' quarters to provide freer communication. To facilitate reception of the expected reinforcements, ladders and runways were deployed, and an embrasure enlarged to admit barrels of powder and supplies. All personnel had been drilled daily for weeks and knew their battle assignments perfectly.

Anderson toured the casemates as frequently as time allowed. Alert to any breach of security, constantly in the sight of his command, and exhibiting a confidence he did not feel, Anderson was satisfied that he had done all he could to prepare for an assault he prayed would not come.

Some five hundred miles directly north, standing at the tall, draped, south window of his office, the president too felt he had done what he had been obliged to do. Gazing across the Potomac to the misty blue hills of Virginia, shyly verdant now, he reflected on his actions. Like Welles, he felt the die had been cast. One could only pray that the forces set in motion were rightly conceived and properly executed. Good old Father Neptune. He hated to deny him his request for a force to defend the yard at Norfolk. Perhaps he should have agreed to let him at least shake the *Merrimack* loose. She would be a dreadful loss. But he was gambling for higher stakes. Virginia was more important than any ship, no matter how formidable. He must take the calculated risk.

Turning from the window he began to pace in his moccasin-clad feet, hands clasped behind, murmuring to himself as he often did when reviewing a decision, justifying a course of action. A lawyer assuming the roles of both plaintiff and defendant. How do you explain, sir, your aggressive stance toward Pickens and Sumter in the light of your passivity in the instance of Virginia?

Ah, entirely different circumstances. As president, my current obligation to the government is to do nothing that would needlessly antagonize Virginia; it is rather to do everything I can to encourage her to remain in the Union. But in ordering supply fleets to Pickens and Sumter I was faithful to my oath of office. How could I possibly explain letting them fall into the hands of the Confederates once having been advised of their intention to take them?

At the same time he felt he had done everything he reasonably could to provide the South with an honorable alternative to war. He had said it best in his inauguration speech: "In your hands, my dissatisfied fellow countrymen, and not in mine, is the momentous issue of civil war. The government will not assail you. You can have no conflict without being yourselves the aggressors. You have no oath registered in Heaven to destroy the government, while I have the most solemn one, to preserve, protect, and defend it. . . ."

Pausing before the fireplace, stooping slightly, he spread his large hands over the glowing logs. The winter chill was still in him. And yet, and yet . . . he agonized. Had he been firm enough? Compassionate enough? Explicit enough? Forthright enough? Surely, if they understood his position, they would know there was no need for war. He had explained time and again, during the campaign, again at the inauguration, and many times since, that his objective was to deprive them of neither their wealth nor their property nor their slaves. "I have no purpose, directly or indirectly, to interfere with the institution of slavery in the states where it exists. I believe I have no lawful right to do so, and I have no inclination to do so." His declared aim was to preserve the Union and to prevent the extension of slavery to the new territories. That had been the platform on which he had run; that had been his position in the debates with Douglas; and those were the principles on which he stood. The face of Jackson looked out from the darkened gilt frame above the mantel. How would he have handled it? More aggressively, no doubt. No pussyfooting, for him.

Really, Abe, how forthright have you been? Down deep where no one has looked and even you fear to tread, do you honestly believe that this nation can exist with slaves in the South and only free men in the North? If that be so, what then was the meaning of your "House Divided" speech?—"I believe that this government cannot permanently endure half slave and half free." Weren't those your very words, sir? And knowing your true sentiments about slavery, sir, isn't it fair to conclude that you are playing with Davis, simply jockeying him into firing the first shot? He pressed the heels of both hands to his temples and cried aloud, "God help us! God help me!"

There was a soft knock at the door. John Hay, the junior of his two young secretaries, came in with an armful of newspapers from cities across the nation, North and South.

"Good morning, Hay." The president's tone was warm and cordial. Young Hay had been an apprentice in his Springfield law office when the president-elect invited him to Washington. Hay's return greeting was lit by the smile of a twenty-three year old who was still somewhat overcome by the privilege of serving in the executive mansion the man whom above all others he revered.

"What are they saying today?"

Laying the bundle on the long oak table, Hay, his brown hair parted on the left side and slicked down except for a stubborn lick that stuck out over his right ear, replied, "Nothing special, Mr. President, just more of the same."

The president walked to the table and gazed at the top sheet. Preoccupied, he turned it. "I see that Mr. Davis is asking for twenty-one thousand volunteers and thirty thousand in reserve." Hay said nothing. He wasn't sure if the president wanted to talk or be left alone. Lincoln rarely dismissed him, leaving it to his discretion as to whether or not to withdraw.

"Is it 'gorilla' or 'baboon' today," asked Lincoln, "and did you ever find out which stands higher on the evolutionary ladder? I am hoping for progress." He could joke about it but he had never really gotten used to it—the hate, the fury, the red pulse of violence seething under the demagoguery. Most vexing was their deliberate misinterpretation of what he tried so painstakingly to convey. Like many who are self-taught, he had reverence for the word, and he placed high value on clarity and precision in expression. To see one's words twisted and debased by political adversaries and in the national press was, he was learning, an affliction particularly reserved for presidents.

Lincoln stood contemplating the stack of newspapers and debated whether to read them through. Of what use would it be to learn that he was still hanging or being burned in effigy in public squares from the Carolinas to Texas? To what avail would it be to know that he was still being depicted as an ape, mindless leader of a Black Republican free-love-free-nigger party bent on ravaging the substance of the South and wiping out millions in slave investment?

The latest favorite rabble-rousing technique of the secessionist speechifiers was to point to Santo Domingo, where slaves had just risen to slaughter their masters, and preach that Lincoln—that devil incarnate—was taking his cue from that wretched Caribbean nation—was panting to free four million slaves, give them all the federal jobs in the South, and spur them to copulation and marriage with white women. At this very moment, they swore, his abolitionist agents and spies were fanning out through Dixie and goading slaves to rebellion. No. Little use in plowing through that stuff. It was enough to give him the hypochondria. Last time he got it, it had laid him low for a week. He couldn't afford the hypo now.

He turned to Hay. "Anything you believe I ought to see?"

"It's pretty much the usual stuff, Mr. President."

"Please be more specific."

Hay, his earnest, boyish features parodied by a long, slender, drooping mustache, hesitated for a moment. "The Southern journals say nothing new—only more of the same. I find yesterday's *New York Herald* the most offensive of the lot." Hay dug into the stack and came up with the edition of April 10: "From an editorial, sir. 'Our only hope now against civil war of an indefinite duration seems to lie in the overthrow of the demoralizing, disorganizing, and destructive sectional party of which "Honest Abe Lincoln" is the pliant instrument.' "

Lincoln walked again to the fireplace and warmed his hands. A log popped, broke open abruptly, and fell off the andiron in a shower of sparks. Addressing the cracked portrait of Jackson, Lincoln said, "Mr. Bennett's *Herald* has been advising ever since the election that I could best serve the nation by stepping down and going home to Illinois. Those New York people can't get used to the idea that somehow, unaccountably, I beat Mr. Seward out of the nomination, and they'll never forgive me for it."

The thoughts of both men turned to the large, high desk near the window, where in one of the many pigeonholes nestled the carefully folded editorial the president had asked Hay to clip from an early March edition of the *Herald*. It was this journal that the retiring President Buchanan spoke of in the few parting words he offered to his successor. "It may not enjoy the largest circulation," he said, "but it is indubitably the most influential in the country for the formation of public opinion."

On the eve of Lincoln's inauguration, the newspaper made its sentiments known regarding the incoming chief executive: "A grand opportunity now exists," declared the *Herald*, "for Lincoln to avert impending ruin, and invest his name with an immortality far more enduring than would attach to it by his elevation to the presidency. His withdrawal at this time from the scene of conflict, and the surrender of his claims to some national man who would be acceptable to both sections, would render him the peer of Washington in patriotism. . . . If he persists in his present position he will totter into a dishonored grave, driven there perhaps by the hands of an assassin, leaving behind him a memory more execrable than that of Benedict Arnold. . . ."

He had kept the editorial by way of a perverse inauguration gift to himself. "If I get a swelled head," he explained to Hay and John Nicolay, his senior secretary, "I can always whip it out for an instant cure."

"Is there anything else, sir?" Hay suspected the president wanted to chat this morning.

"What do you hear around town—down at Willard's and on the avenue?"

"I believe public opinion is swinging our way. People understand that you've left it up to the secessionists. If war comes it's because they want it. I think your 'Send bread to Anderson' campaign has done it. It cuts through the grand verbiage of states' rights versus preservation of the Union, to something people readily understand." The president's head bobbed in that involuntary, nervous gesture that followed when he was pleased. He walked to the window to savor the information. Lord knows, thought Hay, old Uncle needs some good news right about now. The pressures on him this first month would have broken an ordinary mortal. If it wasn't Sumter or Pickens or the navy yard at Norfolk, or the Congress, or the cabinet, or the diplomatic correspondence, it was— and Hay felt that this was the worst in terms of sheer debilitating nuisance—that infernal horde of jackals milling around outside the president's door.

At first Uncle Abe had borne them with good cheer, mixing with them and swapping stories and gossip with the relish of a born campaigner. He had, he frequently reminded his staff, once been one of them. During the Taylor administration he had unsuccessfully sought a job as commissioner of the Land Office. But recently, with the press of events, the crowd out there was becoming too many for him.

He was going less and less to the family rooms for his lunch of biscuit and a glass of milk so that he wouldn't have to run the gauntlet. He didn't miss the food—the man ate less than a normal, healthy sparrow—but he did miss the time with his family. Not so much Mary Todd; Hay suspected they could both manage the absence. But Lincoln felt that Tad and Willie needed him.

These days around twelve o'clock Hay would often see the president reach into his desk drawer and make a noon meal of a bunch of grapes or an apple, which he pared with his pocketknife. Then, crossing his long legs on the desk and steadying a spyglass between his feet, he would munch while he studied the Virginia countryside across the river. Virginia was much on his mind.

"The political pundits," said Hay, his slim figure draped in a new-style frock coat that sported wide lapels and satin-striped cuffs, "are saying that you've been very shrewd, giving the South only the choice of evils. If they start the war they stand to lose many of their Democrat friends in the North, and they'll offend public opinion in Europe. If, on the other hand, they hesitate and refuse to march, then the rebellion will collapse for want of a certain trumpet."

"The immediate problem," said the president, "is the border states, especially Virginia. If she goes, that will leave Washington isolated between two slave states. The game could be up with all the pieces on the board."

Across the President's Park at Navy, Gideon Welles was preparing to take a bold and insubordinate step. To the dashing young officer seated across from him, he said, "You understand, Commander, that what here passes between us must remain between us. I say that for reasons of security, both military and . . . ah . . . departmental."

"I understand perfectly, sir." Commander James Alden did not, in fact, understand perfectly, since Welles had revealed to the young commander neither the subject nor the object of his summons. Alden's patrician features wore a frank smile of anticipation at the prospect of intrigue.

"I and people high in the administration are quite concerned about the fate of the frigate *Merrimack,* now in for repairs at the Norfolk yard. Should any nastiness develop, it would be most unfortunate were she to fall into the wrong hands."

Alden nodded, "I know her."

"It therefore becomes our task, without stirring up the citizenry down there, to remove her to a more, ah . . . shall we say, *congenial* port, such as Philadelphia." Welles reached for his pipe and filled it carefully, taking the time to study the young officer before him. He had never met him before, but the commander came recommended as "reliable." He was, after all, descended of John and Priscilla Alden of Massachusetts, he of the Mayflower Company. As to Alden's competence, that would soon be tested.

"The yard," continued Welles, "is in the command of Commodore

McCauley, whom I don't know but whose loyalty and patriotism I have no reason to doubt. I am told, however, that he is elderly, bereft of energy and decision, and generally unequal to the situation. Is that in accord with your information?"

"I'm sorry, sir, I don't know Commodore McCauley and have no opinion about him."

Welles, dragging on his pipe, nodded thoughtfully. He appreciated the honest reply in spite of the fact that he was fishing for information. It was rumored that McCauley had a bottle problem. He had hoped that Alden would either confirm or deny the rumor. "No matter. Yesterday, McCauley advised by telegram that it will take about a month to get the *Merrimack* into sailing condition. As soon as I received his wire I ordered Engineer-in-Chief Isherwood down to Norfolk to get the ship into good enough shape to be moved—by sail or steam or hook or crook—out of Norfolk.

"And that is why I have sent for you. I want you to go down there, report to McCauley, and explain that you are to take command of the *Merrimack* for the purpose of moving her to the naval station at Philadelphia. I give you no written orders for the reasons of security mentioned earlier. Do you have any questions, Commander?"

"No, sir."

Welles rose and offered his hand. "With any luck—and decent train connections—you should be there by tomorrow, the twelfth." Alden saluted and departed.

CHAPTER
V

At about the time Alden left Washington for Norfolk, General Beauregard received Major Anderson's refusal to surrender.

Beauregard was on the horns of a dilemma. President Davis's orders had been quite clear: He was to reduce the fort if Anderson refused to evacuate. But the general, mindful of public opinion, vastly preferred a bloodless solution. Were he to take Sumter by force, and in the process possibly kill a national hero and his brave band of defenders, the affront to sensibilities at home and abroad would be incalculable. Furthermore, he was aware that the garrison would be starved out in a day or two. Beauregard decided to make another attempt at a negotiated surrender.

Near midnight on April 11 he sent four men in a boat to Anderson with a note saying there would be no "useless effusion of blood" were the major to fix a date and time for surrender.

Anderson, exhausted by the tension and weakened by the diet of half rations on which he had secretly put himself some weeks before, decided to consult with his officers. The meeting lasted three hours, during which Anderson listened more than he spoke. He then arrived at a decision, which was communicated to Beauregard's four emissaries waiting in a cheerless mess hall, where they had been comforted by not so much as a cup of hot black coffee. The major was prepared to evacuate Fort Sumter at noon on April 15, providing he received neither supplies nor instructions to the contrary from his government before that time.

Beauregard's emissaries, having full powers to act, gave Anderson their response in five minutes. They had the honor to advise that General Beauregard would open fire on Fort Sumter in one hour.

Anderson received the notice with a sense of relief. At least the waiting, the petty provocations, the cat-and-mouse game were over. He ordered the sentinels out of their exposed positions on the parapets. Every gate and opening was secured. The men were ordered not to leave the shelter of the casemates unless summoned by official order.

Word spread quickly to the townspeople. The die was cast. In the predawn darkness of a cold and squally morning they poured out of their houses and thronged to the waterfront. The months of rousing speeches against the barbaric North along with the drills and preparations were about to bear fruit. The Yankees were at last to get their comeuppance.

Sumter's sheer walls rising from the dark and choppy waters of the harbor were still invisible. It was half past four in the morning of April 12, exactly an hour after Beauregard's messengers had left the fort.

A stillness gripped the harbor. Even the restless water lapping at the wooden pilings near the shore, breaking on the beaches, surging against the stone jetties, seemed to hush.

From Johnson Island a single mortar shell split the gloom, rising, soaring to the fading stars, its fuse clearly marking the ascent. With exquisite deliberation it reached for its apex and then slowly, reluctantly, arched for the descent. Gathering speed it slammed into the Sumter parade ground, exploding with a flash of light and a muffled roar. It left a neat, conelike crater. It was, said one of the garrison, a capital shot.

Within seconds every available gun in the rebel arsenal of sixteen batteries and seventeen mortars fired. The Civil War had begun.

Worden's northbound train had just crossed the Florida-Alabama line when Captain Adams executed Welles's order. At midnight of April 12, twelve hours after receiving the dispatch from Worden, Adams landed an artillery company of eighty-eight men along with a detachment of one hundred fifteen marines on the gulfside beach of Santa Rosa Island. The Confederates were taken by surprise. There was no attempt to prevent the action. Fort Pickens was reinforced and secured for the Union.

The train chugging up through central Alabama was agonizingly slow, although Worden found the sleepy, sunlit countryside not without charm. It was cotton planting time. The rich, ochre fields, some flecked with tender green leaves, were dotted with darkies—men, women, and children—strawhatted, barefoot, in faded garments of sun-bleached hues. Children, cloth sacks slung across thin shoulders, followed the narrow furrows, scattering fertilizer through shallow trenches. Women, bowing deeply from the waist as though in obeisance to a pagan deity, swung long-handled hoes up and down in endless rhythmic strokes. The men, rein-wrapped in harness to the planter, followed in the dainty steps of the mule—man, planter, and mule locked in a timeless floating embrace. Was this pastoral, sunlit scene the evil? Was it because of this that war might be fought? Thank God it wasn't for him to decide.

The scene stirred memories. Many a shoulder-wracked hour had he, harnessed to the plough, followed in the tracks of the big, high-buttocked horse, whose bay hindquarters were as familiar to him as the faces of his nine brothers and sisters. Once his muscles had toughened to the chore, he liked working in the fields. There was a bond between him and earth and horse, all three reduced to a sun-baked purity.

He had always thought growing plants a miracle. No matter how many springs he witnessed the first shy shoots of corn and hay push through the soil, he felt a surge of gladness at the evidence of renewal. His daddy's farm. Thirty acres. Too small. Couldn't support a herd of cows large enough for a decent cash crop of milk. But it had been all theirs, and there was always food from the garden. Old Ananais used to say, it was a poor farmer who couldn't raise enough food for his family. Yes, food there was, and a way out. It was understood that the children, especially the boys, would seek their living elsewhere. The farm couldn't support them all.

Walking those fields was never too hard, because you carried your dream. He'd always known he'd be in the Navy. Often he would take a book on history or geography or navigation out with him and read it at the end of a plow furrow while the horse caught its breath. At sixteen he had his midshipman appointment.

His eyes refocused on the slaves. How different for these poor devils. No way out. No dreams except bad ones. The same tableau of field, slave, planter, and mule, interrupted by stream, wood, or farmhouse, was endlessly repeated as his train doggedly made its way north.

By four in the afternoon of April 13, having traveled nineteen hours and one hundred thirty miles, the train arrived at Greenville, a dusty little town forty miles south of Montgomery. Worden noticed three men waiting on the wooden platform near the telegrapher's window. They looked as though they had been riding hard. Their nondescript uniforms and sombreros were covered with a film of dust. They boarded the train and came into his car. Spurs jingling, sabers and pistols on their belts, they walked to his seat. One stood next to him, and the others in front of and behind him. The large man in gray who had been sitting to the rear of the car came up, identified himself as Major Chambers of the Army of the Confederate States of America, and advised the lieutenant that he was under arrest. Worden said nothing. The party got off the train at the next stop, Montgomery.

The Confederate capital was wild with excitement. Newspapers were carrying details of the assault on Sumter. Triumphant rebel yells ricocheted off the houses and echoed through the streets. Men cleaned and oiled their hunting rifles. The Confederacy had been baptized in flame. The first long step on the road to independence had been taken.

The local press was also featuring a story on "Lincoln's spy." Worden's arrival had been anticipated. He was a celebrity. A crowd of the curious was gathered at the station. His captors, fearing an attack on their prisoner, formed a wedge about him and pushed through to a waiting carriage. He was taken to the office of the adjutant general.

Davis called an immediate meeting of his cabinet to determine what was to be done with the Union officer. While the meeting was in progress, Worden's guards brought him supper on a tray and told him he was free to write his family or whomever he wished. He penned a short note to Olivia, assuring her that he was being treated well, that he looked forward to early release, and that he was certain he was in no physical danger—an assurance that was not wholly justified, since there was sentiment in the press and on the street for executing him as a spy.

At the conclusion of the cabinet meeting, Secretary of War Walker wired General Bragg that Lieutenant Worden, having been detected conveying secret communications of a hostile nature against the Confederate states, was to be imprisoned. The lieutenant was remanded to the custody of the deputy marshal, in whose rooms he would remain a prisoner for two days. Thereafter he was removed to the county jail, since the military had no detention facilities.

When Worden demanded the reason for his arrest, he received no formal answer. Unofficially he was told by his guards that he was being detained because he and Captain Adams had violated their word of honor regarding the agreement whereby Pickens was to be neither attacked nor reinforced without prior notice.

On April 16, after three days of doing little but lying on his cot in dazed shock, Worden came out of his lethargy long enough to write Walker, swearing on his honor as an officer and a gentleman that he had known of no such agreement. It was to no avail. The CSA had taken its first prisoner of war, and the Union had lost the first of its military to be taken captive in a war that was undeclared and that neither government wanted.

The Montgomery *Advertiser* now identified Worden as "Lincoln's messenger." Another journal, the *Confederation*, reported that he was not being held as a spy but merely as a prisoner of war.

In Washington, the affair of Lt. John Lorimer Worden was hardly a priority matter in light of the developing storm. Welles, who was most directly involved with Worden's imprisonment, felt that the rebels were holding him out of sheer frustration, since their assault on Pickens had been anticipated by a few hours. In any case, neither Welles's sentiments nor those of any other federal official were communicated to the rebels; the Lincoln administration did not recognize the existence of the Confederate States of America.

At Fort Sumter, Anderson and his command took the opening barrage without panic and with a degree of deliberation. The major had done his job well. His men were mentally prepared, dug in, and sheltered. Despite the lack of provisions, morale was remarkably high. The immediate task was to assess damage and determine if any modifications were needed in the defense of the fort. At the first lull, Anderson toured the compound. He found the garrison to a man resigned to a pounding but quietly confident of relief.

Anderson himself was preoccupied by two considerations, fire and food. About the former, he was satisfied that every possible preventive measure had been taken. The fire brigade was alert and knew its job, having been drilled daily since early February. Buckets and vessels of every description had been filled with water or sand and were at the ready. Tanks of water had been distributed to strategic points.

Food was another matter; it could come only from the outside. The garrison had no doubt that a relief squadron was on the way. Every preparation was made to welcome it and to provide for easy access.

A detail had been assigned whose sole function was to report the first appearance of the ships. Anderson's task now, as he saw it, was to make certain his men suffered no needless casualties.

He did not immediately return the rebel fire. The opening rounds were poorly aimed and generally wide of the mark. Aside from a few dents and splinters, there was no injury or damage.

At about six in the morning, the garrison took a breakfast of pork and water, there being not a single biscuit left. At seven, Capt. Abner Doubleday, portly and mustachioed (of whom it was said that twenty-two years ago at Cooperstown, New York, he had laid out the first field dedicated to the new game of baseball), took his station at the south casemate. He aimed a thirty-two-pounder at the Cummings Point battery, stepped back, and shouted "Fire!" The gunner yanked the lanyard, the cannon roared, and an iron ball hissed across the bay and bounced harmlessly off the slanting iron roof of the rebel fortification. The Union had fired its first shot of the war.

As the sun rose, rebel fire began to adjust and become more accurate. Shot began striking the walls of the fort regularly, and mortar shells began to explode with alarming precision over the parapets. Anderson reluctantly ordered abandonment of all barbette guns, which were exposed. And since ammunition was in short supply, he kept only six guns in operation, two for each rebel position. At about ten in the morning, the officers' quarters caught fire. Iron water tanks stored there were perforated by the shell fragments. Happily, the escaping water extinguished the fire.

In the early afternoon, to the loud and elated cheers of the garrison, the sea watch announced a freighter and three U.S. men-o'-war off the bar. The fort dipped its flag in signal: What is the fleet's intention?

Fox could respond with little and do less. The three tugs he had been counting on to land the provisions had not shown up for the rendezvous. Equally distressing, the flagship *Powhatan*, under the command of Captain Mercer, who was responsible for the enforcing aspects of the expedition, had not arrived either. The *Powhatan* carried landing launches and the sailors to man them.

With his executive officer standing by, Fox paced the storm-lashed quarterdeck of the unarmed *Baltic* and swore in frustration. "I have no authority to order fire on the rebel batteries. We're here to provision the damned fort, not to engage in a firefight." He picked up the long glass and studied Sumter. "If they keep taking hot shot and incendiary shells, that place will be a bloody inferno in a matter of hours." He turned to his first officer, "Mr. Sheldon, high tide is in an hour or two, is it not?"

"Yes, sir." Fox considered landing without waiting for the launches or the tugs. But high tide coinciding with bright daylight meant that his deep-draft vessels would be at the mercy of the rebel batteries. They would be smashed to kindling. His own longboats were useless in the heavy sea. He resumed pacing and swearing and praying that the *Powhatan* and the tugs would show up before Sumter was reduced to ashes.

As night fell, Anderson ceased fire in the interest of conserving ammunition. He reposted his sentinels on the parapets to watch for reinforcing and storming parties. But the rebels had no thought of mounting an assault. They were content to fire a mortar shell every fifteen minutes throughout the night—a nuisance factor. At dawn both sides resumed fire, forty-seven rebel guns to six.

At nine the roof of the officers' quarters caught fire. The distance from the source of water, and exposure to shot and shell, made it impossible to extinguish. The rebels, realizing the garrison's predicament, concentrated their fire. The spreading flames began to threaten the magazine. Anderson ordered all hands not at the guns to remove the powder from the magazine, which held fifty barrels; these were distributed throughout the casemates and covered with wet blankets.

A strong wind swept smoke and sparks into every corner of the fort. The men were forced to crouch or lie on the floor and cover their faces with wet handkerchiefs. Suffocating, and blinded by tears and by dense clouds of smoke, they groped, hoisting shot, loading, firing. They took turns crawling to the embrasures for a breath of fresh air.

The pieces of cotton that most had stuffed into their ears were of little use in preventing them from being deafened and stunned. The impact of incoming shells combined with their own, which were now exploding in the burning rooms, caused some to bleed at the nose and ears. Others fell unconscious as though poleaxed. Masonry falling in every direction made of the casemate a dust-choked, trauma-filled chamber from which there was no escape.

Floating flakes of fire began to ignite the beds and other articles of wood and fabric, once again threatening the blanket-wrapped barrels of gunpowder. Fighting for every breath, feeling their way through opaque walls of dust and smoke, dodging flying brick and stone, liable at any moment to be blown to kingdom come, they wrestled all but five barrels to the embrasures and threw them into the sea.

Toward dusk, when it became apparent that no relief was in the offing, Anderson's choice was surrender or sacrifice the garrison. By eight o'clock he made the decision. After forty hours of pounding by more than three thousand missiles, his food supply exhausted, his men sleepless for two days, quarters completely burned, main gates destroyed, magazine doors welded shut by the heat of the flames, the flag shot down and replaced ten times, Anderson accepted Beauregard's terms.

On the following morning, Sunday, April 14, Anderson gave orders for a hundred-gun salute to the flag before it was lowered for the last time. Halfway through the ceremony an ember from the still-smoldering fort fell onto one of the hastily made powder bags, causing a shell to explode prematurely. Five cannoneers were wounded. Another, Daniel Hough, was killed outright. The Civil War had claimed its first dead.

The major marched his men out of the fort, some weeping bitter tears, others smiling grimly, but all heads held high, colors flying, drums beating. They boarded one of the ships of the federal squadron for the journey home. Along the beaches, rebel troops took off their caps in silent salute. There was no cheering. In his trunk Anderson carried the burned and shredded flag. It was his wish that it be used as his burial shroud.

In Montgomery an elated Leroy Pope Walker predicted that the Confederate flag would fly over the dome of the Capitol in Washington before the first of May.

CHAPTER
VI

As Anderson marched his men out of Fort Sumter that Sunday morning, news of the surrender was received in Washington. The president, foregoing church, escorted Mary Todd and the boys to the north portico, brilliant with the forenoon sun of a spring morning, and saw them off in a carriage. The family worshiped at the New York Avenue Presbyterian Church, a few blocks away.

Lincoln, wrapped in his long brown shawl, walked across the cool, shaded park to the War Department, noting that the deciduous trees were either in leaf or were thickening with buds. It was, he thought with some irony, the season of hope.

At the War Department he went to the telegraph room, where amid the nervous clicks of Morse code, he studied the incoming dispatches. He was neither surprised nor, except for the casualties, depressed by the outcome. It had been expected. Once it was known that the relief expedition had failed to get through, the fall of Sumter was a foregone conclusion.

He had achieved the ambiguous objective of seeing the secessionists fire the first shot. The questions now were all political. Had his decision not to surrender the fort been wise? How would the news be received by the nation? By the European powers? By his secretary of state and the majority of the cabinet, who had been opposed to making a stand there? Well, he would soon find out.

Lincoln's senior secretary, John Nicolay, came into the room and advised in his Bavarian-accented English that in accordance with the president's wishes, the cabinet had been summoned for an eleven o'clock meeting. Accompanied by his slender, sandy-haired secretary, Lincoln started for the executive mansion.

After a reflective silence the president said as they walked, "The question, Nicolay, is whether the fall of Sumter will be seen as a victory for the rebels. Will it establish them in the eyes of the world as a legitimate power, a combination so formidable as to attract allies?" The twenty-nine-year-old Nicolay, formal, correct, loyal, and assiduous, remained silent. Obviously, the question was rhetorical. Mr. Lincoln wasn't soliciting his opinion. He was preparing for his meeting with the cabinet.

"And how will it be seen at home? Will this Confederate expression of power intimidate, and discourage attempts to subdue it? Or will it rally our people, convince Republicans and Democrats alike that the time has come to compel this secessionist combination to reform its ties to the Union? And what of the cabinet? Will it stand united and do what has to be done to put down this insurrection?" Nicolay knew that when the "Tycoon," his and Hay's private term for the president, spoke of cooperation from the cabinet, he had in mind one man. Seward.

Nicolay, who had been editor of the Pike County *Free Press* when he accepted Lincoln's invitation to join the administration, ventured a question. "Mr. President, what is the issue? Are the people supposed to rally round the concept of Union as opposed to states' rights?"

"A shrewd question, Nicolay, and one that has to be answered if we're going to win the support of the people." Passing a Norway pine, Lincoln plucked one of the long needles and put it between his teeth. After a moment he said, "I don't believe there are many who would risk their neck for either concept, union or states' rights. The fact is, states' rights is an ancient and honored doctrine held by millions, North and South, to be neither lawless nor disloyal. There's nothing intrinsically wrong or evil about the doctrine. The Union itself is a product of asserting the right to dissolve a political bond that was deemed oppressive."

Both men remained silent as they made their way along the path. The narrow, well-worn footpath reminded Lincoln that each day the question seemed to arise. And each day the dragon had to be reslain.

If states' rights was a legitimate doctrine, why then was secession not to be tolerated? Why couldn't the seceded states honorably follow the path that the thirteen colonies took when they broke with the British Empire? There was only one answer, and like the question it had to be stated and restated, and held up to the light, and turned around and examined until all who pondered the question were satisfied. Clearly, the states of the Union enjoyed the unquestioned right to order and control their domestic institutions. But, at the same time, the Union of the states was perpetual and inviolate. No one state or combination of states had the unilateral right to unmake that union. The Constitution had no provision for its own demise.

He was back to the same worn path. Always, inevitably, inexorably, he was led to the same reasoning, the same simple bedrock proposition. As citizen, man of honor, and chief executive he had no alternative but to remain true to the oath he had sworn that bleak and chilly March morning. When all was said and done, it was a matter of keeping one's word. Preserve, protect, and defend. Simple, clear, unalterable. No way out, even if he wanted one. But would the people follow? Would they be willing to make the sacrifices demanded by what might prove to be a long and savage war—for the principle of preserving the Union?

Punctually at eleven the members of the cabinet and senior military advisers filed into the executive chamber. There was none of the banter and small talk that usually attended the start of a cabinet meeting. The president stood near the door and greeted the men individually. He shook hands with each by way of marking the transition and the solemnity of the occasion. From a cabinet they had become a Council of War. He searched their eyes for a sign that might reveal their state of mind, and he appraised them in light of the new reality.

First, Hannibal Hamlin. Vice president. Maine. Antislave. Solid Yankee rock. But for the grace of God . . . good man if anything happens to me.

Seward. Secretary of state. Silver haired, hawk faced, predatory, omnipresent cigar. War may threaten his supply of Havanas. Mary Todd despises him and his cigars. Self-assured, confident, as befits a former senator and governor from the great state of New York. Probably still clings to the notion of unifying the country through war with Europe. No. None of that. One war at a time. His memorandum makes it clear that he thinks he is best able to govern. Will he stand with me and help to vigorously prosecute the war at hand, or will his political ambitions get in the way? If the latter . . . it won't, mustn't be for long. Does son Fred, assistant secretary, share his father's sentiments?

Salmon Chase. Treasury. Good man. Good lawyer. Ohio. Ambitious. Wants to be president. *Et tu*. He's going to have to raise a lot of money before we're finished.

Caleb Smith. Interior. Indiana. Had to have someone from Indiana. His son assistant secretary.

Gideon Welles. Navy. Good old Father Neptune. The most elaborate wig and the longest beard in government. Voted to relieve Sumter. Connecticut Yankee. Dour, grim, and loyal. Beautiful wife much younger. Frail, but bore him nine children. Three died. That's the worst. I know. Little Eddie, may his sweet soul rest in peace. Uncle Gideon is worried about his ships at the Norfolk yard.

Monty Blair. Postmaster general. Maryland but Union. Antislave moderate in a slave state. Counsel for Dred Scott. Never wavered in his support for reinforcing Sumter. Not an inch to the secessionists. Hard stand. Hard man. Reliable.

Edward Bates. Attorney general. Missouri. Slave state. Border. Critical. Can't lose it. His son assistant attorney general. Remarkable. Three secretaries, three sons. The sins of the fathers. . . .

Talk about sin. Simon Cameron. Secretary of war. The only one I really didn't want. A gift from my blessed campaign managers. But his fifty delegates put me over the top. Pact with the devil. The great state of Pennsylvania—nearest free state to Washington City. Iron, coal, railroads, oil. Need them all. Sumner says he comes "reeking with the stench of a thousand political bargains." Can only wait and see. Either he'll grow into the job or he'll grow into a rope.

Scott. General Winfield. Old, too old. Splendid soldier in his day. Six feet five—got me beat by an inch—and over three hundred pounds. More with the gold braid and the medals and the epaulets. A parade all by himself. Poor old feller. Just trying to stay awake. Gout keeps him up at night.

The president began the meeting with the observation that in firing the first shot on a federal installation that clearly had no aggressive intent, the Southern combination had forced the issue, had given us the alternatives of immediate dissolution of the Union or blood. "I chose the latter," he said. "We must settle this question now: In a free government does the minority have the right to break it up whenever they choose?

If we fail it will go far to prove the incapacity of the people to govern themselves." He paused and looked around the table. This was the moment. If they were going to dissent, now was the time. Silence he would interpret as agreement.

"Mr. President." It was Seward. The silence that fell was absolute and breathless. Everyone knew that what the secretary of state was about to say would have incalculable influence on the government and on the conduct of the war. Savoring the moment and the suspense, Seward straightened some papers in front of him that didn't need straightening, and deliberately flicked the fine gray ash from his cigar. Looking directly at Lincoln he said, "Mr. President, I concur absolutely." Veiled looks darted around the table. The sense of relief was palpable. The secretary of state seemed to be climbing aboard. His three words conveyed more than he spoke. If he hadn't initially agreed with the president's decision to make a stand at Sumter, he was now evidently signaling his support.

Seward, continuing, declared that all available intelligence at State indicated that the prevailing view in London, Paris, and Madrid was that the European powers stood to benefit economically and politically from the failure of the Union, a failure they saw as inevitable. Gesticulating with his cigar, he added: "One has to remember that they see events in a thousand-year context of monarchical systems that derive their power through divine right backed up by a competent military force that compels obedience. They have little faith in public sentiment as a lasting bond of nationality.

"If our Union is shattered," said Seward, "it means to them that the republican form of government everywhere is doomed. It means also that they can continue to build their empires along monarchical lines. And last but not least, it means they can safely ignore the Monroe Doctrine. We note in this regard the Emperor Napoleon's reckless behavior in Mexico; and we see that once again the banner of Castile flies over Santo Domingo. As for England, we know the Confederacy is actively seeking recognition and support in London, and we have reason to believe that the mission finds sympathetic ears."

"Our information at Navy," added Welles, "is that the English have consented to build men-o'-war for the secessionists."

As to the general strategy and conduct of the war (the prospect of a hard and bitter war could not be denied), all were agreed that the most critical point of the contest was the possibility of foreign intervention, a contingency that was obviously central to the South's planning. How else could the rebels hope to overcome their lack of the industries essential to the manufacture of arms, ships, railroads, and the thousand and one things that comprise a war machine? It was no secret. Jefferson Davis himself had been quoted as saying that the South was without machinery and without resources.

The Confederacy was clearly counting on Europe to serve as her industrial reservoir. The quid pro quo? Cotton. The Southern leadership was convinced that cotton was king. The great Lancashire mills of England relied for survival almost exclusively on raw cotton from Southern plantations. Three hundred thousand French textile workers depended on the vital trade exchange with the American South—finished silk products in exchange for raw cotton. Economic self-interest compelled the European powers to supply the Confederacy with the machines of war.

"It must be made clear to the Europeans," said Lincoln, "that we view the present conflict as a domestic insurrection mounted by a conspiracy of willful men. It is not a war between the states. The seceded states are not to be accorded the status of a belligerent power." He looked to Seward to make certain that the secretary of state understood his position.

Seward nodded. "For our part, State will make it known in no uncertain terms that foreign intervention or support will be interpreted as interference in the internal affairs of the United States. In other words, Europe cannot have it both ways. Diplomatic recognition for the Confederacy will mean alienation of the United States."

"The only question that remains, gentlemen," said Lincoln, "is how to respond to the nation, which, of course, includes the secessionists." A declaration of war was out of the question, for diplomatic and constitutional reasons; only the Congress, which was not in session, could declare war.

The president, not unhappy at being unfettered, took the lead. With Nicolay and Hay copying his words on the spot, he dictated a proclamation calling for mobilization of "the militia of the several states of the Union to the aggregate number of seventy-five thousand" for three months' service. Suppressing insurrection was a constitutional function of the militia, which could only be held for ninety days of service outside its own state. The proclamation also convened the Congress for the Fourth of July next; it commanded the treasonable combinations to disperse within twenty days; and it announced that the first object of the military force was to repossess the forts and installations seized from the Union. The proclamation was rushed to the local newspapers and to telegraph offices for transmission to news bureaus all over the Union.

Although it was late in the afternoon when the president adjourned the meeting, Welles hastened back to Navy. It had become his habit to spend most of every evening working at the office, no great sacrifice as long as Mary Jane and the children were still in Hartford.

Waiting for Welles, as he had hoped, was a hand-delivered letter from Chief Engineer Isherwood in Norfolk. Both he and Alden were at the navy yard. There were nine seaworthy men-o'-war in various stages of repair, including the *Merrimack*. Isherwood felt he could have her ready to sail in a few days, assuming cooperation on the part of the mechanics and laborers. It was obvious that there were some rebel sympathizers among the workers and the military, but he wasn't certain they predominated. All depended on Commodore McCauley.

Apparently, in order to ensure that the ships remained at the yard, Governor Letcher of Virginia had ordered vessels sunk in the Elizabeth River between Sewall's Point and Craney Island for the purpose of obstructing the channel north to Hampton Roads. But as far as Isherwood knew, the channel was still viable.

Welles slammed down the letter, swearing. Those blasted Virginians! And their wretched governor—here he was committing a hostile act before their convention voted the secession question. Well, there was no doubt now how they would vote. They were going to secede as sure as God made little apples.

All he could do was hope and pray that Isherwood and Alden proved resourceful enough to free the *Merrimack*. About the other ships, he didn't even dare hope.

CHAPTER
VII

ENTRIES FROM THE DIARIES OF JOHN HAY AND
GIDEON WELLES FOR THE FIRST WEEK OF THE WAR

Monday, April 15 (John Hay)

The president's proclamation was published in today's newspapers.
Although he shows his usual genial and relaxed side to callers, when
he is alone with me or Nicolay his concern is evident. He spends his
time pacing the length of the office—Nicolay and I have a wager on
how long that poor carpet will last—or he stands at the window and
looks across the Potomac.

He's anxious about the people's response to the proclamation. And
he's anxious about Virginia. How will she react to his call for militia?

I am in essential agreement with the analysis of the Prince de Joinville
(French admiral quite knowledgeable about military affairs) who says
that the South through treachery is abundantly supplied with everything of a military character she needs for success, <u>providing</u> the war
can be brought to a rapid conclusion; thereafter, <u>blockade</u> becomes the
crucial factor. If the South can quickly establish substantial military
credentials she will attract an Anglo-French alliance.

Tuesday, April 16 (Gideon Welles)

Received two contradictory hence alarming telegrams today from the yard at Norfolk. One comes from Engineer-in-Chief Isherwood, who advises that he has the *Merrimack* ready for sail. The other comes from Commodore McCauley, who tells me that she will not be ready until tomorrow.

I smell something rotten. I still have no reason to doubt McCauley's loyalty, but why does he disagree with Isherwood, who is obviously competent to decide whether *Merrimack* is ready? McCauley has been quoted as saying that he is reluctant to make a move that might antagonize the Virginia authorities.

Deliver me of timid military men!

Have sent Capt. Hiram Paulding to Norfolk with orders to confer with McCauley for the purpose of defending the yard and ships at Norfolk. Paulding is a gallant officer with a splendid record for personal bravery.

Saw the president this morning. He is bearing up better than one might expect. Like all of us, I think he's relieved that the waiting game is over.

Tuesday, April 16 (John Hay)

A day of glory. The president has most of the answers he seeks with respect to the wisdom of his stand on Sumter and the people's response to his proclamation.

The whole North rises to the call to arms like an awakened and angry lion. One can almost hear the roar of outrage at the insult to the flag at Sumter; one can sense the relief that the cat and mouse game is finally over.

Republican, Democrat, and abolitionist are as one. In thousands of village greens and hundreds of town squares radiant with bunting and resonant with drum and bugle, the people are thronging, pledging money, raising and outfitting companies of volunteers, organizing women's societies to knit and sew and prepare lint and bandages.

We hear that the Sixth Massachusetts Regiment was mustered on Boston Common and readied for transport to Washington twenty-four hours after the proclamation was published. The Tycoon is jubilant.

Volunteer regiments of the foreign born are springing into being as if by spontaneous generation—the St. Patrick Brigade, English and Irish Home Guards, Steuben Volunteers, Garibaldi Guards. Every governor of every free state has wired a promise of troops. Businessmen are already flooding the capital, ready to convert from the soft goods of peace to the iron of war.

In the eyes of the women, one can see that they are steeling themselves for separation and heartbreak. Small boys are putting aside their childish games, and play only at soldiering. It is upon us.

Wednesday, April 17 (John Hay)

Bad news. Even the president can't conceal his disappointment. The Virginia Convention has passed the Ordinance of Secession, 88 to 55. They say Mr. Lincoln's request for state militia prompted the action. The pro-secessionists argued that it would be the grossest folly to provide troops from Virginia that are to be used to fight against everything Virginians believe in. The secession ordinance has still to be ratified by the electorate, but its outcome is a foregone conclusion.

General Scott in his daily report proposes that two or three companies of troops be sent to the Norfolk Navy Yard to defend it against the rebels. Poor Uncle Gideon. "A classic case of too little, too late," he says sadly. Scott also proposes that Col. Robert E. Lee of Arlington, Virginia, be offered command of Union forces in the field. Scott says of him that he is "the very best soldier I have ever seen in the field."

Virginia has seized the customs house and government buildings in Richmond, and has begun to move on the U.S. fort and arsenal at Harper's Ferry, less than fifty miles from Washington.

Revolting development. Turns out that it was only because of the president's trust in Seward that the war steamer *Powhatan* did not arrive at the rendezvous for the provisioning of Sumter. At the last moment, when the press of events was most intense, Seward put a sheaf of papers concerning a variety of matters before the president for signature. One of them countermanded Navy Department orders for the disposition of the *Powhatan*. The Tycoon admits he did not take the time to read the papers, since he presumed they dealt with matters previously discussed. Thus did the *Powhatan* steam down the coast to Pensacola instead of turning off at Charleston. Another reason for the gloom around here. The president said sadly, "If I cannot trust my secretary of state, then I know not whom I can trust."

Thursday, April 18 (Gideon Welles)

Paulding has returned from Norfolk with the news that the *Merrimack* is not ready.

Ordered him back to Norfolk with steam-powered gunboat *Pawnee*, sloop-of-war *Cumberland*, and force of nearly a thousand men (Third Massachusetts and U.S. Marines). He has discretionary orders to defend or destroy. Have president's approval for this move.

Fox is returned from Charleston. Inconsolable. Had no idea why *Powhatan* had not appeared at rendezvous. I was obliged to tell him: "I fear you have to look to the fine hand of the secretary of state for the answer."

"What!" he explodes.

"In a last attempt to prevent the reinforcement of Fort Sumter, Mr. Seward had the *Powhatan* directed, or should I say 'misdirected,' to Pensacola. She is doubtless at this moment riding anchor off Fort Pickens."

"But how is that possible? I saw the departmental orders directing her to Sumter."

"The ways of Mr. Seward are magical and known only to him."

"So," says poor Fox, "I had the mortification of witnessing the surrender of the fort, and losing reputation with the general public for the failure."

"The president plans to send you a letter exonerating you of all blame and taking same on himself."

"But I cannot reveal the letter without injury to the government, at least not until the war is over."

"Welcome aboard."

Thursday, April 18 (John Hay)

General Scott feels the capital is in jeopardy. He expects a rebel attack.

Senator Cassius M. Clay of Kentucky and Senator-Elect James H. Lane of Kansas have organized some of the office seekers in Washington into volunteer battalions. I and Major Hunter have been put in charge of the White House Guards. I tour the mansion a couple of times a day looking as official and martial as I can.

At dusk this evening a company of "Frontier Guards" clad in citizen's dress but carrying very new, untarnished muskets filed into the East Room led by Lane, who brandishes a sword of dazzling splendour. Ammunition boxes are opened and cartridges dealt out.

After spending the evening in close order drill by the light of the gorgeous chandeliers, the guards bivouac on the brilliantly patterned velvet carpet.

Rebel troops have taken the fort and arsenal at Harper's Ferry, about three days' march from the capital, without firing a shot. When the forty-five Union guards heard them coming, they skedaddled, after using gunpowder and fire to blow up millions of dollars' worth of munitions and equipment. We are advised that the rebels salvaged the barrels and locks of about 20,000 pistols and rifles.

Two young women came to the White House tonight to tell me they overheard some men from Virginia swear they were going to do something "within forty-eight hours that would ring through the world." They interpreted that to mean an assassination attempt. I told the president when he was in bed but not yet asleep. He grinned, asked if the ladies were comely, and rolled over.

Friday, April 19 (Gideon Welles)

Chief Engineer Isherwood has returned to Washington with a sad story. He called on McCauley Wednesday afternoon to report that *Merrimack*'s engines and boilers were ready for steam and that forty-four firemen and coal heavers were ready to board. Mc replied that if steam were laid on following morning, "it will be in season."

Fires were started at daybreak Thursday morning. But at nine, when Isherwood reported to Mc that steam was up and everything in readiness, Mc announced that he had decided to retain the vessel, and directed him to draw the fires.

Isherwood thinks McCauley is under the influence of alcohol or rebel officers or both.

When Alden made a separate appeal to McCauley to release *Merrimack,* Mc replied that he would not because he had no crew to defend her in the event of attack, he didn't think she could pass the obstructions in the river, and he could find no pilot to take her out. Alden said she could navigate around the obstructions, and he had a thousand dollars for a pilot who would take her out. But McCauley would not budge. What or who is holding that man?

Alden thinks Mc is terrified and acting irrationally and that traitorous officers have persuaded him that since Virginia passed the Ordinance of Secession, it is wiser for reasons of the ship's safety to keep her at the yard. Alden also thinks McCauley is the victim of a Virginia version of a Potemkin Village deception. The rebels have loaded one company of clamorous "troops" into a single railroad car, which they keep shuttling back and forth on a nearby siding. McCauley believes the yard is about to be overrun by a rebel army.

Friday, April 19 (John Hay)

The president has proclaimed a blockade of all Southern ports. The announcement is regarded by many, including the European powers, as something of an empty threat, since forty ships, most antiquated, cannot hope to patrol 3,500 miles of coastline, to say nothing of hundreds of inlets and harbors.

News received today that troops en route from Massachusetts and Pennsylvania for the defense of the capital have been attacked by a mob in Baltimore. The mayor and the police chief of Baltimore have ordered the destruction of railroad bridges between Baltimore and both Harrisburg and Philadelphia. Washington is now completely cut off from rail communication with the North. We are virtually defenseless. The Tycoon has resumed his pacing.

Saturday, April 20 (John Hay)

Avenues and public buildings in Washington are guarded by city militia. Sentries are posted, and ammunition and muskets have been distributed to clerks in government agencies. (I pray that they will not be called upon to use them; many have never seen a musket before, let alone fired one in anger.)

The president was finishing breakfast when he was advised that General Scott's carriage had stopped under the portico. Knowing of the general's difficulty with the gout, the Tycoon went down to consult with him rather than have the old man try the White House stairs.

Scott had received a message from the mayor of Baltimore saying, "It is my solemn duty to inform you that it is not possible for soldiers to pass through Baltimore unless they fight their way at every step."

"Baltimore," murmurs Lincoln. "Is that city destined to be the cross we must bear?" Scott understood. It was he who had warned the president-elect while he was en route from Springfield to Washington that assassins lay in wait for him in Baltimore.

What should have been the Tycoon's triumphal entry into the capital became instead a surreptitious dash; as a disguised president-elect, wearing a threadbare overcoat and a soft wool cap, accompanied by a single Pinkerton agent, slipped through Baltimore on the cars at three-thirty in the morning. The maneuver was later ridiculed mercilessly in the press as "The Flight of Abraham." The president has since sworn that never again, no matter what the nature of the threat, will he resort to such measures.

Scott advises that the troops could probably fight their way through Baltimore. But Maryland is teetering on the edge of secession. If she should follow Virginia, all could be lost. The president decided to route the troops around Baltimore and through Annapolis.

Scott has received a letter of resignation from Col. Robert E. Lee. The colonel indicated that though he did not believe in secession as a constitutional right, he could not take part in any aggression against his native state or "raise my hand against my relatives, my children, my home." Scott reckons Lee the worth of fifty thousand men.

Sunday, April 21 (Gideon Welles)

Have impressed passenger ships on the Potomac for guard and picket duty. Travel, business, and theatre in Washington City have come to a standstill. Even Willard's is deserted, as if plague-ridden. Thank God Mary Jane and the children are not here.

To compound the isolation, a telegraph operator in Baltimore reports that insurrectionary forces have captured his office. A Washington telegrapher, as his clicking key fades into silence, says, "Of course, this stops all." The president's worst fears are coming to pass. Washington has taken on all the aspects of a city in mourning or under siege; surrounded by a secessionist Virginia and a hostile Maryland, the isolation of the capital is complete.

Those who have private means of transport are fleeing for points north and south. Those who remain keep to their houses, shuttered, locked, and silent, so that it is impossible to tell if the occupants have fled or are within, padding about their darkened rooms in slippered feet.

A rumor that the government plans to conscript the male population for defense of the capital has swept the city. This has almost emptied the ranks of federal employees—like rats deserting a sinking ship. Hundreds have resigned; others simply disappear. Confirms my opinion of "servants" of the federal government. Probably all for the best. At least we've separated the patriots from the traitors.

Monday, April 22 (John Hay)

Flour and grain have been seized and stored in the basements of government buildings, the doors and windows of which are protected by barricades and twenty-four-hour guards. Washington is threatened as it has not been since 1814.

Howitzers have been emplaced in the treasury building, in the Mint, and in the corridors of the Capitol. The senate chamber is occupied by boys of the Sixth Massachusetts. In the House are bivouacked Pennsylvania boys from Reading, Pottsville, Allentown, and Lewistown.

Commodore Franklin Buchanan of Maryland, in command of the Washington Navy Yard, has resigned to go south along with nearly all of his subordinate officers. The yard is left in the charge of Comdr. John A. Dahlgren and a handful of marines.

Robert E. Lee has been appointed by the governor of Virginia to command the state military forces. His resignation has not yet been accepted by Scott, and he is still under obligation to the United States. To my reckoning he is guilty of desertion and treason. Interesting to compare Lee with General-in-Chief Winfield Scott, who is also a Virginian and who was offered command of the Virginia forces before Lee. One can only wish that Lee had learned Scott's lesson in patriotism.

Monday, April 22 (Gideon Welles)

Disaster piled upon misfortune!

This afternoon, determined to hear as many points of view as possible regarding the Paulding expedition to Norfolk, I interviewed Lt. Henry A. Wise, who had been detailed to assist in the rescue of the *Merrimack.*

According to Wise, who was aboard the command ship *Pawnee,* the force arrived at the Norfolk yard on April 20, at ten and a half hours of a clear moonlit night. They were met at the wharf by an obviously shaken McCauley, who advised Paulding that all his Southern-born officers—essentially the entire corps at the yard—had deserted, leaving him alone. At about seven that evening, sensing the yard and the ships to be at great risk, he gave the order to scuttle all ships lest they fall into the hands of the rebels. It was his last act of command; he was now relinquishing authority to Paulding.

Wise, noting that the ships were indeed settling into the Elizabeth River, jumped ashore and ran to the *Merrimack,* which was about three hundred yards distant. He boarded her, and in pitch-blackness ran to her lower decks, where he threw a block into her hold. Judging by the sound of the splash that the water was over her orlop deck, he ran back to report same to Paulding.

Paulding replied that it had been decided to blow up the dry dock and fire the yard and ships. Accordingly he ordered Wise to lay the powder train.

Wise manned a boat, and with a detail from the *Pawnee* returned to the *Merrimack,* where his men gathered combustibles such as cordage, rope, ladders, hawsers, all of which were laid, in the shape of the letter *V,* from the mainmast to one of the gun-deck ports. On top of the combustibles they strung cotton waste saturated with turpentine, leaving the ends hanging outside the ports. The decks fore and aft were flooded with turpentine.

At 2 A.M., all troops safely aboard the *Pawnee* and the *Cumberland,* a rocket flared up from the *Pawnee* signaling Wise and the others to apply the torch. Within minutes ships and wooden structures in the yard were engulfed in flame. But dry dock, machine shops, forges, and guns remained undamaged.

When Paulding was satisfied that the ships were fairly involved, he left the scene with the steam-powered *Pawnee* towing the sailing sloop *Cumberland.* Thus did Captain Paulding elect to destroy rather than defend. With the cities of Norfolk and Portsmouth at the mercy of his twenty-four gun *Cumberland* and his eight gun *Pawnee,* the captain steamed for Washington, leaving the yard virtually undamaged for the rebels.

The arsenal at Harper's Ferry, and now the navy yard at Norfolk. We are the laughingstock of the world. It appears our military are not even equal to the task of destroying our own resources.

Monday, April 22 (John Hay)

The president has withdrawn into himself. I believe he is shaken and confused as never before. He is trying to come to grips with the fact that many on whom he depended owed or thought they owed allegiance to states in rebellion. In whom can he place confidence? Where has patriotism fled? The sense of personal obligation? Honesty, manliness, honor? If clerks and captains and commanders and governors and justices of the Supreme Court prove false, how is he to govern?

As is usually the case whenever reliable sources of information are cut off, rumor and panic rule. People believe what they want to believe and gossip is retailed as gospel. "A rebel army is advancing under Beauregard from Harper's Ferry to invade the capital," goes one story. "No," says another, "Davis has countermanded that order. Good old boys from Massachusetts, Pennsylvania, and New York are on the way via Annapolis, and will be here any hour." No one, including the president, knows the facts, knows which troops, rebel or Union, will be first to reach Washington.

Through all the bad news, except for one occasion, the president broods but maintains an outward calm. Only once, when he was unaware that he was not alone, did he express his anxiety. It was the end of the day and the executive offices were deserted. The president paces the floor of his office in silence for about half an hour when he stops and gazes out the window down the Potomac in the direction of the awaited ships carrying federal troops. In a voice that breaks with anguish, he exclaims over and over again, "Why don't they come? Why don't they come?"

The majesty of a great nation is insulted, and its symbols of authority are in jeopardy. When in the gloom of his office the Tycoon now peers through his glass down the Virginia shore, he sees the Confederate flag flying over Alexandria along with the campfires and tents of a rebel army. His wishful thinking about the state, so many of whose sons have contributed to the birth and nurturing of the nation, has deceived him. Never, deep in his heart, did he believe that Virginia would secede. Father Neptune, who had no illusions, was right.

CHAPTER

VIII

"He just sat there," said Hay, "and didn't even blink. For all anyone could tell, I could have been reading the morning's weather reports."

"He is a cool one," said Nicolay.

"All the more remarkable when you appreciate that he, more than any of them—more than Seward, more than Chase or Cameron or Welles—believes that without public support we can't wage this war for five minutes. He just sat there, took it all in, and didn't change expression."

On the morning in question, Hay had brought to the president's office his usual armload of newspapers. As was his custom he began to quote from them in order of their importance, beginning with New York— always New York, where money and influence were combined as in no other city. Press reaction, especially to the loss of Virginia, was one of anger and frustration with an obviously feeble president and an administration that allowed itself to be victimized.

According to the New York newspapers, a budding movement to depose the president and replace him with a dictator was growing with the support of an influential clique. The idea was finding favor with a number of important journals. The *New York Times* had already found the ideal replacement, one George Law, engineer, canal builder, organizer, financier, and man of action par excellence. Here was a man who could cut through the Gordian knot of Washington politics, root out civil service torpor, and free the government for bold initiative.

When Hay had finished reading the *Times* piece, he turned to the president for comment. Lincoln, sitting at his small, round table and drumming thoughtfully with his fingers, said quietly, "Please continue."

Hay turned to the *Tribune,* where Horace Greeley, preoccupied with the episode at the Norfolk Navy Yard, wrote: "Thus ended the most shameful, cowardly, disastrous performance that stains the annals of the American Navy."

Following the Greeley statement, Hay quoted from the comments of two cabinet members. Attorney General Bates was on record as believing that the government seemed to lack force: "We frighten nobody, we hurt nobody." Treasury Secretary Salmon Chase, in an apparent reference to both Norfolk and Harper's Ferry, implored the president (through the good offices of the press) to remember that the secessionists had anticipated the administration in everything, while "we have accomplished nothing but the destruction of our own property."

Lincoln asked Hay to turn to Southern opinion, remarking dryly that it was time to hear from the enemy. The Southern press was predictably exultant. The *Richmond Examiner*, buoyed by events, saw an opportunity to put a quick end to the war: "There is one wild shout of fierce resolve to capture Washington City, at all and every human hazard. The filthy cage of unclean birds must and will be purified by fire. Our people can take it, and Scott [a native Virginian] the arch traitor and Lincoln the Beast, combined cannot prevent it."

In Mobile, the *Advertiser* saw easy victory for Confederate arms: "The starved, scurvy wretches from the back slums of the cities are not soldiers to meet the hot-blooded, thoroughbred, impetuous men of the South. Dregs and off-scourings of the populace are the forces whom Lincoln suddenly arrays as candidates for the honor of being slaughtered by gentlemen."

In Montgomery, news of Virginia's secession and the events at Norfolk were received with profound joy and relief. In addition to the obvious material and strategic assets the state brought to the Confederacy, her secession lent a moral and spiritual sanction no other state could confer. The very virtues that Lincoln believed would keep Virginia in the Union were those that now lent the insurrection a seal of rectitude and propriety. Virginia, home of scholars and soldiers and patriots and presidents, was the cultural jewel of the South. There was little doubt but that she would take with her other border states that were teetering on the brink.

Among those in Montgomery who had the most reason to rejoice at the turn of events was the stumpy, pudgy little man with the loop of whiskers that ran from ear to ear under his chin, Stephen Russell Mallory. Seated in his handsomely appointed office on the second floor of a converted town house, Mallory was as jubilant as a prudent man of vast experience in politics allows himself to be.

Unlike his counterpart in Washington, Mallory was quite sanguine about the prospects for his navy, which, when Jefferson Davis appointed him secretary of the Navy, barely existed except as a figment of both men's imagination. When Sumter was assaulted, the South had no ships of war, few naval stores, no equipment to produce vessels, very few skilled artisans, no facilities for fabricating engines, and one establishment, the Tredegar Iron Works in Richmond, capable of rolling iron.

By the same token, much less was expected of Mallory than of Welles, who was obliged to think offensively, of invading the South in order to stifle secessionist doctrine. Mallory's responsibility was limited to defending along interior lines. His grand strategy was to defend the Southern coastline, its major ports, and the Mississippi; of course, he must also be prepared to penetrate any blockade the Union might attempt to impose.

In his initial report to his government, Mallory advised that he (like Welles) was looking for ships already built, and was also making arrangements to send an agent to England, where he was to contract for and superintend the construction of ships for the CSA. Mallory had learned that although British law forbade the Queen's subjects from aiding any nation at war with a friendly power, British authorities were, in this instance, prepared to look the other way.

Seated at his Louis Quinze desk, in a handsomely appointed, mahogany-paneled office, Mallory looked with satisfaction on the ambience. For an orphan boy he had not done badly. Like many of humble background who had risen to eminence, he had a proper appreciation for luxury and style, and never took the gifts of the moment for granted. Just as he was aware of his immediate surroundings, he was aware of the building that housed his office; he knew and was grateful to the donor, a wealthy Alabaman who had made a fortune exporting cotton and importing silk from Lyons.

Savoring the moment, Mallory rose and walked to the tall window that stretched almost from frescoed ceiling to carpeted floor. It faced the state capitol, one of the finest examples of classic Georgian architecture in America. It was there on the steps of the portico, Mallory in attendance, that Jefferson Davis had taken the oath of office.

As he reflected on that day, Mallory had reason to give his natural optimism free rein. The welcome news regarding England's willingness to build ships for the Confederate Navy, followed by the coup at Norfolk, was succeeded by another factor, a new element in the equation that fired Mallory's imagination as had nothing else. This new element, so promising as to send the normally restrained and composed Mallory into alternating fits of exhilaration and despair, was in fact older than man and in such common use as to be part of every household. But in marine application, the Confederate secretary of the Navy felt its potential was such as to decide the outcome of the war. The element was iron.

When Mallory was chairman of the U.S. Senate's Naval Affairs Committee some twenty years before, the Navy had experimented with iron for armoring its ships. After many years and many thousands of dollars, the Navy had pronounced the experiment a failure. Mallory, however, remained unconvinced by the Navy's verdict. "The last word on ironclad ships has yet to be heard," he assured the Congress.

As Confederate secretary of the Navy, he was aware of France's use of iron-cased, floating offshore batteries in the Black Sea during the Crimean War. And two years ago, the French, apparently favorably impressed with their batteries, completed the *Gloire,* a wooden frigate bound by a complete belt of armor. Word now reaching Mallory from London told of Britain's *Warrior,* the first warship to be built entirely of iron, its casing an impenetrable four and a half inches thick.

Mallory had a vision. If he could somehow produce an ironclad man-o'-war before the Union could build one, he would, in one grand stroke, redress the imbalance in their respective fleets. But all depended on his winning the race. It was the race that was the reason for Mallory's bouts of exhilaration and despair.

He had reason to believe, on the basis of information provided by the long arm of Confederate intelligence, that the Yankees were not inclined, at least at the moment, to make a commitment to an ironclad warship. He had just received (simultaneously with Gideon Welles, for whom it was prepared) a copy of a report written by John Lenthall, chief of the Bureau of Construction, U.S. Navy. The report concluded: "The necessarily large size, the cost, and the time required for building an iron-cased steam vessel is such that it is not recommended to adopt any plan at present. The subject of ironclad vessels has been freely discussed in the European mechanical journals, but their draft of water, cost, and the time required in the introduction of a new system render it inexpedient at this time to commence such vessels. . . ."

In his report to his government, Mallory wrote: "I regard the possession of an iron-armoured ship as a matter of the first necessity. Such a vessel at this time could traverse the entire coast of the U.S., prevent all blockade, and encounter, with a fair prospect of success, their entire navy."

With a prayer that Welles and the U.S. Navy would accept and be bound by Lenthall's conclusions, Mallory turned once again to contemplation of the prizes offered by the navy yard at Norfolk.

Although capture of the yard did not yield a single seaworthy vessel, Mallory saw it as a godsend nonetheless. In the machine shops, stores, guns, ammunition, dry dock, and even possibly the ships, though they had all been scuttled and burned, he perceived the nucleus of a navy. In his lively, sanguine imagination, all sorts of possibilities began to take shape. And, unlike Welles, Mallory enjoyed the advantage of being able to quickly translate his will into action. The government of the CSA was in its infancy; the channels of its bureaucracy had not yet turned sclerotic.

Within hours of Paulding's abandonment of the Norfolk yard, Mallory had ordered a mammoth salvage operation to begin at once. Simultaneously he ordered a report, to be rendered within ten days, on the feasibility of refloating the scuttled ships. Special attention was to be accorded the *Merrimack*.

A few blocks from the euphoric atmosphere of Mallory's office, one soul in Montgomery, sitting on the iron-framed cot in his cell, received the news of the first week of the war with less than jubilation.

Lieutenant John L. Worden had been imprisoned in the Montgomery County jail for about a week when a guard thrust several newspapers through the bars, and said in a vaguely smarmy manner, "*Loo*tenant, ah believe yawl gonah be innarested inna news this mawnin."

Worden read of Virginia's secession and of the events at Norfolk and Harper's Ferry with a sinking heart. He was quick to appreciate what Virginia and her arsenals meant to the rebel cause. The Confederacy would not be subdued quickly. It was going to be a long, difficult war, and the probabilities were that he would spend it in a jail cell.

Once the initial shock of arrest had worn off, and when it became evident that he was not to be executed as a spy, Worden's sense of anger and frustration began to mount. He was being held unjustly, of that he hadn't the slightest doubt. He had violated neither his word nor any agreement of which he was aware. If Adams had thought Worden was violating an agreement, why then would he have sent him back to Washington via Pensacola? He could easily have returned on a ship of the squadron, or remained aboard the *Sabine* to await developments.

Ceaselessly pacing from wall to wall, and cot to door, he raged, silently, inwardly; it would never do to let his captors see how distraught he was. The reality of being closed within a ten-foot-square space that he shared with a cot, a foul-smelling latrine, and a washstand, he found as astonishing as it was depressing. A few short months ago he was bestride the deck of the *Savannah,* a mighty U.S. frigate of war, as executive officer. And here he was in a cage, a zoo for humans, on display twenty-four hours a day, his freedom and dignity and privacy stripped from him as though he were a savage beast.

It was only after several days that he was able to take pen in hand and, in a burst of fury-driven energy, dash off a dozen letters protesting his innocence. The first had gone to Leroy Pope Walker, Confederate secretary of war, in which he swore on his honor as an officer and a gentleman that he had violated no word he had given or any agreement of which he was aware. Unspoken was his conviction that the United States enjoyed the absolute and unqualified right to reinforce its own installations anytime it saw fit.

Other letters went to Confederate naval officers who were friends and former shipmates, in an effort to enlist their aid. Still other letters went to people he knew in Washington for the purpose of calling attention to his plight, and to make certain that his cause was not lost in the march of events that was overwhelming the capital. But even as he wrote, despairing, he realized the futility of the enterprise.

Having done everything he reasonably could by way of seeking outside help, he turned to consider the options that remained. He realized that all his efforts to gain release had to be accompanied by a real effort to come to terms with confinement. There was no other way. Continuing anger and frustration would destroy him.

What were the alternatives? Either escape or adjust. The outlook for the former was not promising. The jail had only half a dozen cells. He was alone and conspicuous in his. As the Confederacy's first prisoner of war and a naval officer, he was something of a celebrity. Word had come down to the county authorities that this prisoner was to remain under constant, if civilized, watch. Nothing was to happen to him, either by his own hand or of others, that would bring discredit on the new nation of the Confederate States of America.

His guards, accustomed to dealing with drunks, horse thieves, and murderers, were not sure how to treat him. They settled, for the most part, on a rather elaborately courteous manner, the net effect of which was heavy-handed irony. Security was tight, with one singular exception. They had offered him the privilege of walking freely about town were he to give his word of honor that he would not try to escape.

Worden had declined the offer and expressed his reasons in a letter to Olivia: "I see in their invitation a remarkable inconsistency inasmuch as the alleged reason for arresting me in the first instance was that I violated my word. Further, they know that as an officer I am honor-bound to take advantage of the first opportunity to escape. I believe their offer false and insincere, made for reasons of public—possibly international—opinion." He didn't tell Olivia that the net result of his refusal was that they kept him in virtual solitary confinement.

In a subsequent letter, he warned her that "all mail, incoming and outgoing, is censored on the grounds that, as an 'inhabitant' of this capital, I am in a position to transmit information of a sensitive nature."

On a more positive note, he advised that the authorities permitted him the privilege of purchasing groceries at the local market through the good offices of an obliging guard. He did not mention that prison fare, which was brought to him on a grease-stained wooden tray, was cheerfully admitted by his captors to be execrable; nor did he tell her that he didn't take advantage of their offer to purchase food, because he preferred to remain under no obligation to his jailers.

One of his guards, a coarse, brutish fellow, couldn't keep his eyes off Worden's watch and pocketknife, scarce commodities in the industry-poor South. He never tired of making it clear that were Worden to "sell" them to him, the lieutenant would enjoy privileges beyond his fondest dreams. When Worden learned that the privileges, which the guard never detailed, did not include an opportunity to escape, he lost interest. He would never voluntarily part with watch and knife, since he felt they would prove invaluable were he to attempt escape.

"I am given no duties to perform and have no obligations," he wrote. "Boredom would be a problem, except that some of the good townsfolk have taken it upon themselves to keep me well supplied with reading material. In truth, my situation could be far worse."

But reason and rationalize and try as he might, Worden could not accept imprisonment. He did not know if he was less suited to incarceration than other men; he knew only that he could not come to terms with it and would not survive prolonged confinement.

His thoughts were interrupted by the guard who had brought the newspapers. "Luncheon is served," he announced grandly. Setting the tray, bearing a bowl and two slices of bread, on the washstand, he withdrew.

Worden studied the mess in the bowl: watery split-pea soup with several floating chunks of red, undercooked ham veined with streaks of white gristle. The bread was covered with an oleaginous film. He pushed the tray back along the floor and under the bars.

Lying back on his cot, he continued his meditation. At forty-three, and after twenty-seven years in the Navy, Worden had seen himself, on the eve of war, as a mature officer, fired by no dreams of glory, no fantasies of fame and public adulation. He approached his job with neither an inflated nor a falsely modest appreciation of his role. His duty was to help preserve the peace and train to defend his country at war, along with thousands of others. With this role he had been content. That he was still a lieutenant was, he admitted, a source of some embarrassment and mild discontent. But since money was not a pressing problem, and Olivia had no driving ambition to be the wife of a commodore, he was able to look forward to his next promotion with equanimity.

War, however, does unpredictable things to men, professional military included. Rather like an aging lover, Worden found, to his not unpleased surprise, that certain fires he thought had long since been extinguished had in fact merely been banked, and were very much alive in the form of burning embers. Ambition was rekindled. The true irony of his discovery was borne upon him as he lay on his mattress of corn husks in an Alabama jail.

But personal ambition was actually the least compelling of the reasons that prevented Worden from coming to terms with imprisonment. He was a descendant of Puritans, the first of whom had come to the New World from England early in the seventeenth century. Along with the blood of his forebears, he had inherited their conscience. The ideals of sacrifice and devotion formed the twin pillars of his profoundest beliefs. The thought of languishing in jail while others were sacrificing their lives and their fortunes was intolerable.

He remembered having read as a youth, while standing in his father's field waiting for the big old bay to catch his breath, a line he thought of surpassing beauty. He had never forgotten it. Writing about the ancient Germans in his *Decline and Fall of the Roman Empire,* Edward Gibbon said that "they despised life when it was separated from freedom." The German barbarian, however, saw freedom as a means to indolence and license. Worden, standing at the end of the furrow, wrapped in harness to the plow, began, on the spot, to develop his own definition. After considerable reflection, he came to the conclusion that freedom meant neither indolence nor license, but was rather the uninhibited right to dedicate oneself to a vocation of one's choice.

He chose the Navy. It proved a felicitous choice. In the rigorous discipline of the service, he saw no inconsistency with his view of himself as a free man. He also found that there were few things more to his liking than a stout deck under his feet, the fresh salt air in his lungs, and a clean, unlimited horizon before his eyes. More than half his lifetime had been spent on the great seas of the world. He asked nothing more than to spend his remaining years in the same way.

The metallic scratch of key in lock told him that the guard was bringing his evening meal. Time had gotten away. Worden glanced at his watch; it was five o'clock. There was the inevitable wooden tray with the grease stain that seemed to resemble a short man or boy holding a horse by its halter. The dish reposing on the horse's rump held a bit of hoecake and sorghum. He nibbled at the cake but soon put it aside. The sorghum, a cold, lumpy porridge, he didn't attempt.

Made drowsy by hunger and lack of exercise and fresh air, he rolled over on his cot for an uneasy sleep. Although he slept a great deal, it was in the form of short naps made unpleasant by dreams of distress.

He awoke at about nine, as always unrefreshed and vaguely disoriented, and washed in the small enamel basin. Stripping down to his underwear, he prepared to retire. It was the best part of his day. He was doing what he normally would be doing at the end of the day were he not in prison—going to bed.

Settling under the thin blanket over which he had thrown his tunic, he arranged the candle for reading and turned, as was his nightly custom, to the Bible. He read in no particular order and favored neither testament. His habit was to choose a book or passage at random. Although he would have denied it if questioned, he tended to see a certain mystical design in the selection that came to hand on any given evening.

This evening his fingers found the story of Moses in the Book of Deuteronomy. Although he had read it many times, this time he felt a special poignance in the words of the Lord: "For thou shalt see the land afar off; but thou shalt not go thither into the land which I give the children of Israel."

Worden saw a certain relevance to his own situation. Of course, he was not Moses; he had led no one on a forty-year exodus through the wilderness, nor had he received the Law on a mountaintop. And, certainly, participation in what appeared to be a civil war was not to be confused with admission to the promised land.

Still he saw a parallel. It was not entirely by chance that his fingers had found that passage. He had spent twenty-seven years laboring in preparation for the moment his country called. All his adult life had been spent training to come to his country's defense. But now, in her hour of need, he lay locked away, impotent. He drew no comfort from the fact that God had denied Moses, his magnificent and faithful servant, entry to the promised land. God had allowed Moses to play his role. That he was denied his earthly reward was cause for sorrow. But of infinitely greater tragedy would have been God's denying Moses his vocation.

That was the core of Worden's frustration. He was being denied his vocation. It was as though he had lived his life in vain.

He refused to believe that providence would be so capricious as to prepare him for a role and lead him to the opening scene of what was surely the most crucial turn in his country's history since its birth, only to bar the door to his participation. He resolved that he would not rest until he was out of jail. He must make every possible effort to free himself. But how? What could he do that he had not already done?

His last best hope was Olivia. She loved him as he cherished her. She needed him as he needed her. She knew him better than he knew himself. She would understand that prolonged confinement was intolerable, an impossibility for reasons both spiritual and physical.

Only Olivia knew about his illness. Only she knew how it ravaged him. Only she could nurse him through the bouts of fever and chill that left him so enervated and uncoordinated that the simplest physical act, such as walking or bathing, became a task of monumental difficulty.

During one of his tours, either in the Caribbean or the Mediterranean, he had contracted a disease that clung with a tenacity that left even specialists in tropical medicine baffled and defeated. Beyond giving it the name "relapsing fever," they could do little else. Under healthful conditions in a temperate climate, he functioned well and suffered no symptoms. But his chances of surviving an Alabama summer in confinement were, at best, doubtful.

Olivia understood. Beautiful, wise, gentle Olivia. Reclining on his straw-filled mattress, a smile lit his eyes. The women in the family—sisters, cousins, aunts—spoke of his and Olivia's courtship and marriage as though it had the quality of legend. "Ah, yes," they would say over their sewing or their quilting, telling their women's tales, "those two, Olive and Jack, like lovers they were, in a storybook." And after twenty years he still delighted in saying to her that he never thought of their attachment as the stuff of fairy tales. "I just felt for you what any sailor feels for his girl." And after twenty years, he would grin and she would blush.

Olivia came of a wealthy and socially prominent family who made their home, appropriately enough, at the top of Quaker Hill, a lovely and wooded eminence of small farms and sprawling estates, situated near the Village of Pawling in New York's Dutchess County. There the Toffey family of six children, three boys and three girls, lived with their parents in a rambling, white frame house that accommodated them in quiet rather than spectacular luxury. The Honorable Daniel Toffey, paterfamilias, was a wealthy cattle merchant and politician, having held numerous town offices and served in the state legislature.

The Worden family lived some twenty miles west, near the banks of the Hudson, in the undistinguished little village of Swartwoutville. They were introduced at church, the only place they could reasonably have met since the likelihood of their meeting in a social setting was remote. As a young suitor, Worden tended to see Olivia's wealth as an obstacle rather than an attraction, although he knew the instant he saw her that she was to be his beloved. Olivia would later claim that she knew long before him, and what, pray, had taken him so long to propose?

To this day he had not confided to her the reason for his apparent irresolution. He dreaded confronting her father to ask for her hand. What if he should refuse the petition of a lowly midshipman? As it turned out, the old gent was delighted, wondering too why young Worden hadn't gotten a move on.

They were married at the Quaker Hill Meetinghouse as soon as he became a passed midshipman. And despite or perhaps because of (he was not closed to the possibility) his long and frequent absences, their marriage flourished, giving them four beautiful children.

He knew that once he sanctioned it, Olivia would mount a tireless campaign on behalf of his release. Sweetly feminine, cool and white-gloved with a will of finely tempered steel, he was persuaded that she was capable, in the cause of preserving their family, of prevailing against a government—or two.

CHAPTER

IX

Summer has never been kind to Washington. It descends abruptly in a humid, suffocating cloud that sucks breath and strength, that leaves clerks and congressmen, presidents and emissaries stunned and gasping and speculating on the reasons the capital of a great nation was placed in an environment so patently inimical to the strenuous pursuits and cool deliberation demanded by the business of government.

The summer of 1861 was no exception. The Potomac, with its marshes, stagnant pools, swamps, and tidal basins lapping the edges of Constitution Avenue and, on occasion, flooding Pennsylvania Avenue, compounded the distress and discomfort that plagued the city.

Family privies were widely used. Hotel toilets emptied into back lots or at best drained into the canals and creeks that ringed the city. Young John Hay, with his gift for expression, likened the prevailing city stench to the odor of a thousand dead cats.

Flies and mosquitoes were a constant nuisance. Much of the drinking water came from contaminated wells. Epidemics of typhoid, tuberculosis, malaria, and dysentery exacted a heavy toll. In Europe, Washington was regarded as a hardship post; visiting diplomats were encouraged to leave their families at home.

For Abe Lincoln the unpleasantness of that summer, his first as president, was exacerbated by the pressures of an impatient and clamorous press and public. The Union's response to his proclamation and call to arms had been magnificent, spontaneous, and wholehearted. There was scarcely a village or a town in the North that hadn't given of its men and resources. For the three-week period ending May 8, loans and contributions from citizens for war purposes were estimated at $23 million. The government's credit, Secretary Chase was pleased to report, was virtually without limit. Patriotic passion was at its peak. The people had had enough of rebel belligerence, the latest example being the move of their capital from Montgomery, Alabama, north to Richmond, Virginia. Richmond! Just 122 miles from Washington. That was nerve. It was time to teach them a lesson, show them that they were dealing with a resolute and formidable Union.

Why then the delay on the part of the federal government? Here it was the end of June and the administration seemed to be sitting on its collective hands. Why was there no action? Why weren't the troops put to the task for which they had been recruited? The sentiment of the people was let's get on with it and get it over with so we can return to our normal peacetime lives.

Horace Greeley ran a series of fiery editorials for a month in the *Tribune,* exhorting the administration to seize the initiative: "Forward to Richmond! Forward to Richmond! The rebel Congress must not be allowed to meet there on the 20th of July. By that date the place must be held by the National Army."

The president summoned his Council of War on June 29. He declared that unless the administration heeded the prevailing public sentiment, the government was in danger of losing its popular support. "And that, gentlemen," he added, "is to lose everything. The capital, I am assured, is secure, at least for the present, thanks to the arrival of troops from New York, Rhode Island, and Massachusetts. It appears that now is the time to go on the offensive."

Simon Cameron spoke next. He reviewed the War Department's latest intelligence on the Confederate military posture, informing the council that, "General Lee, who is now acting as Davis's military adviser, is assembling two armies." Walking to the map of Virginia on the wall, and pointing, he said, "One is in the Shenandoah Valley, not far from Harper's Ferry, about fifty-five miles northwest of Washington, under command of General J. E. Johnston. The other, under General Beauregard, is massing some thirty miles southwest of us, at Manassas Junction." A strategic rail point lying on an open plain, Manassas Junction was a nexus for rail lines running in all directions and was heavily used in the movement of rebel troops.

Manassas, the president pointed out, lay between Washington and Richmond. It seemed the logical target for an offensive. Taking it would appease public opinion and put Union forces a step closer to the rebel capital. "And bloodying General Pierre Gustave Toutant Beauregard's nose," interjected Seward, "will make victory that much sweeter."

With a deep rolling rumble General Scott cleared his throat and roused his massive bulk. He begged to differ with the president and with the secretary of war. Now was not the time and Manassas Junction was not the place for an offensive. The general didn't believe in little piecemeal wars that would bleed the country dry without yielding a decisive victory; and he didn't have much faith in militia or volunteers as a fighting force. He had a plan of his own.

Scott believed in the blockade concept. His strategy called for closing off all Southern ports on the Atlantic and gulf coasts, while simultaneously building up the regular army. When the army was thoroughly trained it would, supported by a fleet of fast river steamers, fight its way down the Mississippi, garrisoning the strategic points all the way to New Orleans. The Confederacy would then be completely surrounded and cut off from its western extremities. Thereafter, a gradual constriction of the noose would compel surrender with the least loss of life and expenditure of resources.

"How many men and how long to achieve victory?" asked the president.

"Three hundred thousand and three years."

"But something must be done now, and it must be done with the seventy-five thousand troops of the militia whose ninety-day enlistment terms begin to expire in a few weeks."

Hold off, counseled Scott and General McDowell, at least until fall or winter, when the regular army will have been brought to strength and be better trained for an offensive campaign. Offensive operations, especially, require thoroughly trained forces. Another ninety days will make a difference.

The president and the cabinet demurred. The people and the popular press were clamoring for action. "And while it is true," said Lincoln to Scott, "that you are green, they are green also." Military strategy bowed to political necessity. Scott and McDowell agreed to formulate a plan for the capture of Manassas Junction.

Before the meeting adjourned, McDowell warned all present: "We cannot count on keeping secret our intentions. The spies are alive and well informed as to every movement, however slight, we make."

The plan devised by Scott and McDowell for the capture of Manassas was deliberately neither sophisticated nor complex. Wise generals do not burden green troops and inexperienced commanders with elaborate strategies. In the time-honored canon of military tactic, it called simply for bringing to bear at a specific point in time and space a force superior in weight and numbers to that of the opposing enemy.

The crux of the plan called for Union Gen. Robert Patterson to preoccupy Gen. J. E. Johnston by every available means, including show of force and use of force, in order to keep Johnston in the Shenandoah Valley and thereby prevent him from coming to the aid of Beauregard. McDowell, then, whose army outnumbered Beauregard's by 30,000 to 20,000, would be free to advance on Manassas with a considerably superior force.

The first pitched battle of the Civil War was about to be joined.

General Robert Patterson was uneasy and confused. He was bivouacked with his Army of the Upper Potomac at a village with the arresting name of Bunker Hill, in Virginia's northern Shenandoah Valley. The sixty-nine-year-old Patterson felt that he should be making a move, but he wasn't sure where.

His orders were clear and unambiguous. General-in-Chief Winfield Scott had charged him with the task of holding J. E. Johnston, commander of the Confederate Army of the Shenandoah, precisely there, in the Shenandoah Valley near the town of Winchester, until McDowell prevailed at Manassas. Patterson had been advised by Washington that he outnumbered Johnston by a ratio of three to two, and the fact was that his army did stand at 18,000 to Johnston's 12,000.

But Patterson had little faith in Washington's estimates. His own officers, on the strength of reconnaissance, were reporting that the rebel force was equal if not superior in number. And Patterson totally discounted the intelligence offered by residents of the valley, who tended to confirm Washington's view. The natives were not to be trusted. They were, after all, Virginians, albeit of the western variety.

Contributing to Patterson's sense of unease was the order that had come from Scott at the end of June, directing him to detach all his regular army units for transfer to Washington. There had been no explanation with the order. The reasons for sapping his strength were quite beyond him. Washington City was secure from rebel attack. Why then did they need additional regular army units? The troops already there, he heard, were doing nothing but parading by day and carousing by night. What on earth or in hell could be on Scott's mind?

Patterson was infuriated and depressed by turns. After brooding on the matter for two weeks, he came to the conclusion that the order was simply a consequence of Scott's poor judgment, a factor in the Union command that was increasing cause for concern. Apparently the combination of age, infirmities, and the press of events was just too much for the old man. The general in chief was showing distinct signs of senility.

Without the regular army units to stiffen the ranks of his volunteers, Patterson felt exposed and vulnerable, especially with respect to artillery. Manning guns of large caliber demanded long periods of training and teamwork of a standard that was simply not to be found in the ranks of ninety-day militia.

Then, too, there was the matter of his opposite in command, Gen. Joseph E. Johnston. Patterson knew him to be one of the best of a talented crop of professional officers. A West Point graduate of the same class as Robert E. Lee, Johnston had served with distinction in the Black Hawk, Seminole, and Mexican wars, receiving three brevets for gallantry and meritorious service.

Patterson, a major general in the Pennsylvania militia, had also served his country with distinction in the War of 1812 and in the Mexican War, but he was not a professional soldier. Rather he was a businessman who had retained ties to the military. He did not presume to be the equal of Johnston in military matters.

The final cause of Patterson's diffidence was the question of timing. There was no telegraphic communication between him and McDowell. He could not be certain of the exact date McDowell was striking Manassas and therefore wasn't sure when he could safely disengage Johnston. He wasn't interested in opposing the talented rebel general a minute more than was necessary. Patterson had his own ax to grind.

Patterson was obsessed with the strategic and political importance of Harper's Ferry. He dreamed of recovering it for the Union in the first great victory of the war, and it was there that he wished to take his troops. He had Scott's approval for the move once he had fulfilled his obligation vis-à-vis Johnston.

After days of inaction and dithering indecision about making a move toward Winchester, where Johnston made his headquarters, Patterson received welcome news. A wire from Scott dated July 16 advised that McDowell was planning to advance that very day.

Patterson was relieved and delighted. He saw his mission with respect to Johnston as having been essentially accomplished. If McDowell was advancing today, he would carry the junction tomorrow. A skirmish with Johnston's cavalry had just demonstrated that the rebel army was still encamped at Winchester; even if Johnston were to decamp immediately, there was no way he could be at Manassas in time to influence the battle. Patterson estimated the distance between Winchester and Manassas at forty-five miles as the crow flies—a three- to four-day march.

Patterson concluded that he was thus spared the necessity of engaging an army he deemed superior in number, better positioned, and better supplied. He made immediate plans to withdraw east toward Harper's Ferry, thereby enlarging the distance between himself and Johnston from thirteen to twenty miles.

Scott's telegram to Patterson was correct as far as it went. McDowell was indeed advancing on July 16. The advance, however, was from Alexandria, some thirty miles from Manassas.

Green troops and mid-July Virginia heat are not made for quick marches. New boots and tender feet mean blisters. Packs grow heavy on soft, white shoulders. Men were dropping from heat exhaustion. Those still on the march, choking from the heat and dust, tied bandannas over their noses and mouths. Water discipline was nonexistent. The troops drank at will, with the result that every pond or stream was occasion for breaking ranks to refill canteens. Fifty men from Col. William Tecumseh Sherman's brigade took off at the sight of a blackberry patch to fill their stomachs and their mess gear. Other troops began to jettison equipment, first haversacks then blanket rolls. Even the horses, chafing under heavy military harness and maddened by the flies that stung their lathered hides, bolted at the scent of water.

It took McDowell two full days to march his army approximately twenty-five miles from Alexandria south to Centreville, a village about three miles north of the center of the rebel line.

McDowell was disappointed. He had originally planned to engage the rebels on the relatively open ground east of Centreville, but intelligence and scouting reports revealed that Beauregard had pulled back to a position that afforded more cover. The rebels were dug in along an eight-mile stretch of the south bank of a winding, sluggish stream that covered the approaches to Manassas Junction like an undulating umbrella. Meandering on a southeasterly course to the Potomac, the stream was in places quite narrow and fordable, nothing more than a glorified ditch. But its banks were wooded and steep, and the rebels were concentrated at the several bridges and fords. The name of the stream was Bull Run.

When McDowell reached Centreville, rather than mounting an immediate attack, he decided to bivouac to better organize his forces.

Forty-three-year-old Gen. Irvin McDowell had earned an excellent reputation as a loyal, first-rate officer. A West Point graduate of the same class as Beauregard, the six-foot, massively built McDowell had won the brevet of captain in the Mexican War, and had advanced steadily up the career ladder. A renowned trencherman, but with a strong antipathy to alcohol, he enjoyed the confidence of the cabinet and of Mr. Lincoln, who appointed him brigadier. Only General-in-Chief Winfield Scott was less than pleased at McDowell's appointment to command the Army of Northeastern Virginia. Scott's major objection was McDowell's lack of experience in handling large bodies of troops.

Having established his command at Centreville on July 18, and satisfied as to the state of his forces, McDowell sent a skirmishing detail to probe the center of the rebel line at Blackburn's Ford.

Beauregard was ready for it. As the federal force broke through the tree line on the north bank, it was met by a wall of small arms fire. Yankee bodies fell; Bull Run was tinged with Yankee blood. McDowell's men pulled back. Beauregard was pleased; he had fired the first shot of the war at Sumter, and now he had drawn first blood at Bull Run.

Beauregard had been ready for the Yankees at least as early as July 16, when he received a ciphered message from Mrs. Rose O'Neal Greenhow: "Order issued for McDowell to move on Manassas tonight." Mrs. Greenhow, a tall, olive-skinned beauty of supple, graceful figure, the charming widow of a State Department official, was the center of a circle of well-born Washington ladies whose avocation was spying for the Confederacy. Allan Pinkerton himself, head of Lincoln's secret service, later established her perfidy. Standing in a pouring rain on the shoulders of an aide, peering through a first-floor window, Pinkerton witnessed an exchange of information between Mrs. Greenhow and an obviously smitten young Union army captain detailed to the local provost marshal station.

But even if Beauregard hadn't been forewarned by the raven-haired widow, he would have known the attack was imminent. It was surely the worst of many poorly kept secrets of the war.

McDowell decided that his army, having been bloodied at Blackburn's Ford, would benefit from a couple more days of regrouping and rest. He ordered the advance for the early morning hours of Sunday, July 21.

His strategy was set. His force was divided into four divisions. One was to attack the Stone Bridge, part of the major east-west road that crossed the stream. Two divisions were to flank the upper, or northwest, end of the rebel line in a turning movement. The three divisions would then link up on the south side of the Run and march on to Manassas Junction, about four miles farther south. The fourth division was to be held in reserve while paying special attention to the lower fords to the southeast.

The plan was sound; the troops were rested and eager for action. They outnumbered the enemy. All McDowell needed was the fortunes of war on his side.

Saturday, July 20, dawned hot and humid, and the omens turned sour. The Fourth Pennsylvania Infantry regiment along with a battery of artillery attached to the Eighth, New York, announced that they were leaving the scene. Their ninety-day terms of enlistment had expired.

Toward midday a vexed McDowell was further dismayed to see a horde of Washington civilians descend on Centreville. They came on horseback; they came in carriages, gigs, buggies, and wagons—senators, congressmen, and journalists joined by hundreds of curiosity seekers. It was a summer weekend junket, and they came with their wives and children and servants. Sporting binoculars and picnic baskets, brandy and cigars, they came to watch the ultimate sport, the men in top hats and frock coats, the ladies in crinoline and with gay ruffled parasols. Among the spectators, Simon Cameron; the secretary of war was predicting a smashing victory for the North. They kept coming through the night of the twentieth to the morning of the twenty-first, impeding troop movement, unsettling the troops, and intensifying McDowell's heartburn. He had eaten the better part of a spoiled watermelon Saturday evening.

He would, no doubt, have been more discomfited had he been aware that Saturday night General Johnston slipped nine thousand of his twelve thousand troops into support positions behind Beauregard's line. McDowell's numerical superiority had vanished.

Released by Patterson's withdrawal, Johnston promptly marched his men from Winchester, twenty-five miles south, to Strasburg, a rail point on the Manassas Gap Railway. From Strasburg it was a fifty-mile train ride to Manassas Junction. The maneuver marked the first time in history that a large body of troops was moved by rail into combat. Three thousand men were still on the way when the battle began.

The two Union divisions that were to execute the turning movement were two hours late, enabling the rebels to reinforce their defensive positions. But turn it they finally did. The division assigned to force the Stone Bridge moved punctually at six. They jammed the bridge, a human wall, taking rebel fire point blank. But cross it they did. At terrible cost.

Both sides fought bravely. The federal troops were gallant, being forced to the offensive at all points. They forded the stream in several places, in water sometimes chest high, holding their rifles above their heads. They scrambled up the steep and wooded bank to be met time and again by deadly small arms fire.

Boys from New England, New York, and Pennsylvania left their broken bodies on the banks, their limbs in the trees; blood seeping from torn flesh mingled with the winding stream and, swirling with the current, drained down to the Potomac.

Shortly before noon McDowell had seventeen thousand troops, including four batteries of artillery and seven brigades of infantry, across Bull Run. Galloping along the Union line, he waved his cap in the air, shouting, "Victory! Victory! The day is ours!"

The federal assault was proving irresistible. By one o'clock only one rebel position remained between Union troops and Manassas Junction—a ridge, known as Henry House Hill, protected by a line of pine thickets. It was defended by a brigade of Virginians under the command of Gen. Thomas Jonathan Jackson. It was this same Jackson, the orphan boy who managed to gain entrance to West Point; who carried in his saddlebags a Bible along with a volume of Napoleon's maxims on war; who would neither write a letter to his beloved wife nor read one from her on the Sabbath; but who "with the blessings of an everkind Providence" would on the Sabbath fight and slay an enemy ready for deliverance. At Henry House Hill that day he earned his sobriquet.

General Barnard Bee of the Confederate Third Brigade rode up to Jackson with the cry, "General, they are beating us back!"

"Then, sir," replied Jackson, "we shall give them the bayonet."

Bee galloped back to his brigade of men from Tennessee, Mississippi, and Alabama, shouting, "Look, there stands Jackson like a stone wall. Rally behind the Virginians!" Then he fell from his horse, shot dead.

Jackson posted his men in a line of battle along the edge of the pine thickets and assembled four artillery batteries of twenty-six six-pounders where their fire commanded the level surface of the plateau.

At half past one, McDowell himself, galloping, swearing, screaming, shook loose two batteries of eleven Parrott rifles and emplaced them opposite the Confederate batteries. The Parrotts were the new ten-pounders with a range of 1,950 yards, manned by regular army units. It had become apparent to both commands that the action at Henry House Hill would determine the outcome of the battle.

At the murderous range of 330 yards, the rival batteries slugged it out, profaning the summer Sunday afternoon with the screech and terror of exploding death. Neither side gave an inch.

At about half past two, Captain Griffin, commander of one of the Union batteries, noticed, some 200 yards to his right, a body of infantry advancing. He quickly decided to meet it with canister when a staff officer identified it as a supporting regiment. The men were wearing blue uniforms. With no wind stirring, regimental flags were limp and indistinguishable.

On command, the blue-clad infantry advanced a few paces. The front ranks dropped to their knees, and the regiment, which was the Thirty-third Virginia, poured volley after volley into the ranks of the Union batteries. The few gunners and support personnel left standing remained motionless for an instant, paralyzed with horror. Then they too were cut down.

Still the Union troops came. They stepped over their dead and wounded, avoiding the bleeding bodies and the scattered limbs strewn across the plateau up to the brow of the hill. They ignored the maddened, galloping, riderless horses, many bleeding from their nostrils; others, bellies slashed, lay pawing their blood-rich guts. The din of rebel artillery and screaming men and animals masked the crack of rifle fire.

To the advancing Union troops only the sharp spurts of orange flame marked the rebel infantry concealed amongst the trees. Jackson's men were well trained and frugal with ammunition. Almost every flash of orange was followed by a staggered, slumping body in Union blue.

Simon Cameron's brother, a colonel, was cut down leading a charge a few yards from Henry House, leaving his regiment, the New York Seventy-ninth, leaderless.

Grim old Union Col. Sam Heintzelman, bearded, unkempt and bitter because at fifty-six he was still a colonel, had his forearm shattered by a bullet. Doctor King galloped to him and tried to dislodge the slug while both men were still mounted, Heintzelman swearing and fuming at the delay.

On the blood-soaked ground amid the twitching, kicking, still-harnessed horses, an artilleryman from New York mutely held up two bleeding stumps where his hands had been, as a rebel cavalryman, saber raised, galloped toward him.

The brunt of the fighting now fell to the Pennsylvania brigade, which had only three regiments, the fourth having decamped the previous day.

At four o'clock, Jackson's brigade broke out of the tree line, and with rebel yells and fixed bayonets charged the blue line on the plateau. At the same moment the remainder of Johnston's Army of the Shenandoah, three thousand troops fresh off the train, attacked the naked flank of the Union forces.

The Yankee line sagged. Minutes later it broke.

The retreat was orderly at first. But when the Union troops recrossed Bull Run they encountered the Washington sightseers. The terror of the women at the prospect of being captured by rebel troops was communicated to their men. Panic seized the spectators. They streaked for Washington, leaving picnic hampers, bottles of wine, and carriages overturned in their haste.

The hysteria spread to the troops, and the retreat became a rout. Abandoning their packs, and in some instances their weapons, the troops turned tail and ran. A lucky Confederate shell scored a direct hit on a fleeing wagon as it was crossing the narrow Cub Run Bridge, thus closing off the main escape route. The rout became a stampede.

The troops didn't stop at Centreville; they poured through it on their way to the Potomac. Some ten thousand terms of enlistment were due to expire in the next few days. These men were not about to regroup and return to fight.

The rebel command, joined by Jefferson Davis up from Richmond, conferred. Jackson, the light of battle sparking his dark eyes, urged attack and pursuit. "Now!" he cried, he whose spiritual guide was Jesus of Nazareth, he who was already gaining a reputation for shooting deserters more swiftly and with less ceremony than any other general, North or South. "Now is the time to strike, pursue them to their Yankee capital, capture the government and end it all!" But Davis and Beauregard demurred. The Confederacy too had sustained heavy losses; the army was in disarray. They needed time to regroup. Davis prevailed. The rebel force did not press their advantage.

CHAPTER

X

In Washington that Sunday morning of July 21, the president awoke with the first light, as was his custom, aware that McDowell had begun his offensive. By eleven o'clock when he went to church with his family there was still no news. Lincoln betrayed no visible signs of anxiety or stress.

After church he returned to the executive mansion with Mary Todd and the boys and, foregoing lunch, walked through the park to the War Department, where the first telegrams had begun to come in.

The early reports were inconclusive. Toward three in the afternoon, telegrams began arriving with greater frequency and the news fluctuated. The president walked across the street to army headquarters at 17th and F, where General Scott had his office. Scott was asleep, lying on his back on a cot, snoring heavily, his gouty leg resting on a chair. After a moment of hesitation, the president asked an aide to awaken the general to discuss the reports.

Sitting up, Scott dismissed these first reports as meaningless. Changes in wind currents and variations in echoes made it impossible for a distant listener to determine the course of a battle. Nevertheless, he expressed confidence: McDowell's plan of battle was sound, and he outnumbered the enemy. The president left and Scott lay back to resume his nap.

When the president returned to the War Department he found that dispatches had been arriving every ten to fifteen minutes and were growing more optimistic. The rebel line had been driven back several miles, its rear at Manassas Junction. One of Scott's aides brought a telegram reiterating the news that McDowell had driven the enemy before him, adding that he had ordered his reserve division to cross Bull Run. The aide said that General Scott was satisfied with the truth of the report and that McDowell would capture the junction if not this evening then certainly by noon tomorrow. The president ordered his carriage for his usual evening drive.

At six o'clock he had not returned when Secretary Seward came to the executive office, haggard and breathless, the color drained from his face. "Where's the president?" he demanded hoarsely of Nicolay and Hay.

"Gone to drive."

"Have you any late news?" Nicolay read to him the telegrams announcing victory. "Tell no one," panted Seward, "the battle is lost. McDowell is in full retreat and calls on Scott to save the capital. Find the president and tell him to come immediately to General Scott's."

A half hour later Lincoln listened in silence to Nicolay and Hay's report, and without change of expression walked across the park to army headquarters. He was handed a telegram sent by a captain in the corps of engineers: "General McDowell's army in full retreat through Centreville. The day is lost. Save Washington and the remnants of the Army. The routed troops will not re-form."

Scott angrily dismissed the message. He had in hand two contradictory reports, one putting the rebels in retreat beyond Bull Run, the other reporting McDowell in hopeless and disorganized retreat this side of Bull Run.

A few minutes later a telegram from McDowell confirmed the disaster, but said that he would hold at Centreville. Fifteen minutes later a second wire came from McDowell: "The larger part of the men are a confused mob, entirely demoralized." He planned now to make a stand at Fairfax Courthouse.

After several hours a third telegram advised: "Many of the volunteers did not wait for authority to proceed to the Potomac but left on their own decision. I think now, as all of my commanders thought at Centreville, there is no alternative but to fall back to the Potomac."

The president conferred with Scott about measures for the defense of Washington, then returned to the White House. It was almost midnight. He had been active for eighteen hours and his day was not yet over. Reclining on the sofa in his office, he began to receive the first of the civilians to return from the battle scene, those fortunate enough to hold onto their horses and carriages.

Tales of horror and stampede abounded. Several of the congressmen said they had tried to stem the tide of retreat, brandishing pistols at the fleeing troops, but they were swept aside as if by a tidal wave. Among the civilians captured by the rebels was Congressman Alfred Ely of New York, who was now on his way to a Richmond prison. Strewn along the twenty-mile route to Washington were uniforms, blankets, haversacks, canteens, rifles, broken harness, overturned wagons—the loot to the rebels incalculable.

Mostly the president listened, said little, and took notes with pad and pencil. But to one excited witness who claimed complete victory for the Union, he drawled, "So, it's your notion that we whipped the rebels and then ran away from them."

There was no sleep for the president that night. He continued receiving visitors into the small hours of Monday morning, recording each version of the battle, each opinion as to the cause of defeat, and each recipe for future victory. Over and over again he heard that the troops lacked discipline, leadership was inadequate, communication poor. The system of using volunteers for short, fixed periods of time was worse than useless. How can one expect a man to be daring and brave in battle when he knows he is to be mustered out in a few days?

When the stream of callers stopped, he put aside pad and pencil, removed his gold-rimmed eyeglasses, and wrapped himself in his long brown shawl. In stockinged feet he walked to the window; there he stood looking into the blackness, listening to the rain beating on the White House eaves.

Alone, Lincoln began to grieve. It was his time to weep and to mourn. He mourned through the dark hours as only a president and commander in chief, with a full sense of responsibility and an awareness of the political and military options, can mourn. He sorrowed with harrowing questions, tortured answers, tormented speculation, terrible what ifs. Gray remorse and leaden guilt poisoned his innards.

It was apparent even at this early hour that the casualties in dead and wounded would run to the hundreds if not thousands; he didn't distinguish between North and South. American boys lay dead and dying on the plains before Manassas and on the banks of Bull Run. Why?

To what avail? What had been accomplished? How could the carnage possibly be justified? Bull Run was no step toward resolution of the conflict, no step toward ultimate victory for the Confederate States of America. The Union must and would prevail. Would Bull Run have to be fought again and again and again?

Scott was right, his strategy correct. Little piecemeal wars would simply bleed the country white. Manassas had been neither the time nor the place for a confrontation. As president he had pandered to the pressure of public opinion, and now boys lay dead and dying. But dear God, what choice did he have? If the Union was to be preserved, if the evil institution of men enslaving men was to be ended, men had first to die. But for this death-obsessed man, this simple answer was unacceptable. He had in his lifetime known too much death.

It began when he was a child, seated at the family hearth. The first oft-told tale was of the death of his grandfather, slain by Indians, leaving Abraham's father an orphan at six. When Abraham was ten, his mother, Nancy Hanks, died; she was thirty-four. The chores of keeping house and doing for the menfolk fell to Sarah, his twelve-year-old sister. When he was nineteen, working on a ferryboat on the Ohio River, Sarah, then twenty-one, died in childbirth. She had been a second mother to him.

He was a young representative from Sangamon County serving in the Illinois statehouse when the news came that his friend Ann Rutledge was dead of "brain fever" at twenty-two. It was then that the poem by William Knox began to come so readily to mind:

> 'Tis the wink of an eye; 'tis the draught of a breath
> From the blossom of health to the paleness of death,
> From the gilded saloon to the bier and the shroud;
> O, why should the spirit of mortal be proud?

In 1850 when he was a congressman, he and Mary Todd suffered the unkindest cut. After two months of illness their four-year-old son, Eddie, died—their beautiful boy in the cold, unfeeling ground. Lincoln did not think he could bear the hurt, and Mary Todd never really recovered. Thereafter she became anxious in ways she had never been, especially when the welfare of her husband and sons was at issue. She suffered dreadful headaches and harbored unreasonable fears about poverty.

The bouts of melancholy, from which Lincoln had suffered since he was a young man, began to intensify. The condition was referred to as "the hypochondria," deep cycles of depression that lasted for days, sometimes weeks. When he was suffering from the hypochondria, it was not unusual during a conversation—it didn't matter with whom—for his speech to gradually lower to a whisper and finally trail off to silence. A pained look as of dim, unwelcome remembrance would cloud his eyes. For minutes at a time he would sit thus, closed off by an impenetrable wall, remote, lost. When he returned it was often with an anecdote or a small joke by way of apology for his absence.

Lincoln's opiate was work and humor. "He used humor," an acquaintance said, "to whistle down the sadness."

"I tell you the truth," the president confided to an old friend from Illinois, "when I say that a funny story, if it has the element of genuine wit, has the same effect on me that I suppose a good, square drink of whiskey has on an old toper; it puts new life into me."

That gray Monday morning after Bull Run, Hay found Lincoln on the couch, hollow eyed, gaunt, wrapped in his long, fringed brown shawl, putting his notes in order.

A steady, drenching rain had set in about midnight. With the dawn, gray and wet, the retreating troops reached the bridges over the Potomac and began straggling into Washington. Baffled and humiliated, mud-caked and exhausted, they dropped in their tracks—in the middle of the street, on the sidewalks, on the steps of houses—some still clutching rifles. There they lay, the rain pelting them, small rivulets forming in the mud caked on their uniforms and on their pain-etched faces. Those residents who were sympathetic (most of Washington exulted in the rebel triumph) began to move among them with hot soup and bandages.

At State, Seward, haggard and disheveled, looked down from a window through the gloom to the soldiers of the Grand Army, a ghostly battalion shuffling down Pennsylvania Avenue through the mist. His thoughts did not dwell on the military disaster. His concern was with its effect on opinion in Europe.

The president, having washed and dressed and breakfasted on an egg, his first food in twenty-four hours, sat at the small round table in his office, drafting a memorandum on the basis of his notes made on the battle. It was a nine-point program for the future conduct of the war, and it began: "1. Let the plan for making the blockade effective be pushed forward with all possible dispatch. . . ."

Throughout the South that Monday morning, the soft July rain seemed to enhance the jubilation. Celebration was the order of the day as church bells pealed the news of the glorious victory. The Battle of Manassas clearly demonstrated the superiority of Southern gallantry and the gentleman warrior over the scurvy wretches of the Northern slums.

Victory in the war's first pitched battle bestowed on the Confederacy a sudden legitimacy and respectability. The rebel command scented a triumphant outcome to the war. It was just a question of time before King Cotton brought England and France to the side of the South. And while it was true that the Yankee blockade was a threat, happily it had proved to be no more than that. Leroy Pope Walker showed his contempt for it by ordering eighteen thousand new Enfield rifles from England.

Every Southern city of any size was planning its Bull Run Ball. And from Richmond came rumors and whispers about an invincible iron ship that would soon smash the Yankee Navy and end the threat of blockade forever.

CHAPTER

XI

The Sunday evening of Bull Run found Secretary Welles in his office at the Navy Department. Earlier in the day when the issue was still in doubt he had stopped by the telegraph room at the War Department for the latest reports.

Finding the president and several members of the cabinet, notably Seward, Chase, and Blair, in attendance, Welles chose not to remain. Advising Mr. Lincoln that he would be in his office if needed, he walked the few yards from War to Navy, sat at his desk, and tried to concentrate on cleaning up some of the correspondence that had accumulated in reproachful mounds.

On top of one of the piles that contained letters from unofficial sources, he noticed the lucid, flowing script of Mrs. John L. Worden. After seeing twenty letters, he reflected, one gets to recognize the hand. Without reading it he knew it was another plea for intercession on behalf of her husband, who, according to Mrs. Worden, was desperately ill and was, with no legal or moral justification, being detained by Confederate authorities. Why didn't the federal government intercede on his behalf? With a flush of guilt Welles knew that he could not respond to this letter any more than he could to the previous eight or ten that he had let go unanswered. What was there to say? After agreeing that the detention was unjust, he could only explain that he was powerless to do anything about it. As a member of the cabinet he could not negotiate Worden's release, because the Union refused to deal with the rebel government.

Poor Worden. He wondered how he was getting on. Not very well if unofficial reports were to be believed. He didn't stir from his cell, although he was supposed to have liberal exercise privileges. And despite the fact that his jailers allowed him to purchase whatever provisions he chose, he ate next to nothing. Rumor had it that he had lost a dreadful amount of weight, and that if he were not released soon, he wasn't likely to last much longer.

Welles wished there was something he could do. In their one brief meeting, the tall lieutenant with the quiet manner had inspired his confidence and respect. He felt somewhat responsible for Worden's plight, since it was he who had sent him on the mission—a mission well accomplished. At the same time, he felt that Worden had demonstrated poor judgment in trying to return to Washington through Pensacola. In any case, there was nothing to be done now. His hands were tied. The government refused to negotiate with the Confederacy on the ground that it lacked legitimacy. It simply did not exist. It had no status as a nation or as a belligerent, and could therefore be dealt with only through unofficial channels.

The rebels were willing to exchange Worden for a captured Confederate officer of the same rank, but only if negotiations were conducted on a formal level as between two sovereign states. Both the president and Seward were strongly opposed to any action that might be construed as acknowledgment or recognition of the CSA. If the Union were to compromise in this instance, it was argued, what then could be expected of foreign powers?

As it was, Queen Victoria had already accorded recognition of sorts to the rebel government when she declared the "royal determination to maintain a strict and impartial neutrality in the contest between the United States and certain states styling themselves the Confederate States of America."

"The United States," trumpeted the *London Times* on the occasion of the royal pronouncement, "has ceased to be."

The royal determination to maintain a strict and impartial neutrality, thought Welles bitterly, apparently did not prevent Her Majesty's subjects from supplying ships and guns to the rebels. England's next step, probably when her mills ran out of raw cotton, would more than likely be outright alliance.

In any case, the president's policy of strict nonrecognition of the CSA was probably the correct course. Worden, at least for the present, would have to remain in a Montgomery jail.

Welles turned his thoughts away from the lieutenant to the day's events, ruminating on his action of that afternoon when he walked out of the telegraph office, advising the president where he could be reached. Had that been wise? Politic? Considerate? Could he have been of aid and comfort to Mr. Lincoln by remaining with him? He tried to persuade himself that his behavior had been quite proper. There were plenty of others there, cabinet and military. The battle had been strictly an army operation. There was no point getting underfoot. If Mr. Lincoln wanted him, he knew where to find him. Once summoned he could be at his side in two minutes. He thought of the other cabinet secretaries as mousing around the president, currying favor, seeking to become his confidant. The one cabinet member who most certainly should have been there, Secretary of War Simon Cameron, was conspicuous by his absence.

Welles had very strict notions about what was seemly behavior with respect to the chief executive. One went to him when summoned or in an emergency. Otherwise one kept one's distance.

The fact was, he was uncomfortable with the men who surrounded the president. He was not one of the clique who met regularly with Mr. Lincoln on an official and a social basis. His perception of himself in Washington was that of rara avis, an admittedly political animal who was not easily and naturally gregarious. He envied those who were, those fortunate types who could slip gracefully into the company of men wherever they were, geography and political persuasion notwithstanding.

Seward was of that happy fraternity. With his rich cigars, his brandy-loosened wit, profane and brilliant, and with the piercing but humor-edged cynicism of one who has known the underside of politics as party leader and as governor and senator of a great state ("I've seen everything twice," he liked to say), Seward fit right in with the old friends from Illinois and the old boys from the president's early days in the Congress. The secretary of state spent evening after bibulous evening in the convivial company of men who had risen to eminence playing the political game, even at times on opposite sides.

Although the president neither drank hard liquor nor used tobacco, his appreciation for lively company and a good story, in the hearing or the telling, was already legend. It was after hours in the executive chamber that the president found ease and sustenance, surrounded by his cronies, scratching his elbows as he gleefully delivered the "snapper," reveling in the knee-slapping laughter of men who had traveled the same road. And it was for this company that Welles for some reason was not qualified. That he was not one of them was certainly not entirely his choice. On the other hand they had never declared him unwelcome. It was rather one of those delicate, unspoken understandings on the part of both Welles and the president's men (not the president) that somehow all would be happier—or perhaps less constrained—were Welles to withhold his honored presence.

Yet, like them, he too had traveled the political road. He had served for nine years in the Connecticut legislature; was state comptroller for three terms; postmaster of Hartford; and chief of the navy's Bureau of Provisions and Clothing. He had made the race for Congress and the Senate but been defeated both times.

Welles pushed aside the stacks of correspondence and, tilting back in his swivel chair, crossed his short legs on the desk. Reclining comfortably, he lit his pipe and reflected on Gideon Welles as others saw him, in an effort to understand why he seemed to be on the periphery rather than at the center.

At fifty-nine he probably cut a slightly ridiculous figure. When he jogged about the capital on his horse for after-hours exercise, conspicuous with bushy white beard and elaborate brown wig, he was beginning to feel self-conscious if not a bit foolish. New England behavior apparently didn't travel well to the nation's capital.

As a public servant he was meticulous (to others, probably fussy), demanding (tyrannical), thoroughly honest (fanatical), loyal (to Abe Lincoln), and conscientious (to a fault). Some, he knew, called him "the old lady at the Navy Department." The president, referring to him as "Father Neptune," liked to tell the story of a dying sailor whose last wish was that he might see his grandmother, to whom he was devoted. The lady being unavailable, a messenger was dispatched to the Navy Department to implore Secretary Welles to don petticoats and impersonate her. But Welles regretfully declined, offering the excuse that he was examining a model of Noah's ark, with a view to its introduction in the U.S. Navy. Not really very funny. But then, Western humor is primitive.

On the positive side, his private life afforded, as far as he knew, no cause for criticism. A dedicated family man, loving husband to a beautiful wife (fifteen years his junior), devoted father to their six children (it could have, should have, been nine). Three times he had to tell her, his darling, his throat so constricted with grief that he could barely get out the words, that her . . . their baby was. . . . He still couldn't say it. Didn't know how to tell her, standing there at her bedside, mopping his face with a handkerchief, apologetic as though somehow it was his fault . . . if only he had. . . . Three times she had lain there, a week—two—three—each time longer than the last, hollow eyed, uncomprehending. Their beautiful babies. But he couldn't think about that now.

Could Mary Jane be part of the problem? At forty-four her beauty had mellowed to a glowing loveliness—poised, ripe, charming. If there was gossip, it was probably not the men. It was their wives—old battle-axes—who were offended by the disparity in their ages and their evident happiness. Old busybodies. The Beauty and the Beast. Well, Washington would have to take them as they were. That was another thing old Abe and Seward had in common—troubled wives. Mary Todd with her headaches and her fears about the safety of her boys and about poverty. And Frances Seward plagued by depression, convinced that her nerves and her vascular system were going to pieces. No wonder the president and Seward sought each other's company. The alternative was an evening with a shrewish wife.

What was it particularly about Washington that made him persona non grata? He had never had that difficulty back home. There he was accepted for what he was, a hardworking, honest newspaperman and politician.

But the total persona—virtues, faults, warts, and all—whatever it was, did not commend him to the society he coveted here and now. Whatever it was that enabled him to succeed in Connecticut just didn't stand up in the nation's capital. And at his age he was not about to change. But he was also too honest not to admit that it hurt, especially when he saw Seward, patently one of the president's most dangerous and outspoken political enemies, enjoying the privileges of crony and confidant. Although the secretary of state had presumably made an about-face and was now one of Mr. Lincoln's supporters, Welles had always been that . . . at least since that windswept March night at the Hartford station.

When earlier in the evening an aide brought him news of the defeat at Bull Run, his first thought was of the president. How was he taking it? He hoped it wouldn't lay him low. Everyone was aware that he was worn, run-down, nerves stretched like piano wires. Of late he barely slept and only picked at his food. The pressures on him were more than mortal man should be expected to bear. He hoped the president wouldn't snap under the strain and succumb to one of the deadly summer fevers that seemed to be felling half the capital.

There was no question in his mind but that Lincoln was the linchpin of the government. It was he who held it together, he alone who had no personal ax to grind. His motives were solely and exclusively dedicated to victory and to the preservation of the Union. Without him. . . . Welles could envision no government without him. Certainly no member of the cabinet was qualified to take his place. Vice President Hannibal Hamlin was one of the few well-intentioned and able men in the cabinet, but he was hardly equal to the task. All the others were self-serving mediocrities.

As for Bull Run, it was a shocker. No one really expected defeat. It was obvious that radical changes would have to be made in the leadership. From planning to supply and combat, the battle had been exclusively an army operation. He could not help but derive a small glow of satisfaction from that.

The more he thought about it, the more convinced he became that Bull Run could turn out to be a blessing. For one thing, it was going to clear the air and wake people up to the nature of the enemy. The South was a determined and resourceful foe. If she was to be beaten, bitter sacrifice must be the price. It was going to be a long and tragic war with a people who were fighting to preserve their rights, their homes, and their sacred honor. Bull Run had demonstrated how formidable a combination they were.

With the recent secession of Arkansas, North Carolina, and Tennessee, the Confederacy was now a compact nation of eleven states, with a territory more than double the size of any European power except Russia, and a population of five and a half million whites and three and a half million Negroes. She had a seacoast that stretched more than three thousand miles from the Chesapeake to the Gulf of Mexico, with a number of fine harbors and many navigable rivers. Her interior waterways would be of inestimable value in the transport of foodstuffs and materiel. And she had the advantage of fighting along interior lines.

There was no way the federal armies could force their way into the South, fighting every step of the way, trying to beat each state into submission. There wasn't time enough, men enough, money enough.

Welles sighed and knocked the dottle from his pipe. Certainly the defeat would force a review of strategy. Neither side could afford many more Bull Runs. Scott's strategy of total blockade or "Anaconda" proposal looked more and more attractive. The old man had made sense. And he was not without influence on the president. If Scott's plan were adopted, it would mean a vastly expanded role for the Navy. Welles sighed again, sat up in his chair, put the pipe in its drawer, and picked up the nearest pile of letters.

In the course of the next two days Welles's speculations were confirmed when he received a copy of the president's memorandum directing that the blockade be accorded first priority. His reaction was mixed. He was gratified by his implied elevation to a position of central importance in the war effort, but he was at the same time made uneasy by the unreadiness of the fleet.

He summoned Fox to his office and showed him the president's memorandum. "You know," said Welles, "what the first question will be at the next cabinet meeting."

Fox nodded. Stroking his black beard he replied after a moment, "I believe you have a reasonably good story to tell. The blockade is now credible. Even Her Majesty's government has agreed to respect it."

"Yes," said Welles, "but that doesn't stop those damned limeys from selling their blockade runners to the rebels. I understand those steamers are really slick—fast and easily concealed. They're playing hob with the fleet."

"Look on the positive side. Every one of our steam-powered ships of the line is back home and in the blockading squadron. There's not one in a foreign port. Every private steam-powered ship that can be fitted for a gun is being bought, borrowed, or commandeered. We've got commission brokers in every state of the Union—including your brother-in-law in New York—scouring the rivers and the seas for likely ships. We've got seven sloops of war and twenty-three gunboats under contract for construction." As Fox warmed to the task, his dark eyes took on their characteristic glint. "I believe," he concluded, "you ought to walk into that cabinet meeting with your sails full and your pennants flying."

Welles smiled. "I do appreciate the morale builder, Captain, but the fact is, at this moment, we have twenty-four blessed steamers to enforce a blockade that stretches from Hampton Roads to south Texas, some thirty-five hundred miles of coastline. What does that work out to per ship per mile? About a hundred and fifty miles per ship? Not a very formidable force."

"It's growing."

Though he was admittedly not of sanguine disposition, Welles actually had legitimate cause to feel uneasy—cause that transcended his concern about the inadequacy of the blockading squadron. There was on the horizon a black cloud that seemed to be growing larger and more ominous every day. It was as though the time-honored rules of the game were about to be changed. Nagging at the secretary was the sense that something new, something revolutionary was in the offing. And he felt ill-prepared to deal with it. He recognized that he was seriously deficient in matters of marine warfare, especially as they related to technological advance.

When early in May he had been informed of Stephen Mallory's recommendation to a Confederate congressional committee that it urgently consider the construction of ironclad vessels of war, Welles found the news interesting but little cause for alarm. He knew that the South, with her lack of industrial resources, was not in a position to produce a steam-powered ironclad. Nor was it likely that she could persuade England or France to part with the one or two prototype vessels they had developed.

Welles's interest was nonetheless piqued. If Mallory felt that strongly about ironclads, there must be something to them. Welles had the virtue of knowing his own limitations. He was only too well aware that on the subject of naval architecture he was way out of his depth, and he freely admitted that Mallory was by far the more experienced and knowledgeable, particularly in the matter of ironclads.

It was Mallory, as chairman of the U.S. Senate's Naval Affairs Committee, who had headed the inquiry into the Stevens battery. In 1842 the Hoboken engineer won a government contract to build an ironclad battery or war steamer. Congress appropriated a quarter of a million dollars for the purpose. In 1856, fourteen years later, the battery was still incomplete and another quarter of a million had been spent. Stevens petitioned for an additional $812,000 to finish the job. Stevens's problem was that each time he came up with an armored hull, a new gun appeared that was able to pierce it. The Navy refused to endorse his request for the additional appropriation. Congress was happy to save the money, and the project was abandoned.

Immediately after Sumter, at Welles's suggestion, a board of naval officers had been convened to reexamine the rusting Stevens hull. The board subsequently rejected the ironclad battery as a candidate for completion and commission because it felt that she would draw too much water and as a consequence would lack the maneuverability and speed vital for naval operations.

But here was Mallory, intimately acquainted with the history of the failed experiment, insisting that his government pursue the concept. Moreover, there were England and France in hot competition to construct ironclad men-o'-war. There must be something to them, something more than was indicated by the Bureau of Construction's Lenthall report. As secretary of the Navy, Welles felt obliged at the very least to give his government the opportunity to reevaluate iron as a shipbuilding medium. That would not, he knew, prove to be a simple task.

To begin, a good part of the senior officer corps was predisposed to reject the concept, and their opinion would weigh heavily with the Congress, which would have to appropriate the funds for any kind of investigation or experiment. Welles, on the contrary, put little stock in the opinion of the officer corps. Their judgment did not persuade him that the concept of ironclad warships was impractical or unworkable. He had been exposed to the navy bureaucracy long enough to realize that the service, especially the top brass, did not take kindly to change of any sort. And when such proposed change contradicted an opinion recently rendered by a naval board composed of their peers, it was doomed without question.

Welles had done what he usually did when confronted by a question of a technical nature. He summoned his assistant secretary. "What do you think, Fox, shall we recommend construction of an ironclad?"

Fox considered the question for several moments. "I don't see," he said slowly, "how we can expect the Congress to approve an appropriation in view of the negative recommendation on the Stevens battery."

"For heaven's sake, man! The Stevens battery was designed twenty years ago. I expect the technology has improved since then."

"I'm not so sure. I haven't seen anything since to persuade me that the concept is viable."

"You're like all the others," said Welles. "Twenty years in the service has left its mark." Fox smiled. In their discussions they had fallen, by unspoken mutual consent, into role-playing, Fox speaking for the career officer bound by military tradition, by the conservatism peculiar to the seafarer, and by a bone-deep distrust of change; Welles, who had never spent a day at sea, represented the eternal landlubber condemned to the thankless task of introducing new ideas in a hostile environment.

"Really," said Fox, "the viability of iron at sea has never been demonstrated to the satisfaction of the department. You're fighting an uphill battle. Anyone can see that wood is naturally buoyant; it floats. Iron is another matter."

"What about the English and French batteries in the Crimean War?"

"Inshore ironclad batteries are one thing. Oceangoing ironclad vessels are another. Certainly, one can put an iron belt around a wooden hull and it will float. But the question is, how thick can the plate be? Thick enough to take a twelve-inch shell? And if so, how much dead weight does that mean? How much water will she draw? How maneuverable will she be?"

"We'll never know," said Welles, "until we build one."

"Well, the Congress will not be in a mood to spend for a vessel that has not been proved, and they won't be inclined to spend for another experiment. And the brass aren't going to go out of their way to lobby for it. They'd rather stay with what they know. And you can't blame them. This is hardly the time to be introducing a whole new fighting environment."

"The brass!" exclaimed Welles. "If they had their way we'd still be without steam propulsion. Canvas is really the only thing they trust. They think steam is a passing fancy. After some thirty years and millions of miles they're still not sure steam is here to stay. How many times have you heard them (Welles roughened his throat to a whiskey-coarsened growl), 'Give me a trim three-master, a proper gale, and we're the equal of anything afloat.'

"You know the old saw," Welles switched again to his whiskey voice, " 'I'm willing to be hacked to pieces by cutlass, riddled by bullets, blown to bits by shot and shell, but I'm damned if I'm prepared to be cooked alive by an exploding steam boiler!' "

"Well," said Fox, "you have to say this for sail: One doesn't have to take up space storing fuel; one doesn't have to be concerned about staying within range of a coaling station; and sail has never been known to scald anyone to death."

"And," finished Welles, "without smoke, your canvas and your decks remain sparkling white." He dismissed the subject with a resigned shake of his head. "Let's get back to the question of ironclads. Do we or don't we recommend building at least one?"

They had agreed to study the question further and meet during the second week in June, at which time they would decide. Should they decide affirmatively, there would be enough time for the president to incorporate their proposal into his Fourth of July message to the Congress.

Coincidentally, it was when Welles and Fox met again in June that they learned that the *Merrimack* had been raised and was in dry dock at the Norfolk yard. They assumed that if she was salvageable, the rebels would rehabilitate her as an auxiliary motor and sail frigate. "In what sort of condition could her engines be, after soaking in that saltwater?" mused Fox.

On the subject of ironclads they had decided on what they felt was a modest proposal. Mr. Lincoln readily accepted it and included it in his July message to the Congress.

The presidential message was substantially a petition for the legal sanction and the means to put down the rebellion. He asked for four hundred thousand men and four hundred million dollars. In the bill of particulars was the recommendation of the secretary of the Navy.

Welles's recommendation, which was published in the *New York Times* (thus assuring that the rebels would be apprised without delay of the department's intent), noted the attention that other governments were giving ironclad steamers and called for the appointment of a proper and competent board to inquire into the matter. Playing the bureaucratic game to the hilt, he added, "And it is for the Congress to decide whether on a favorable report they will order one or more ironclad steamers or floating batteries."

Fox's forebodings were proving correct. The Congress had readily approved most of what the president had asked for by way of legal sanction and funds. But here it was July 18, two weeks after the president had delivered his message, and not a move had been made in either house on Welles's proposal. The Congress was clearly in no hurry to act on the question of ironclad vessels for the Navy.

Welles understood too well the reason for the impasse: his relationship with the chairman of the Naval Affairs Committee, Senator John P. Hale of New Hampshire. The two men were barely on speaking terms. The senator had previously approached Welles on behalf of some friends and constituents who were offering to sell their services to the Navy in a manner the secretary considered less than savory. Welles rejected Hale's approach in terms so harsh and peremptory that thereafter the chairman became the department's severest critic instead of its staunchest friend in the Senate.

Welles was desperate. He had a sense that time was running out. Mallory was nothing if not resourceful. If anyone could, he would find a way to beg, borrow, steal, or even build an ironclad.

Then Welles got lucky. He found impetus for a Union-built ironclad in a most unexpected quarter. On July 18, a Pinkerton agent handed him a copy of Stephen Mallory's most recent report to President Davis on the subject of the *Merrimack*. It had cost $6,000 to raise her. To rehabilitate her to her former condition as an auxiliary motor and sail frigate would require approximately $450,000. There was, however, an attractive alternative. For an expenditure of $172,523, they could make of her an ironclad warship. Mallory assured Davis that in an ironclad *Merrimack* the CSA would have an invincible vessel, one that would be able to "contend successfully against the heaviest of the enemy's ships and drive them from Hampton Roads," anchorage of the U.S. blockading squadron. The Pinkerton report added that Mallory, apparently without waiting for anyone's approval, or for an appropriation, had given the order to proceed immediately with the rehabilitation and refitting of the *Merrimack* as an ironclad.

So the *Merrimack,* torched to her waterline, mired in the mud and brackish water of the Elizabeth River for forty days, a glistening, slimy, charred hulk, with engines, machinery, and boilers on the verge of turning to rust, was to be reborn as the first ironclad warship of the Confederate Navy.

Once again Welles felt the cold knife of panic invade his bowels. His fears that Mallory would somehow be able to produce an ironclad were realized. And it was already well on the way.

On the following day, Senator James Grimes of Iowa, moved by news of rebel intentions, introduced a bill directing the secretary of the Navy to appoint a board of three skillful naval officers charged with investigating plans for armored steamships or steam batteries.

On August 3 the Congress passed a measure endorsing appointment of a board, and it appropriated a million and a half dollars for construction of one or more armored batteries on the condition that the board report favorably. The president approved the measure the same day.

Welles immediately wired copy for a classified advertisement to newspapers throughout the Northeast. He expected the ad to appear in the editions of Wednesday, August 7. Wednesday was the traditional day for notices of government requests for bids. Unhappily, the copy did not reach the papers in time for the August 7 editions. It was published on the following Wednesday, August 14.

Under the headline "Iron-clad Steam Vessels," the notice stated that the Navy Department was open to offers for the construction of one or more iron-clad steam vessels of war, either of iron or of wood and iron combined, for river service. The vessel was to be of not less than ten nor more than sixteen feet draught of water; it was to carry armament of from eighty to one hundred and twenty tons weight, with provisions and stores for from one hundred sixty-five to three hundred persons, for sixty days. The vessel was to be rigged with two masts and wire-rope standing rigging. Respondents were asked to notify the department of their intention to bid before August 15 (virtually impossible), and to present their propositions by Tuesday, September 3, now only twenty days hence.

CHAPTER

XII

At precisely 8:30 on Wednesday morning, August 14, a stocky, strongly built man with full side beards, wearing a well-cut dark frock coat, velvet vest, snowy white shirt, and black cravat, sat down to breakfast in the dining room of his home at 95 Franklin Street in lower Manhattan. Although he was fifty-eight, his military bearing, air of vitality, and high color were that of a much younger man, the probable consequence of two hours of calisthenics on arising, a cold sponge bath, and robust Swedish genes.

With practiced fingers he tucked an immaculate linen napkin into his collar with one hand and with the other reached for the morning *Tribune,* which lay crisply folded to the right of his place setting. His housekeeper, Miss Ann Cassidy, a shapely, fair-skinned young woman, walked noiselessly in from the kitchen and laid a dish of cool, wine-colored fruit compote before him along with a tall tumbler of water cooled to twenty degrees below room temperature, in accordance with precise instructions from her employer.

"Good morning, Captain Ericsson," she beamed, her handsome features and red hair lit by the morning radiance. "Lovely day!" Circling behind him she deftly removed one of two loaves of napkin-covered bread from the mantel and placed it on a plate within the captain's reach.

He preferred that bread be left to mature to a prescribed degree of staleness before it was served.

"Good morning! Good morning!" he responded heartily but somewhat absently, being absorbed in the front page of the newspaper, which consisted almost entirely of classified advertisements. His eye was momentarily arrested by a striking notice that ran almost the length of the page in the middle column. Headed, "Barnum's American Museum," it read: "The manager is highly gratified in being able to announce to his patrons the engagement of the most wonderful and extraordinary novelty [the line "wonderful and extraordinary novelty" was repeated four times in bold type] ever offered to the people of New York, a living Hippopotamus from the River Nile in Egypt. . . ."

The captain was not interested in such novelties. His eye flicked to the adjacent column on the right, headed "Proposals." In an eight-inch-long advertisement, the Navy's Bureau of Construction was calling for bids to build twelve side-wheel steamers. Side-wheel! He grunted in disbelief. The Navy dies hard. The captain continued scanning down the column to the next notice, a twelve-inch appeal from the Navy for "machinery for screw steam sloops." Interesting. But not for him. One should be grateful, though, that they've progressed to the screw propeller.

His eye continued its downward course and came to rest on a two-and-one-half-inch block near the bottom of the page, headed "Iron-clad Steam Vessels." He read this notice with great interest, reread it, shook his head in wonderment, then read it again, muttering, ". . . three hundred men . . . one hundred and twenty tons . . . two masts. . . ."

Miss Cassidy brought in a bowl of steaming oatmeal and, noting the untouched fruit, said, "Captain, are ye not hungry this morning?"

"Yes, yes, of course," he mumbled and, putting the paper aside, hastily spooned up the compote. Taking up the paper again he read and reread the specifications as he downed his porridge, two soft eggs with bread, and a cup of hot, very strong tea, muttering this time, "They're mad," or simply, "Imbeciles!"

Having finished breakfast, he repaired to his study, a generous room lit by two large windows facing south and stretching almost from ceiling to floor. The windows were neither shuttered nor curtained; the captain believed in the salutary properties of sunlight.

The room was furnished with three heavy, beautifully carved walnut tables, one of which held an inclined drafting board. Scattered about were six matching dining chairs, a swivel chair, and a piano stool. The furniture, though substantial and of first quality, was without gloss except where use had lent it a patina. On the floor was a once-handsome Oriental carpet, now a patchwork quilt of pieces obviously joined at different times over the course of the years. The walls of the room, once white, were grayed and dingy.

The captain had found that the odor of fresh paint and varnish induced in him symptoms of a severe cold, and therefore both were banned. He was also opposed to heavy housecleaning and to repairs in his study because of the violence they did his working routines. Miss Cassidy was able to have the carpet repaired only by rushing in a weaver, who replaced the threadbare parts when the captain was out at the machine works or the foundry.

Ericsson sat at one of the tables and received his secretary, a young man with whom he discussed the chores of the day. He then summoned one of his three assistants, to whom he gave instructions for relay to the Delamater Foundry and to the model maker.

The brief meetings concluded, he removed his coat and, raising the piano stool to a convenient height by placing it on a wooden shipping crate, set to work at the drawing board. He drew quickly and with marvelous facility. The designs for pistons, cylinders, and flywheels flowed in a steady stream from his pencil. His only tools were an immaculately sharpened pencil, of which there were a score, neatly arranged at the side of the board, and a triangular scale. He never erased and rarely retraced. His facility was all the more remarkable for the absence of the middle finger of his right hand, the hand with which he drew.

The ambience was remarkably quiet; the captain abhorred stray noise. The tranquility was not a coincidence. He had taken the precaution of buying his neighbors' rights to their dogs, and he had bought all the chickens in the neighborhood for the privilege of wringing their necks.

At half past one, after four hours of uninterrupted work, he removed his boots and cravat, loosened his collar, and stretched out for a short nap on one of the tables. For a pillow he used a handy dictionary.

Rising at two, he worked until four, when dinner was served. He returned to his study after dinner and continued at his drawing board until seven, when he stopped for tea and toast, which Miss Cassidy brought on a tray. Resuming, he worked without interruption for another four hours. Shortly after eleven he donned his coat and walked out onto dimly lit Franklin Street for his three-mile constitutional.

Since his house was situated at the southern tip of Manhattan, near the confluence of the East and Hudson rivers, it was his custom to alternate direction. He turned either directly west, where the banks of the Hudson were only a few blocks distant, or southeast to the East River, which coursed about half a mile from his doorstep. In either event, his walks invariably took him to the waterfront and the harbor. The sea was a magnet. Had the captain been of a romantic bent he would have said that the blood of Vikings ran in his veins. But he was by predilection and conviction a confirmed utilitarian, and if asked why his walks led to the harbor, doubtlessly would have replied that since his work usually concerned things nautical, he was drawn to the sea.

On the evening in question, the captain turned left or west as he exited his house near the corner of Church and Franklin. Walking at a pace that might be described as somewhat brisker than a stroll but more leisurely than a march, he traveled streets that were clean and, except for the occasional clip-clop of an equestrian or horse and carriage bearing home a late-night reveler, quiet and deserted.

The neighborhood, a residential enclave of New York's comfortable, middle-class merchant community, was favored with pleasant, two-story houses constructed in the Federal style, red brick and neat, white wood trim predominating. The summer evening was agreeable, the gentle breeze from the Hudson cool and refreshing.

Crossing Church, West Broadway, Hudson, and Greenwich, the captain came to West Street, which served as the New York bank of the Hudson River. There he turned south, walking along the seawall toward the tip of Manhattan, savoring in dark silhouette the occasional sloop or frigate riding at anchor, lanterns fore and aft gleaming in the dark.

Breathing deeply and occasionally swinging his arms, Ericsson luxuriated in the exercise, in the fresh air, and in the release from his drafting board. It was always thus, he reflected; during these after-work walks he felt a bit like a grade-schooler on recess. That was life's secret: enjoying the things that one did of necessity—work, food, exercise, sleep. His life was taking a definite turn for the better. He was more in control. If it weren't for Amelia . . . ah, Amelia. No. He would not think about her. There was nothing he could do. To dwell on her would be weak and unproductive.

By way of transition to the subject he wished to contemplate, he thought fleetingly of Miss Cassidy, Cassidy of the luminous red hair, the translucent skin, her firm, lithe body moving under that simple sheath of a housedress.

But it was that two-and-one-half-inch block at the bottom of the first page of the *Tribune* that he was determined to think about during this evening's walk—"Iron-clad Steam Vessels." Writing the proposal would not be difficult. The work was done. But it would mean getting involved with the U.S. Navy. Not a pleasant prospect. The U.S. Navy. If it weren't for the Navy, Amelia would probably still be. . . . Nevertheless he had to do it. That much he owed to the country and to himself.

At Battery Park he looped around the squat, thick-walled red-stone circle that was Castle Clinton, the old Dutch fort that once guarded New York harbor and was now the nation's principal immigrant depot. It was here, not too long ago, that he—and she—came to this land.

Turning back north now, he passed the grand colonnaded mansions that adorned State Street, the splendid Gothic pile of Trinity Church, tallest structure in Manhattan, and, a few blocks farther north, the more modest but beautifully elegant St. Paul's Chapel, where George Washington had worshipped.

He was home by midnight, and at half past the hour sound asleep in a bed whose legs were encased in numerous thicknesses of felt to prevent vibration from a pump engine installed across the street; the bed itself was softer only by a degree or two than the walnut table on which he napped.

Thus did Captain Ericsson spend his days, the routine broken only infrequently by a visit to one of his suppliers, or by dinner at the Union Club, a block east of his residence, where he met with one or two close associates. He worked at his drawing board twelve hours a day, 364 days a year, observing only Thanksgiving, which he celebrated with a family of old friends.

For fifteen days, in odd hours and during his nightly walks, Ericsson brooded over the two-and-a-half-inch classified notice in the *Tribune*. On August 29, having decided on the most expeditious way to respond without directly denigrating the Navy's specifications, he interrupted his work long enough to write, in his own hand, a letter offering to construct a vessel for the destruction of the rebel fleet at Norfolk and for scouring the Southern rivers. He sought "no private advantage or emolument of any kind." Alluding to rumors of the reborn *Merrimack*, he noted that land batteries were not able to resist steel-clad vessels, and hence, "our great city is quite at the mercy of such intruders and may at any moment be laid in ruins." In a postscript he added: "It is not for me, sir, to remind you of the immense moral effect that will result from your discomfiting the rebels at Norfolk, nor need I allude to the effect in Europe if you demonstrate that you can effectively keep hostile fleets away from our shores."

The letter was addressed "To His Excellency Abraham Lincoln, President of the United States."

CHAPTER

XIII

Nicolay and Hay were convinced that the fall of Sumter was the signal for every crank, charlatan, fanatic, and would-be brigadier or admiral in the nation to sit down and write a letter a day to the president. The mail came by the wagonload. It engulfed, swamped, inundated. They dared not let it accumulate lest it literally push them out of house—they were both quartered at the executive mansion—and office.

They agreed the only way to handle the problem was for each of them, whenever he could snatch a moment from the day's routine, to pluck a few of the more plausible-looking envelopes from the mound of canvas sacks. The rest of the mail was consigned directly to the trash. The few letters they deemed worthy of a hearing they referred to the appropriate agency. Only the barest fraction reached the president. Ericsson's was not among the chosen. Nor did his letter come to the attention of the three-man board appointed by Secretary Welles to examine proposals for ironclad vessels.

Commodores Joseph Smith and Hiram Paulding and Comdr. Charles Davis shared a single attitude toward their assignment: They were far from pleased and were openly uncomfortable in the task. The aged Smith, senior officer and chief of the Bureau of Yards and Docks, speaking for the three-man board appointed to evaluate bids for the construction of iron ships, confessed to Welles that they were approaching the job with a lack of confidence born of ignorance. What, after all, did they know about ironclad construction?

Welles responded that he had information to the effect that a small army of men was working night and day to ready the *Merrimack* for sea, and that it behooved the commodore and his colleagues to educate themselves without delay.

Late in the afternoon of Tuesday, September 3, the deadline for submitting presentations, the board made the first of three awards. It granted a contract to Cornelius Scranton Bushnell of New Haven, a businessman of influence and substance who counted among his assets a shipyard on the Quinnipiac River and the friendship of his Connecticut neighbor Gideon Welles.

Bushnell was not averse to turning a dollar, and was at the same time firmly committed to the Union and dedicated to the effort of maintaining the integrity of the blockade. Therefore he should have felt a happy sense of serving his own and the nation's interest when, having just signed the contract, he walked out of the Navy Department offices into the soft September evening.

But Bushnell was not altogether pleased. He had several reservations about the *Galena,* the ship he had contracted to build. It was to be a steam-powered, essentially wood-hulled gunboat, plated with a double layer of iron bars over her vulnerable areas. Given the time limit imposed by the board, which was quite sensible of the progress of the *Merrimack,* the *Galena*'s design, admittedly a compromise, seemed the most expedient alternative.

The reason then for Bushnell's qualified sense of achievement was that the ship, at best a hybrid, was not likely to be a credit to her builder. Nor, given the best intentions and an around-the-clock work schedule, could the *Galena* be ready in time to meet the *Merrimack,* whose hull and machinery were already in place. Compounding his misgivings were the warnings of several knowledgeable naval officers who expressed doubt that the *Galena* would be able to carry the weight of the armament prescribed without foundering. And even assuming she could, they felt the added weight would leave her so clumsy and slow as to disqualify her for combat.

Turning east on Pennsylvania Avenue, Bushnell, a fine-looking, large man with regular features and a short, dark beard, pondered his next move. It was apparent that before he proceeded with construction he needed some definite answers with respect to the ship's seaworthiness.

Like most visitors in Washington on government business, he was staying at Willard's. As the threat of invasion subsided and the capital resumed its normal rhythms, the hotel had once again become the nerve center of the city. Its bars, parlors, lobby, corridors, and dining rooms swarmed with office seekers, financiers, contractors, military officers, and correspondents—anyone who wished to see or be seen, or to catch up on the latest inside information.

Approaching the entrance, Bushnell noticed standing on the steps, enjoying an after-dinner cigar in the late summer twilight, Cornelius H. Delamater, a portly, gregarious soul in his forties, whom Bushnell knew to be the owner of a foundry and machine works in New York. As owners of noncompeting establishments in the same industry, the two had a nodding acquaintance warmed somewhat by the coincidence of their sharing the same given name. "Good evening," said Bushnell cordially.

"Good evening to you, sir." Delamater had been in Washington for about a month, and had come to the capital for two reasons. The first was to find out why his company had been awarded no government contracts when it appeared that every foundry and machine works on the northeast coast had more government work than they could handle. His second reason was, of course, to repair the omission. He was reasonably optimistic about his prospects, and had written to his associate, Capt. John Ericsson, a few days after his arrival: "I am treated well; have had two evening interviews with Mr. Secretary Welles, one of them alone in my own room."

Delamater knew that Bushnell had made a presentation to the ironclad board that day, and he was curious as to the outcome. However, he felt he did not know him well enough to put the question directly and therefore made the general inquiry, "How does business go?"

Bushnell hesitated before responding. Like most astute businessmen, he shared information only for cause, and he was most selective of those with whom he discussed business affairs. Should he tell Delamater of the award? Why not. He had been constrained to no secrecy by the Navy. And even if he had, secrets did not remain so for long in this town. And he did need help. One never knew. "Very well, indeed," he said. "I have had some good luck today." He told Delamater of the award to build the *Galena,* adding, "But I am somewhat concerned. Several navy men have expressed doubt that she can carry the stipulated iron, and since I am not an engineer I have doubts as to her seaworthiness."

Delamater did not hesitate. "I know just the man to answer your questions. His name is Ericsson, Captain John Ericsson of New York, and he is the most competent naval engineer I know. He'll settle the matter definitely and with accuracy." Bushnell resolved to stop in New York the following day on his way to New Haven.

At eleven the following morning he was on the steps of 95 Franklin Street. Miss Cassidy ushered him to the studio, where the two men quickly established credentials. Without further prologue Bushnell laid out the plans for the *Galena* and put his questions. Ericsson asked that he leave the plans and call again in twenty-four hours, at which time he would have his answers.

Punctually at eleven the next morning Bushnell was advised, "She will easily carry the load you propose and stand a six-inch shot at a respectable distance." Bushnell was delighted. He had no doubt as to the validity of Ericsson's opinion. The captain obviously knew whereof he spoke.

Bushnell was rolling up the plans for the *Galena* and preparing to leave when Ericsson said, "Do you have a moment, sir, to examine the plan of a floating battery that I guarantee is absolutely impregnable to the heaviest shot or shell?"

Taken aback by the unqualified nature of the captain's claim, Bushnell replied, "That, sir, is the problem that has been occupying me for the past three months. Given the time constraints, the *Galena* is the best we have been able to come up with." Ericsson left the room for a moment and came back with a dust-covered wooden box of a size that might accommodate a pair of shoes. From it he took a pasteboard model and plans for a craft the likes of which Bushnell had never before seen. He was nevertheless immediately struck by it.

The deck, a long rectangle rounding to a point at bow and stern, was perfectly flat or flush and, with two exceptions, clear of all structures including masts and rigging of any sort. The exceptions were a cylindrical revolving iron turret squarely amidships, and near the bow a tiny cube large enough, the captain explained, for the wheel and for the head and shoulders of two men who stood on a platform below the deck. The iron-covered deck overhung the hull fore and aft, thus providing protection for the anchor and for the rudder and propeller.

But the truly exotic aspect of the vessel was that most of it lay underwater; in a rough sea her deck would be constantly awash, being only a foot and a half above the waterline. The lower hull slanted sharply inward to her flat bottom; thus crew and machinery were surrounded by a wall of water. The lack of superstructure meant radically reduced weight. She therefore drew only ten and a half feet of water—the navy specifications allowed a limit of sixteen—easily allowing her to navigate coastal waters and most rivers.

"Her design is so simple," said Ericsson, "that within ten weeks after commencing construction I can have her under the rebel guns at Norfolk."

Noting the thickness of the dust covering the box, Bushnell asked, "How long ago did you design her?"

"What I call the subaquatic or partially submerged system of naval warfare has been one of the hobbies of my life. I first began to think about it as a child watching the behavior of timber rafts in our Swedish lakes. I found that the raftsman in his elevated cabin experienced very little motion even as the seas were breaking over his nearly submerged raft. Those seas at the same time worked the traditional sailing vessels nearly on their beam ends."

He pulled open a drawer in one of the walnut tables. "You may be interested in this." He handed Bushnell a gold medal affixed to a tricolor ribbon, along with a letter bearing an imperial seal, dated 1854. Letter and seal were from the Emperor Napoleon III in gratitude for "the new system of naval attack which you have submitted." His Majesty, however, rejected the offer on the ground that "the result to be obtained would not be proportionate to the expense or to the small number of guns which could be brought into use."

"That was during the Crimean War," said Ericsson. "I had actually designed the system years before with an eye toward protecting Sweden from Russia, whom I consider her traditional and inevitable enemy."

Bushnell continued to examine the model, turning it in his hands. It was trim and clean lined. Unlike the *Galena* it was all of a piece; no hybrid this. Function, design, and materials coincided perfectly. It had been conceived as a fighting machine, to mete out punishment while remaining minimally exposed. Bushnell's thoughts raced. The Navy had to have it. He would happily sacrifice the *Galena* if it became a question of one or the other. How cooperative would this man be? What did he want for his design? There was little time for bargaining or for long, complex negotiations. Obviously the inventor treasured the thing and rightly so. He had shown it to no one except the emperor, had made no subsequent attempt to market it, apparently holding it against the day when it would be most eagerly sought. This was the day. Either Ericsson had to take model and plans to Washington and make a presentation to the board, or he must entrust it to an agent, preferably himself. But they had barely met. Why should the captain trust him? How could he persuade him that he would represent him fairly? One thing was in his favor: He suspected the captain was not disposed to drop his work and fly off to Washington.

Bushnell was an old hand in situations of this sort. He understood the value of silence at certain pivotal moments. Walking to a chair, he sat, placed the model on a table, and continued to study it, toying thoughtfully with the turret for a moment or two before looking up at Ericsson. From the tentative smile in the eyes of both men it was apparent that they were thinking complementary thoughts.

"Take it," said the Swede, "and good luck." Bushnell wasted no time. He quickly gathered up model and plans for both vessels, pumped Ericsson's hand, and rushed off to catch the first train, not for Washington but for Hartford, Connecticut. He had long since learned, especially when dealing with the government, that the quickest way to an objective was not necessarily the shortest. He knew that Welles was spending a few days at home to help his wife prepare for the family's move to Washington, where he had at last found a suitable house. Bushnell had planned to return to New Haven and there initiate construction of the *Galena*. But that project was, for the moment, placed on the back burner.

The first train he was able to catch out of New York brought him to Hartford the following morning. Bursting into Welles's study, he found the secretary in the classic attitude of movers. Standing with a perplexed expression amidst a sea of books and papers that had been torn from their accustomed niches, he was trying to decide what to leave and what to pack.

"Gideon!" cried Bushnell. "Fear not!" And laying the wooden box before Welles with a rather theatrical gesture, declared, "I have found a battery that will make us masters of the ocean and moreover will discourage our European friends from even the thought of further adventure on this side of the Atlantic."

Welles, glad for the excuse to sit down, invited Bushnell to do the same and said, "Cornelius, you look a bit peaked. May I offer you something to drink?"

"Thank you, thank you, no time now. Plenty of time for that later. Do please open the box."

More astonished than curious by his friend's extravagant claims,

Welles removed and examined the model. He was not immediately taken with it, never having seen or imagined anything like it. All he saw was the flat, unencumbered deck, strangely free of spar and gunwale, with only the turret and the tiny cube to relieve the unbroken plane. The Navy's specifications had clearly called for two masts and wire-rope rigging. "Who designed her?"

"Captain John Ericsson of New York."

"How many guns has she?"

"Two, in the turret." Welles knew the *Merrimack* mounted forty before she was scuttled. He didn't know how many the rebels were planning for her now.

"How large is her crew?"

"About fifty-seven." The Navy had specified 165 to 300.

"Her draft?"

"Ten and a half feet." Welles's interest was piqued. He had been frustrated for months by the inability of his blockaders to maneuver in shoal water.

"Two guns," he said dubiously.

"But don't you see, Gid, those two are worth ten of the traditional kind. These revolve and can fire in any direction regardless of the ship's heading. The guns mounted on the other vessels are, for the most part, fixed, and can only fire when the ship is in the proper attitude. Also, the guns in the turret are protected. As soon as they fire, the port closes and the turret turns."

Welles regarded the model a bit more favorably. Actually, he was persuaded more by Bushnell's enthusiasm than by anything he saw. He had reason to respect his friend's judgment. "Ericsson . . . Ericsson," he mused, "Captain John Ericsson. Why does that name sound familiar?"

"I believe he's worked for the department before. But that was some time ago."

Welles nodded. "In any case, the board has chosen a second entry, but they have not yet selected a third. I think you ought to get back to Washington as soon as you can and present this . . . has it a name?"

"He calls it a 'subaquatic system of naval warfare.' "

"Well, whatever it is, I would get it there as soon as possible. You realize we are three days past the deadline. Let's hope they won't be too stuffy about lifting it."

After the travel-worn Bushnell departed, Welles sat thoughtfully for another few minutes. Then, donning his hat and coat, he announced to Mary Jane that he was going out for about half an hour. Walking the few blocks downtown to the local telegraph office, he sent the following wire to an aide: "Urgent prepare dossier Capt John Ericsson New York engineer stop Arrive Washington Tuesday September ten Welles."

En route to the capital Bushnell stopped at 95 Franklin Street to tell Ericsson that Welles was on their side. The captain was delighted, but warned, "You have a long, hard fight ahead. Remember, you can never convince a sailor."

In Washington, Bushnell's first move was to summon to his room at Willard's two friends and associates from Troy, New York, John A. Griswold and John F. Winslow, partners in a large and thriving iron mill. It being a warm, late-summer Sunday, they were pleased to accept Bushnell's invitation to a drive in the suburbs. Having been engaged by Bushnell to supply the armor plate for the *Galena,* they were anticipating a discussion regarding prices and terms. The two partners, both tall, sharp-featured, and bewhiskered men in somber garb, were experienced in the recondite world of government business and were, not by coincidence, close friends and supporters of Governor William Seward.

After riding for about fifteen minutes northeast on Vermont Avenue to the pleasant, tree-shaded environs of the Soldiers' Home, far from the tumult and the ubiquitous ears of Willard's, Bushnell instructed the driver to slow the horses to a walk, and then he turned to his guests. He described Ericsson's battery in superlatives, and said that it was essential that it be built and built quickly, and that in the interests of national survival the naval board had to give its immediate approval. Though Welles was for it, for a variety of reasons, not the least of which was the craft's exotic design, he was not sanguine at the prospect of board approval. For that reason influence of the strongest sort had to be brought to bear. The partners murmured sounds of understanding.

"Whom do you have in mind?" asked Griswold.

"The president."

The partners nodded thoughtfully but without enthusiasm. "How can we help with Mr. Lincoln? We're not his confidants."

"Mr. Seward is." The partners exchanged glances. "Gentlemen, we can't afford the time for a waiting game, for the niceties and formalities of elaborate negotiation. I'm going to be quite candid. I hope you will do the same. I believe in Ericsson's battery. I think it can save the blockade, the *Merrimack* notwithstanding. Further, I believe it will make money for its sponsors. If it succeeds, the government will want more.

"Captain Ericsson has given me carte blanche to negotiate on his behalf. I am prepared to offer you a fifty percent interest in the vessel, keeping one fourth for myself and one fourth for Ericsson. I ask in return that you help me secure a letter of introduction from Governor Seward to the president."

At ten the following morning the three men were received by the secretary of state, who claimed to be delighted by this opportunity to see two old friends and to make a new one. Offering cigars, the urbane, silver-haired Seward put them at ease and, puffing on his Havana, sat back to listen to their plan. Bushnell did the talking.

First he acknowledged the central role of the blockade in the war effort. He saw the *Merrimack* as a very real threat. One rebel ironclad, he felt, was capable of devastating the Union's blockading squadron. A counter was desperately needed. The only eligible candidate that he knew of was Ericsson's battery. Though admittedly a fraction of the rebel ironclad's size, he felt it would prove her match and more in battle. Equally important, the Ericsson battery could be completed in time to meet the *Merrimack*. But there was no time to lose.

Seward agreed. He was happy to do anything he could by way of maintaining the blockade and obliging two important constituents.

From State, armed with the letter of introduction, the three men proceeded directly through the park to the executive mansion. Even had they not bothered to secure the letter from Governor Seward, chances are the president would have received them. Mr. Lincoln was fascinated by the artifacts of war. His door was always open to gunsmiths and inventors who came to present their weapons and their schemes. Like a small boy playing hooky he liked nothing better than to walk out of the executive office with a new rifle as an excuse to break the routine. Using a woodpile on the south lawn as a barrier, he would pin a piece of notepaper to a log and blaze away. He was trying to persuade the Army to accept the new breech-loading rifles, which he thought superior to the muzzle-loaders. And of late he had been spending afternoons at the navy yard, where he followed the development of the new Dahlgren gun with keen interest.

The president, pacing in his beaded moccasins, interrupted a letter he was dictating to Nicolay and invited his visitors to sit at the long rectangular table. Bushnell removed the pasteboard model from the shoebox and spread the plans before Lincoln.

The president took to Ericsson's battery immediately. Twirling the turret, he remarked that he had an affinity for flat-bottomed boats, having piloted one as a young man down the Mississippi to New Orleans. He said that although he exercised no power in the matter, he would be happy to meet them at the office of Commodore Smith the following morning at eleven.

Smith's office, on the first floor of the Navy Department, was small and modest. Most of the dozen officers in attendance, along with Winslow and Griswold, were forced to stand while Bushnell made his presentation to the board. A makeshift chair, actually a wooden crate, was found for the president, who listened attentively but said nothing. Only two board members, Commodores Smith and Paulding, were present, Commander Davis being off on assignment. The board members and Fox, who was sitting in for Welles, expressed no opinion after Bushnell delivered the presentation. The other officers were unanimous in their opposition to the plan.

The negative comment was strong, unequivocal, and, on occasion, heated. The vessel would prove unseaworthy and unstable. There weren't enough guns. The concussion from shot taken on the turret would knock the gun crew senseless. Ventilation was inadequate. Buoyancy was dubious.

For an hour Bushnell stood and took the criticism. When it was exhausted, Smith turned to the president and asked his opinion. Lincoln rose from his low perch and said, "Well, all I have to say is what the girl said when she put her foot into the stocking, 'It strikes me there's something in it.' Good morning, gentlemen." He made his way out of the crowded room.

No decision was reached. Smith declared he would convene the full board the following morning, Wednesday, when Commander Davis would be present. Bushnell was invited to make his presentation once again.

Nine o'clock that evening, about eight hours after the board had adjourned, Secretary Welles arrived in Washington, wearied by the long train ride from Hartford, and unhappily alone. Mary Jane and the children were not quite ready to accompany him, and he felt that he couldn't wait. His presence was demanded by events in Washington.

Instead of proceeding to his newly acquired house, he went directly to the Navy Department. No one was there except the duty officer and the sentries. But reposing neatly in the center of his desk, along with a note from Fox summarizing the result of Bushnell's presentation, was the report he had requested, looseleaf bound in a gray hardcover binder. It was about four inches thick, much more reading than Welles had bargained for. After a moment of indecision he stuffed it into a small satchel and, hailing a hack, drove the half mile to his house, which was in the northwest quarter of the city near Connecticut Avenue.

Refreshed by a hot tub and a supper, prepared by his Negro housekeeper, of cheese omelet with corn bread and half a bottle of wine, he settled into bed with a grateful sigh. It had been a long day.

The report began with a brief introduction: "The narrative herein is largely a digest of the documents appended. Sources are therefore generally reliable. Where source is undocumented and open to question, it is so identified." Welles flipped to the back of the binder and noted to his relief, for he was determined to finish the narrative before morning, that most of the contents consisted of department documents such as transcripts of hearings, official reports, contracts, and correspondence. The narrative portion was relatively brief. He turned to the first page and began.

The subject, Capt. John Ericsson of 95 Franklin Street, New York City, was born in Langbanshyttan, Vermland, in southwest Sweden, on July 31, 1803. His father, Olof, was part owner and superintendent of an iron mine. As a child, subject exhibited an interest in and talent for drawing, designing, and constructing machinery, especially of a mining variety.

When he was eight years old, the continuing war with Russia occasioned widespread economic hardship in Sweden, which had been forced to cede Finland and the Aland Islands in 1809. Subject and family were compelled to remove to Forsvik, about a hundred miles to the southeast, where Olof found employment as a construction foreman on the Gota Canal. Subject has openly and consistently expressed strong anti-Russian sentiment.

Through his twelfth year he appears to have acquired an excellent albeit informal education via volunteer tutors. He attended no formal school until he and his brother Nils were appointed cadets in the Mechanical Corps of the Swedish Navy. While with the corps, subject rendered drawings for the archives of the Gota Canal and served as a leveller.

By way of attesting to his early ability, department source relates that at age fourteen subject was in charge of six hundred troops working on the canal, although he was still too short to reach the eyepiece of his levelling instrument without the aid of a stool.

At age seventeen subject entered Swedish Army with rank of ensign. Won distinction in athletics (wrestling and weight lifting) and as an artilleryman.

At about age twenty-two he fathered a son by a woman (unidentified) to whom he was betrothed but not married. Son, Hjalmar, was left in care of subject's mother.

Securing leave from Army, subject left Sweden for England, the apparent and expressed purpose being to further his career as an inventor/engineer. There he made a connection with machine manufacturing house of John Braithwaite in which he became a junior partner. Subject was occupied during this period with designing more efficient steam engines. He successfully developed the first steam-powered fire engine.

In 1827 subject was charged with desertion by Swedish military on the ground that he had overstayed his leave. The Swedish crown prince intervened. Subject was honorably restored to service and promoted to rank of captain, which he resigned forthwith, choosing to remain in England. He has, however, continued to retain the title, and continues to express strong affection for his native land.

In subject's twenty-sixth year, his firm entered a competition sponsored by the Liverpool & Manchester Railroad for the best steam locomotive. Twenty-two weeks were allotted for construction. Subject learned of competition when only seven weeks remained until the test trial. Of five entries two survived, one, The Rocket by George Stephenson, engineer employee of the railroad; the other, The Novelty, built by subject.

Following is partial account of the trial as reported in *London Times* of October 8 and 16, 1829:

> But the speed of all the other locomotive steam carriages on the course was far exceeded by that of Messrs. Braithwaite and Ericsson's beautiful engine from London. It was the lightest and most elegant carriage on the road yesterday, and the velocity with which it moved surprised and amazed every beholder. It shot along the line at the amazing rate of

thirty miles an hour! It seemed, indeed, to fly, presenting one of the most sublime spectacles of human ingenuity and human daring the world ever beheld.

> The definite trial of Messrs. Braithwaite and Ericsson's locomotive carriage (The Novelty) was fixed for this day. The load having been attached, the engine started on its journey shortly after one o'clock. It performed two trips with great celerity; but when running down the course for the third time the pressure of the steam was too great for the boiler, which unfortunately burst. [It was later established that the boiler did not burst. The steam escaped because of "green joints."—department source.] This accident put an end to the trial and The Novelty was taken from the course.
>
> The trials which have taken place have satisfactorily proved the superiority of the principle on which The Novelty is constructed. The machine was, however, too hastily and slightly fabricated—defects which Messrs. Braithwaite and Ericsson can easily remedy in any future engines which they may construct for railroads.

The Stephenson engine was declared the winner of the competition.

At age thirty-three, in 1836, subject married Miss Amelia Byam, nineteen, by all accounts a charming and musically gifted lady of good family but of uncertain parentage.

Subject continued to work on perfecting engines and inventing devices, one of which was a machine for taking depth soundings from a moving ship. In 1836 he was granted a patent (U.S. and England) for the screw propeller as a motive power for steamships, which until that time relied exclusively on the paddle wheel.

Subject demonstrated propeller for the British Admiralty on a small ship specially built for the purpose. Their lordships rejected the device as impracticable. (The British Navy did not adopt the screw propeller until eight years later when it employed a motive system designed by subject.)

The firm of Braithwaite & Ericsson failed in 1837. Subject spent a short (undetermined) term in Fleet Street prison as a foreign debtor.

In London subject made the acquaintance of U.S. naval officer Capt. (later Senator) Robert F. Stockton of New Jersey. Stockton commissioned subject to construct screw steamer *Robert F. Stockton,* seventy feet in length, ten-foot beam, three-foot draught, propelled by fifty-horsepower engine, equipped with sail. She sailed to New York in May 1839 with a crew of five for tug duty on the Delaware and Raritan Canal, where she is still in service.

In November 1839 subject and Mrs. Ericsson came to the United States, ostensible purpose of captain's visit being to introduce the screw propeller to the department. According to department source, visit was encouraged by Captain Stockton, who was negotiating with government for construction of steam propeller warship.

In September 1841 department issued Captain Stockton orders to superintend construction of said warship (later named USS *Princeton*) at the Philadelphia Navy Yard. Subject was immediately engaged by Stockton to provide design and working drawings.

The *Princeton* was the first warship to employ (1) screw propeller; (2) engines so arranged as to be below decks and below the waterline, thus protected from enemy fire; (3) engines coupled directly to the propeller shaft for maximum efficiency and reliability; (4) engines fast enough to turn propeller directly without intercession of cogwheels or gearing; (5) forced draught for furnaces, thus making them independent of smokestacks, which are easily shot away; (6) disappearing, or telescopic, chimney for concealment in combat; (7) automatic range finder and self-acting gunlock; (8) improved gun carriage for checking recoil.

In a letter to Captain Stockton dated July 28, 1841, subject leaves matter of payment for use of patent rights to aforesaid devices to the sole discretion of the government.

The two twelve-inch guns mounted on the *Princeton*'s bow and stern were the largest in the fleet. One, the "Peacemaker," was designed by Captain Stockton. The other, the "Oregon," was designed by subject, who brought it from England, where it had been fabricated. The Peacemaker, the heavier of the two, a foot larger in diameter at the breech, was, according to contemporary press accounts, the largest mass of iron ever brought under the forging hammer.

In 1843 while subject was superintending construction of the *Princeton* in Philadelphia, Mrs. Ericsson returned to England. Undocumented reports have it that she found both the subject's habits of work (long hours and frequent absences) and the rude atmosphere of New York intolerable. Although subject is quoted as having said, "My wife is jealous of a steam engine," the parting was said to have been without acrimony. It was understood that Mrs. Ericsson would return to New

York. As of this date she remains in London. The department has established that subject sends her and his mother remittances on a regular basis. He also supports his son, whose education is in the care of subject's brother. Subject also subsidizes the education of a number of needy members of the Ericsson clan.

In a dispatch dated February 5, 1844, Captain Stockton advises the secretary of the Navy that the USS *Princeton* has been completed and has been delivered to the department. Dispatch also enumerates her innovations as stated above. Subject is nowhere credited nor does his name appear in said dispatch.

USS *Princeton* was subsequently ordered to the Potomac for two demonstration cruises for the benefit of members of the government. On the afternoon of February 28, the ship was completing the second of the two exhibition tours. Aboard were several hundred notables, including President Tyler, members of the cabinet, members of both houses of Congress, ranking military, and, in many instances, their respective families.

Subject was not aboard although the printed programme for the day indicates he was to have accompanied ship from New York. Reason for his absence has never been documented by an independent source. According to subject he was at the Wall Street wharf at the hour appointed by Captain Stockton, expecting to be conveyed to the *Princeton* by one of her longboats. However, the ship steamed by without stopping.

By way of salute and demonstration, the larger guns of the ship were repeatedly discharged during the exhibition tour. At a point some fifteen miles below Washington City, opposite Mount Vernon, Captain Stockton acceded to the request of the secretary of the Navy, Mr. Thomas Gilmer, for a last salute from the Peacemaker. Said gun, bearing a fifty-pound charge, burst, killing and wounding upward of twenty people. Among the dead, Secretary of the Navy Thomas Gilmer; Secretary of State Abel Upshur; Commodore B. Kennon; Col. David Gardiner, state senator from New York and father of President Tyler's fiancée; and a personal servant of the president. Among the wounded were seventeen members of the ship's crew. Captain Stockton, who was standing immediately to the right of the breech, suffered only superficial wounds.

To a request from Captain Stockton that subject appear at the Court of Inquiry convened a week after the incident, subject refused as follows (full text appended): "How differently should I have regarded an invitation from Captain Stockton a week ago! I might then have had it in my power to render good service and valuable counsel. Now I can be of no use."

Captain Stockton made it known to the court that subject was responsible for disaster and that his refusal to appear was prima facie evidence of his guilt. Court exonerated Captain Stockton of all blame on the ground that he had in the design and manufacture of his gun consulted a number of recognized experts, including the subject.

On March 14, 1844, subject submitted to the secretary of the Navy an invoice in the amount of $15,080 for services rendered in connection with the invention, design, and construction of the USS *Princeton*, including per diem expenses of 230 days at $5 per day ($1,150).

Said claim in the amount of $15,080 was disallowed by department on the negative recommendation of Captain Stockton, who held there was no contract for the subject's services.

Despite subsequent favorable ruling by the U.S. Court of Claims, and the strong support of Senator Stephen R. Mallory and the Senate Naval Affairs Committee, of which he was chairman, subject's claim has not as of this date been honored except for per diem claim of $1,150.

In 1847 the Royal Academy of Sciences of Stockholm elected subject an honorary member. In 1848 subject became a naturalized citizen of the United States. In 1850 the Swedish government elected him a Knight of the Order of Vasa, and in 1852 the Royal Military Academy of Sweden elected him an honorary member.

During the period of the aforesaid awards, subject was principally engaged in developing the caloric engine, which utilizes heated air rather than steam for motive power and relies on a heat transfer and regenerative, i.e., reuse, principle. The principal advantage of this engine is that, since no water is required for its operation, the nuisance and hazard of the steam boiler is eliminated.

Subject succeeded in raising half a million dollars from a number of sponsors for the purpose of constructing a ship, *The Ericsson*, which used the caloric engine as a means of motive power.

On a trial trip in March 1854, several miles north of Sandy Hook, *The Ericsson* foundered in a storm. It was subsequently raised by the department in a salvage operation under the command of Commodore Joseph E. Smith. Informed opinion holds that the caloric engine is not and never will be a satisfactory substitute for the steam engine as a means of propulsion.

Subsequent to said salvage operation, subject has had no further contact with the department. Subject is reputed to be possessed of strong will and, when provoked, ungovernable temper.

Welles, whose eyes were half closed, let the report slip slowly from his left hand onto the floor while with his right he groped for the key to the wick of the lamp and turned it down. Within a minute or two he was sound asleep.

CHAPTER

XIV

Rested, breakfasted, and sanguine as always, Bushnell made his way to Welles's office the following morning at half past ten.

Welles greeted his friend with a joviality he did not feel. "Well, Cornelius, good morning! Going to have another go at our navy brass?"

"Indeed, I am, Gideon, and I am looking forward to the encounter. The meeting, I'm sure you know, is scheduled for eleven this morning. And this time it's with all three members of the board."

"How does it look to you?"

"Despite all the negative comment, I'm confident. We don't have to convert the whole Navy, only the three members of the board. We have a sound plan. It's not expensive as weapons systems go, certainly there's a need for it, and Ericsson says he can be ready in ninety days. Why then wouldn't the board approve?"

"I couldn't agree with you more. But . . . ," Welles shrugged, "I've learned that logic and reason don't always prevail in matters of this sort. In any case, is there anything I can do for you?"

"Yes. It might be helpful if you were to sketch briefly the backgrounds of the board members. I like to know something about the people I'm dealing with."

"Certainly, I'll be happy to tell you what I know. First, Smith. He's the senior officer on the board. Probably the most diffident. Can be pushed either way by either of the other two. Not much formal or theoretical education. Learned shipbuilding as a boy in his father's business. Midshipman at nineteen. Brave sailor. Old man—seventy-one. Tired and anxious. I suspect he'd rather be home puttering in his garden.

"Commodore Paulding. I think he's probably for it. Sixty-four, better educated, surer of his judgment. Gallant sailor, spectacular combat record—except for that fiasco at Norfolk. He's currently chief of the Bureau of Detail . . . heavy responsibility, selecting officers for war-time duty. Slated for command of the New York Navy Yard. Good man to have on your side.

"Then there's Davis, Commander Charles Henry. Fifty-four, Harvard educated, science and mathematics. The department's resident genius. Not a line officer. Involved mostly with astronomy and navigation. He's an executive at the Bureau of Detail. Hasn't said much. I don't know which way he's inclined. I think he's your swing vote."

A few minutes before eleven, Bushnell made his way to Smith's office. When Welles followed a minute or two later, Bushnell was standing at a lectern that rested at the end of the table at which the three board members sat. Two rows of chairs had been set up to face table and lectern. The room had the look of a small lecture hall.

Welles took a seat at the end of the back row, settled back, and lit his pipe with a nonchalance he did not feel. Glancing around the room, he noticed that the president was not in attendance.

Bushnell, having the benefit of a previous presentation and another evening of study, was even more persuasive this time. He made a clear and compelling case for the ironclad battery.

Although Welles did not express an opinion, he was, on his second exposure to the Ericsson battery, more favorably disposed. He couldn't know if it would prove effective, but he felt that it was an ingenious and sophisticated machine deserving of an opportunity. From a political standpoint it was essential that the challenge posed by the *Merrimack* be met by a prompt and substantive response. Perhaps the other two vessels selected by the board would ultimately prove superior to the Ericsson system. But the fact was they could not be ready in time to meet the *Merrimack*. Ericsson said he would build his battery in ninety days.

The comments that followed the presentation were essentially a rehash of the previous day's hearing. All expressed opinion was negative. Several officers were heated and hostile in their criticism. Others, though apparently more objective, were nonetheless unalterably opposed. Welles listened with a mounting sense of unease. It was becoming obvious to him that the issue was not being decided on its merits. There were too many skeletons in the closet. He wondered what would have happened if the several plans had been submitted to the board anonymously.

When comment was exhausted, Commodore Smith announced that the decision would be made public the following day. After the meeting, in a brief exchange with Welles, Bushnell expressed confidence. He tended to dismiss the comments from the audience. As he saw it, of the three board members, he had one positive and one maybe. He left for Willard's, for a few drinks and lunch with Winslow and Griswold.

Fox, walking upstairs with Welles, was not sure how the vote would go. He thought Davis was probably of the Isherwood-Lenthall school. John Lenthall, the Navy's top architect, was on record with a negative recommendation for ironclads. He had made his considerable reputation designing tall, graceful, and swift sailing ships of wood. He believed ironclads drew too much water, cost too much, and would take too much time to introduce. One didn't change horses in midstream. Fox didn't altogether trust Lenthall, who was a protégé of Stephen Mallory. Lenthall was also on record as believing it impossible to tow the *Merrimack* out of the Norfolk yard.

And Engineer-in-Chief Isherwood, Fox declared to Welles, thought ironclads pure humbug, nothing but a scheme to line the pockets of a few greedy opportunists. But then Fox himself was not all that sure about ironclads either. He wanted to believe in them out of loyalty to Welles and because he too felt that the *Merrimack* demanded a substantive response. He also wanted to see Ericsson succeed. Gustavus Vasa Fox, like Ericsson, was a Swede.

On Thursday, September 12, for the third consecutive morning, Bushnell presented himself at the office of Commodore Smith. Only Smith and Paulding were present. Smith, though courteous as always, didn't waste any time. He advised Bushnell that the board had rejected the Ericsson plan.

Bushnell was not prepared for rejection. He was staggered, hugely disappointed, and uncharacteristically at a loss for words. Smith and

Paulding were, with reservations, in favor. But Davis was unalterably opposed, and Smith would not make an affirmative recommendation to the department unless the board was unanimous in its approval.

"What," asked Bushnell, "are Commander Davis's objections?"

"Want of stability was the reason he gave," replied Paulding, "but, off the record, you must know how most of the department feels about Ericsson since the *Princeton* disaster. Last night the air was full of croakings about 'the wild Swede,' and the department being about to father another Ericsson failure."

Indignantly Bushnell declared that Ericsson had never failed the department, that, on the contrary, he had built for the department the first steam war propeller, that the bursting of Stockton's gun was no fault of Ericsson's. Indeed, the "wild Swede" had taken the precaution of shrinking onto the breech of his own gun three-and-a-half-inch-thick reinforcing hoops made of the best American wrought iron. He had tried to persuade Stockton to use the reinforced gun for the exhibition firings, but Stockton wouldn't hear of it.

And as for the caloric engine, it had proved a triumphant success. Hundreds were in use driving printing presses; hoisting gear for warehouses, docks, and ships; irrigating land and supplying villages with water. In short, the engine was in use and in great demand wherever a limited, economical, safe, and independent motive power was required. Bushnell happened to know too that Ericsson and Delamater had made upwards of three hundred thousand dollars on just the little three-horse pumping engines that worked like a charm. True, the caloric engine couldn't drive an oceangoing ship, but that was because no one had been able to develop a metal that could accommodate the tremendous heat generated.

Bushnell was eloquent, impassioned, and sincere. He argued the pressing needs of the country and the crucial role of the blockade, and even alluded, albeit delicately, to the unmistakable favor with which Mr. Lincoln had regarded the battery. After an hour his persistence if not his eloquence bore exiguous fruit. He wrung from the commodores agreement that they would recommend Ericsson's battery be constructed if, and only if, Davis joined with them. Tucking plans and model under his arm, Bushnell made straight for the office of Commander Davis, just down the corridor.

Commander Charles Henry Davis, Boston born, son of a solicitor

general of Massachusetts, came of pure New England stock and was
of the bluest of the bluebloods. A product of the Boston Latin School
and Harvard University, Davis was handsome, distinguished, and had
perfect manners. It was said that, as a recognized authority in mathematics and navigation, he suffered from no inclination to underestimate
his abilities.

Bushnell gave the commander the benefit of a shortened version
of his plea to Smith and Paulding. Davis heard him through without
comment. When Bushnell finished, the commander regarded him coolly
for a moment and then, paraphrasing Exodus 20:4, said with a gesture
toward the model, "You may take the little thing home and worship
it; it would not be idolatry, since it was made in the image of nothing
that is in heaven above, or that is in the earth beneath, or that is in
the water under the earth."

Stung and angry, not trusting himself to reply to the Harvard-educated
sailor, Bushnell retreated and slowly made his way upstairs to Welles's
office. The two friends greeted each other in silence; then they nodded,
mutely acknowledging the disappointment they both felt.

"Cheer up, Cornelius. You've succeeded at least in isolating the major
obstacle. There's only Davis to be won over."

"Yes, but he's a cool one and a beaut."

"There must be some way to make him see the error of his ways."

"You know how difficult it is to get a resident genius to recant. By
reason of his status he can't be wrong. He's convinced that either the
vessel lacks stability, or that Ericsson is unreliable, or both. And no
one around here is knowledgeable enough to persuade him differently."

The idea occurred to both men simultaneously. "Yes," said Bushnell,
"but how am I going to get him to come to Washington? He's sworn
never to set foot in this city unless and until the government pays his
bill for the *Princeton*. And then you know how precious his habits are.
He hates to stir from that studio."

"It's worth a try. He's obviously best able to represent his plan. And
as far as engineering and mathematics are concerned, I wouldn't hesitate
to pit him against our genius."

"I agree. And the man is a magician. I believe he could charm the
birds out of the bloomin' trees if he put his mind to it. Anyone who
can persuade a gaggle of hardheaded money brokers to sink half a million

into an experimental ship—and have them vie for the privilege—can, in my opinion, talk anyone into anything."

"Well then," said Welles, "what are you waiting for?"

Bushnell started for New York that evening. From the moment he boarded the train, his thoughts were fixed on one question, How am I going to get him—a man who can be infuriated by the mere gleam of navy brass—to go to Washington with the facts I have to relate?

By the time his train reached Baltimore, Bushnell had an idea. Reviewing in detail the meeting wherein Ericsson entrusted model and plans to him, he recalled the glow of pride in the inventor's eye as he exhibited the gold medal sent by Louis Napoleon. Before the train reached the outer limits of Philadelphia, Bushnell had decided on his approach to Ericsson.

Arriving in New York late in the day, he decided not to rush to see him. He treated himself to a good dinner and a full night of rest at the Astor House, a gracious old hostelry on lower Broadway, a few blocks south of Franklin Street. At nine o'clock the following morning, in the glow of a late summer sun, Bushnell, composed and refreshed, presented himself at Ericsson's door.

The captain did not wait for Miss Cassidy to admit him. Seeing Bushnell, Ericsson went himself to greet him. "Well, what's the news?"

"Glorious!"

"Yes, yes, but what did they say?"

"Commodore Smith says it is worthy of the genius of an Ericsson."

The glow of pride evoked by the gold medal shone once again. "And Paulding, what did he say?"

"He said, 'It's just the thing to clear the rebels out of Charleston.' "

Triumph flushed the inventor's cheek. "And Davis, what about Davis?"

"Oh, Davis wants two or three explanations that I couldn't give him. Secretary Welles proposed that you come to Washington and explain these few points to the board in his room tomorrow."

"I'll go; I'll leave tonight." At six in the evening Ericsson crossed the Hudson by ferry and caught the night train to Washington. It was Friday, September 13. Bushnell elected not to return with him. It was not that he was superstitious. He just didn't fancy being present when Ericsson learned the true disposition of the board.

After an uncomfortable night in an ill-ventilated, overheated car, crowded as trains to a wartime capital inevitably are, Ericsson arrived early Saturday morning and went directly to the Navy Department. Only Welles and the three board members were in the secretary's room. Travel-worn, but borne by the expectation of a warm welcome, Ericsson bid everyone a cordial good morning. Then he learned that his plan had been rejected. The captain was not adept at concealing his feelings. The disappointment was visible.

His first inclination was to withdraw. If these navy imbeciles didn't appreciate a gem when it was offered, why indeed cast pearls before swine? He didn't need this nonsense. His studio was comfortable and sunlit. A good living was assured. His little caloric engines were making him wealthy. He swallowed. To his surprise and mortification he heard the sound of his own voice, "Why?"

Commodore Smith, speaking for the board, explained that it was felt the vessel lacked stability. "Stability!" exploded Ericsson. "That's her great merit." His blood was up. He dug into the small valise he was carrying and, fingers trembling with restrained fury and fatigue, laid before them a drawing of a transverse section of the battery. Establishing the vessel's center of gravity, he demonstrated that to heel the craft over a single foot, six hundred ninety men of average weight would have to stand at the extreme edge of the deck. Estimated crew was fifty-seven. "There is not now," he declared, "in the service of the United States any vessel of equal size that can compare in stability to the vessel under consideration."

Welles asked how much it would cost to complete her. "Two hundred and seventy-five thousand dollars," replied Ericsson. After a pause he added, "Gentlemen, I deem it your duty to the country to give me an order to build the vessel before I leave the room."

He goes too far, thought Welles. Smith, pleading the need for time for further deliberation, asked the captain to return at one o'clock. Ericsson used the opportunity to go to Willard's and seek out Delamater. In his friend's room he washed, changed his shirt, and quickly drew another diagram to demonstrate the stability of the battery. He suspected the subject was going to come up again.

Shortly before one o'clock, in the corridor leading to Welles's office, Ericsson encountered Commodore Paulding, who invited him to his room where he requested clarification of certain aspects of the captain's earlier demonstration. After Ericsson complied, Paulding graciously declared, "Sir, I have learned more about the stability of a vessel from what you have said than I ever knew before."

At one o'clock, Smith said that no decision had been reached, but if the captain would call on Secretary Welles later in the day, he would have his answer. Two hours later Welles briefly advised him that the board had reported favorably. He suggested that Ericsson return to New York at once, get the project started, and send Bushnell down in a week for the formal contract. Welles neglected to mention that Commander Davis consented to recommend the battery on the condition that the secretary assume the risk and the responsibility.

On Monday, September 16, as Ericsson in New York was engaging the first of seven subcontractors, the Ironclad Board rendered its official report to the secretary of the Navy. With true military regard for securing the rear, they began by qualifying: "Distrustful of our ability to discharge this duty, we approach the subject with diffidence, having no experience and but scant knowledge in this branch of naval architecture." Then, acknowledging that the construction of ironclads was "zealously claiming the attentions of foreign naval powers," the report held that opinions differed among naval and scientific men as to the wisdom of the policy. They allowed that for "coast and harbor defense, ironclads are undoubtedly formidable adjuncts to fortifications on land. As cruising vessels, however, we are sceptical as to their advantage and ultimate adoption. Wooden ships may be said to be but coffins for their crews, but we are clearly of the opinion that no ironclad vessel of equal displacement can be made to obtain the same speed."

The board recommended three vessels for construction: two essentially conventional sail-rigged, steam-assisted, iron-belted gunboats and the Ericsson battery. The latter was not approved as a seagoing vessel but rather as one that "may be moved from place to place along the coast in smooth water."

On Friday, October 4, as the keel plate of the battery was passing through the rollers of the iron mill, Bushnell arrived at Welles's office for the formal agreement. Donning a pair of oval, wire-rimmed spectacles that he used only for close reading of important documents, Bushnell noted that in accordance with the advertised specifications, the Navy's contract was still demanding "masts, spars, sails, and rigging." Ericsson would make short work of that, but still it was an annoyance. The department could always claim that "Ericsson et al" had not conformed to the agreement. The vessel was to be paid for in five installments at various stages of construction and at the discretion of the department. Twenty-five percent was to be withheld from each payment as security for the completion of the vessel. She was to be ready for sea duty one hundred days from the execution of the contract, or by Sunday, January 12, 1862.

Signatories were Ericsson, with Winslow, Griswold, and Bushnell as sureties; for the department, Welles. At the very end of the contract was a postscript that surprised and dismayed Bushnell. When the vessel was ready for sea and the government took possession, said possession was not to be interpreted as acceptance. The test of the battery's qualities and properties was to be made thereafter in actual combat, "the reservation of twenty-five percent to be withheld until the test is made." Further, if the vessel failed the test in the opinion of the government, Ericsson and his associates were bound "to refund to the United States the amount of money advanced to them on said vessel."

"Ericsson and the others will never stand for this," said Bushnell.

Welles shrugged, "It was the only way I could get the contract through the board. When it was learned that Ericsson's battery had been recommended, all kinds of hell broke loose. It was 'the wild Swede' all over again. People around here have long memories. They're like the Bourbons of whom it was said, 'They forget nothing and they learn nothing.' " Bushnell agreed to take the agreement back to New York and try it on the others.

When he read the postscript clause to Ericsson, poring over his drawing board, the Swede couldn't have cared less. The bit was in his teeth. He was spending sixteen hours a day turning out designs for the hundreds of parts of the battery, and was at the same time supervising and driving his subcontractors. His reaction to the clause was an airily preoccupied: "Perfectly reasonable . . . yes, quite proper. Indeed, I hope her commander will be ordered to hold his powder until he is as near the rebel batteries as he can get."

Bushnell, with a sense of mingled awe and disbelief at this display of sublime self-confidence on the part of his newly acquired associate, went up to Troy to secure the signatures of Griswold and Winslow. The former signed with reluctance. But Winslow refused. He was adamant and he was indignant. "It's preposterous," he sputtered. "Since when is a contractor obliged to guarantee that a weapons system will prevail in battle? There's no precedent for that kind of arrogance. If the Navy tried that on every contractor, it would never get a ship built."

Wearily, Bushnell returned to New York. "Give him a week," growled Ericsson without looking up from his work. "If he still won't sign, get somebody else." Ericsson wanted to keep Winslow in the project if at all possible. He was not unaware of the iron mill owner's access to "certain members of the administration," and to sources of capital. As it turned out, Winslow came down to New York in a week and signed.

CHAPTER

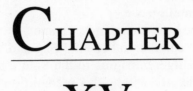

As Winslow in New York was with misgivings signing his name next to that of the secretary of the Navy, Welles in Washington was pursuing one of the more pleasurable aspects of his job. Welles loved to read the newspapers. And since he was obliged as secretary of the Navy to be thoroughly informed on world affairs, it was with a happy sense of combining vocation with avocation that he turned to the accumulated pile of papers on his desk. The daily press, domestic and foreign, was one of two main sources of information, and by far the more important. The other source, Mr. Pinkerton's Secret Service, was barely organized.

As an old newsman, Welles followed current events with an aggressiveness and energy matched by few others. Keeping up with the news was no passive, casual perusal of the press for this passionate little man. A former editor, he was especially aware of the difference between fact and fiction; and nothing roused his ire more readily than editorial opinion masquerading as news. At home, when cries of disbelief, hoots of derision, and barks of sarcastic laughter would ring through the walls of his study, Mary Jane and the children would turn to each other and say, with knowing smiles, "Papa is reading the newspapers."

In his office on this day, Welles began, as was his custom, with the New York papers, because they had the best foreign coverage. The

Herald was his first selection. On page four of the edition for October 8, he noted that in Lancashire, England, the shortage of raw cotton had idled a thousand spinners. Thousands more in the industry were working reduced hours. "Yes," said Welles to himself, "that is in accord with departmental intelligence."

In the same column he read that in the opinion of the *London Shipping Gazette,* a respected commercial sheet, "England and France, having already conceded belligerent rights to the South, cannot, in common consistency, much longer withhold a recognition of independence." " 'Belligerent rights'! 'Common consistency'!" bellowed Welles. "What the devil does that mean!"

He knew from a number of departmental reports and press dispatches that the silk manufacturers of Lyons were desperate. Their stocks of the fabric most prized by the wives and daughters of the Southern cotton planters were mounting daily, choking their warehouses and factories because their ships were unable to penetrate the blockade.

Welles permitted himself a small glow of satisfaction. Apparently the blockade was beginning to work. But the true test of its effectiveness was the extent to which it cut off war materiel exported from the Continent for consignment to the rebels. It was the lack of guns and ammunition that would finally defeat the South.

Turning to page six he read that the French and Spanish governments, having decided to intervene in the affairs of Mexico, were sending fleets and troops to the gulf, a direct contravention of the Monroe Doctrine. Welles nodded in confirmation. The move had long been rumored and came as no surprise. In large measure it was, he surmised, a probe to test U.S. capabilities and resolve. Well, if the Europeans are indeed coming to this hemisphere, we can do precious little about it, Mr. Monroe notwithstanding. Mr. Lincoln's doctrine is one war at a time.

He picked up the *Herald* for October 9. Little reason for cheer. In a lengthy article of rebuke to the government, a correspondent reported that the English steamer *Bermuda* "has been allowed to slip through the fingers of the commander" of the federal blockading squadron at Savannah despite the *Herald*'s warning two weeks previous that she was clearing at Liverpool. "Idiot!" hissed Welles. "She could have been clearing for any port in the world." The *Bermuda,* continued the article, conveyed to the rebels, inter alia, six to seven thousand Enfield rifles, cartridges for the same, army shoes, blankets, ammunition, quinine, and eighteen rifled cannon of large size and long range.

Welles was aware of the incident. The rebels had simply outsmarted the Union command. By firing guns and creating a commotion, they had diverted the Union force, thus allowing the *Bermuda* to slip through. "So," he muttered to himself, "the blockade is effective against the Lancashire spinners and the Lyons silk manufacturers, but it was ineffective at Savannah. The *Herald* giveth and the *Herald* taketh away. . . ."

The article continued, "Our readers were made aware yesterday that the *Merrimack,* one of the ships sunk at Norfolk and subsequently raised by the rebels, is now in a state of complete repair and clothed with steel armor."

"Not true, rumor monger," shouted Welles. He had recent reports from several different sources all confirming that the ship was still in dry dock, and that the Tredegar Iron Works in Richmond was having difficulty turning out two-inch iron plate. The rebels were scouring the northern Virginia countryside for scrap iron, tearing up railroad track for the *Merrimack*'s casemate. Also plaguing the rebels was a shortage of rolling stock, which further complicated the delivery of iron to Norfolk.

But that the *Merrimack* was a real and imminent threat there was no doubt. She was already having an impact on morale. Port city mayors all over the North were pleading for protection from the "monster" that they were convinced would ravage their defenseless cities unless preventive measures were taken. Even more alarming, naval commanders of sound judgment and impeccable credentials were beginning to warn of the *Merrimack*'s prowess.

On Welles's desk was an ominous note from Lt. Joe Smith addressed to his father, the commodore. Young Smith, executive officer aboard the fifty-gun sailing frigate *Congress,* was on patrol duty in Hampton Roads. He wrote affirming the serious nature of the threat posed by the rebel ironclad, adding, "I have not yet devised any plan to defend us against *Merrimack* unless it be with hard knocks."

Also on Welles's desk was a letter from Commodore Louis Malsherbes Goldsborough, flag officer in command of the Atlantic Blockading Squadron. At the thought of Goldsborough a smile softened Welles's features. The commodore was one of those people of whom no military force can have enough. He had entered the Navy as a midshipman at the age of seven, and legend had it he was weaned on ship's grog and a belaying pin. Apparently his rearing in the Navy hadn't stunted his physical growth. At fifty-six, after forty-nine years in the service, he stood an immense six feet four and weighed more than three hundred pounds. With a red, red beard, a foghorn for a voice, and a manner that discouraged even a thought of contradiction, the commodore was (behind his back) referred to by his men as "Old Guts."

Welles had recently written Goldsborough to say that it was essential that the Navy "put forth all its strength, and demonstrate to the country and to foreign powers its usefulness and capability in protecting and supporting the government and the Union." In response, writing from his flagship, *Minnesota,* sister ship to the *Merrimack,* Goldsborough assured the secretary that he was making every effort to seal the South's Atlantic ports, but at the same time he warned that the *Merrimack* was undoubtedly going to complicate his task. All intelligence indicated that she would prove "exceedingly formidable." Confederate opinion considered her impregnable.

As Welles pushed the letter into its file envelope, there was a rap on his door. It was Fox. "Do you have a minute?"

"Come on in . . . what's on your mind?"

"Just a progress report from our wunderkind in New York."

"Ericsson?"

"The same. He's sent Commodore Smith a batch of copies of working drawings for the hull and some of the machinery, including the rudder and screw."

"Do they meet with the commodore's approval?"

"You know old Joe. He said the other day he thought these newfangled ironclads were going to 'bilge' his reputation. Down deep he doesn't trust them. God gave us wood for ships."

"I have a letter from his son. He says he doesn't know how he's going to defend against the *Merrimack*."

"On the subject of *Merrimack*," said Fox, "I have just learned that her executive officer is one Lieutenant Catesby ap Rogers Jones. I know him well. Shipped with him. As bellicose and brave as a fighting cock."

"Sometimes it seems that all the good ones have gone South."

"Well, if it's any comfort, Ericsson is working night and day—even his subcontractors are working round the clock. He plans only one day off in the year. Even Christmas is a working day. His one holiday is Thanksgiving. Seems he lost the middle finger of his right hand on Thanksgiving some years ago. He was superintending a job at Delamater's when a workman reached out to steady a connecting rod. Ericsson put out his own hand to caution the man and his finger dropped to the floor. He stuck it in his pocket and said that that was reason enough to quit work. He's observed the holiday ever since. Tough old bird."

"Speaking of tough old birds," said Welles, "I have a letter from Goldsborough."

"What does he say?"

"Much the same as young Smith. Thinks the *Merrimack* will prove *très formidable*."

"Have you heard," asked Fox, "the latest story about Goldsborough?"

"More than likely, but I'll listen."

"Seems the hour for chapel service had struck, and the chaplain, not seeing the commodore, assumed he was going to skip devotions that morning. He commenced the service and a few minutes later in stalks Old Guts. The Goldsborough thunders, 'Sir! God ain't on the ship til I get there!'"

Some hundred and fifty miles to the south, in Hampton Roads, standing on the stout planking of the *Minnesota*'s quarterdeck, Commodore Goldsborough was, as it happened, engaged in a humanitarian gesture. "Send a letter to the rebel bastard," he growled to a yeoman. "Tell him we've got his and they've got ours and they both want to be exchanged. And don't forget to tell the son of a bitch there's nothing official about this. Let's just swap and be done with it."

"Aye, sir." Sniffling in the morning chill, the yeoman/amanuensis went below to the commodore's cabin. Folding down the hinged cover to an oak drop-front desk, he sat and dipped a steel nib into a glass inkwell. Without removing his fingerless wool gloves, he wrote in a highly ornate but nonetheless legible hand:

> U.S. Flag Ship "Minnesota"
> Hampton Roads, Octo. 10th, 1861

Sir:

By a letter from Lt. Sharpe (now as you are doubtless aware, a prisoner in New York) to his wife, forwarded to Norfolk today by a flag of truce, I perceive that he is very anxious to be exchanged. Without any specific authority on the subject of exchanging prisoners, I venture nevertheless to say to you that I think he may be exchanged for Lt. Worden of our Navy, who, I understand, is still confined at Montgomery.

Lieut. John L. Worden sailed with me some years ago, and I am on terms of intimacy with his family. Hence the reason of my feeling deeply interested in his behalf. Will you be good enough to inform me whether this suggestion be acceptable to yourselves or otherwise?

Respectfully

Your Obt. Servt:

L. M. Goldsborough

Flag Officer

Commdg Atlantic Blockading Squadron

Brigadier General Huger

Commdg Forces

Norfolk, Va.

Olivia Worden's pleas on behalf of her beloved had, at last, found fertile soil.

CHAPTER
XVI

When General Beauregard opened fire on Fort Sumter, Commodore Joseph Smith was seventy-one years old. He had served in the Navy for fifty-two of those years. The commodore had been blessed with a long and distinguished career, having accomplished everything a devoted sailor in the service of his country might reasonably wish.

As a young lieutenant in the War of 1812, at the critical battle of Lake Champlain when the United States desperately needed a victory, he was assigned the duty of winding his ship so as to bring to bear on the British the firepower of an undamaged broadside. Although wounded, he remained at his post under fire and accomplished his task. The Congress awarded him the Silver Medal for gallantry. Thereafter he saw combat duty in the skirmishes with Algiers, where once again he served with distinction. During the long period of peace that followed, he saw extensive sea duty with the Mediterranean and Pacific squadrons. In 1846 he was appointed to the important and prestigious post of chief of the Bureau of Navy Yards and Docks, the agency that provided the shore facilities responsible for developing and maintaining the seagoing forces.

Thus in 1861, after more than a half century of service, the last fifteen years of which were spent as bureau chief in a difficult and onerous position, it is little wonder that the gallant old sailor was looking forward to retirement with covetous and weary eyes. When he was a young line officer, the tall ships with the billowing white sails—eagles of the sea, swift, graceful, and deadly—were the pride of the fleet.

At about the time he became bureau chief of Yards and Docks, the Navy was convulsed by the first radical change in naval architecture in its history. Steam engines, boilers, furnaces, and gritty coal were rudely displacing soaring white sail. And this revolution was followed in quick succession by another technological upheaval. The ungainly and vulnerable side paddle wheel was replaced by the more efficient underwater screw propeller.

And now the elderly commodore was obliged to contend with still another momentous change. The very essence of ships was to be transformed. Iron was to displace wood. It was almost too much to contemplate. And it came on the eve of his long-awaited retirement.

It had all been planned. After some rest and travel with his wife of forty-three years, he would settle down in Washington for further service with the two institutions he most revered, the Episcopal Church and the U.S. Navy. For the former he would continue as a senior warden; for the Navy, he was to become a member of the Retiring Board. Happily, the family name would continue in the active lists in the person of his son, Joe.

But the war intruded, exploding all dreams of retirement, rudely compelling the old man to remain at his post, a position uniquely suited to a young, forward-looking officer committed to the technologies of the future.

Smith neither trusted nor was he in sympathy with the concept of employing iron as a shipbuilding material. And was it not an unreasonable fate that demanded of a seventy-one-year-old officer, in a time of terrible crisis for his country, that he revolutionize the Navy in which he was nurtured? Was it not indeed a cruel stroke of fortune that obliged an elderly and by now infirm officer to cast off the ageless essence of every vessel that had ever gone to sea, in favor of an iron boat that, as Commander Davis put it, was like nothing in heaven above or in the earth beneath or in the water under the earth?

As Smith saw it, he was laying his reputation (built in more than a half century of honorable service) on the line to endorse a two-gun "iron pot" conceived by a wild Swede who was associated with, if not responsible for, the worst peacetime disaster ever to befall the U.S. Navy.

For the commodore to report favorably on Ericsson's plan and to award him a contract took an act of courage easily comparable to that which had won him a Silver Medal for gallantry under fire. And, unhappily, Smith was not the kind of man who, once having made a decision, could shut it out of his mind and turn to other matters, trusting to a benevolent providence or to the good offices of men for a favorable result. Tormented by the fear of failure and ignominy, he worried and stewed and fretted.

From the day Ericsson was advised to proceed with the construction of his battery until the day it was completed, Smith wrote him no fewer than twenty-four letters, supplemented by countless informal notes and word-of-mouth messages, all of which reflected Smith's lack of confidence in the project. Were Ericsson a man of lesser faith in his own ability, the strain of the work and the sense of responsibility, combined with the incessant—and there is no other word for it—nagging, would have broken him down.

On September 25, the commodore wrote: "I am in great trouble from what I have recently learned, that the concussion in the turret will be so great that men cannot remain and work with the guns. . . ."

On October 11, he reverted to his favorite theme: "I understand that computations have been made by expert naval architects of the displacement of your vessel and the result arrived at is that she will not float with the load you propose to put upon her, and if she would she could not stand upright for want of stability nor attain a speed of four knots. . . . I am extremely anxious about the success of this battery. . . . I want to go to New York, but I am now so afflicted with rheumatism I can but barely walk."

On October 19, a new concern: "Your plan of ventilation appears plausible, but sailors do not fancy living underwater without breathing in sunshine occasionally. I propose a temporary house be constructed on deck, which will not increase the weight of the vessel more than eight to ten tons. . . ."

On October 21, the tormented commodore wrote: "The more I reflect upon your battery, the more I am fearful of her efficiency."

His next concern was that the heavy iron plating of the overhanging deck would settle or warp the infrastructure of wood beneath "so that her deck would after a time become much curved and finally break."

In a letter that followed two days later, Smith asked: "How is a man of five feet eight or ten inches in height to steer or work in a conical iron pilothouse only five feet high?" (The answer was that the pilot stood on a platform below deck so that only his head and shoulders were in the pilothouse, which was actually rectangular.)

To the commodore's stream of queries and complaints Ericsson replied as graciously as time permitted. He tried to reassure the old man. The captain was neither rude nor a boor, especially to one to whom he felt he owed a debt of gratitude. Ericsson never forgot that it had been Smith who detailed a crew to raise the foundered caloric ship that bore his name. Ericsson was not the sort to forget a favor.

Only once, when Smith wrote repeatedly about his twin bugaboos, stability and buoyancy, did Ericsson show a hint of impatience. "There is no living man," he wrote, "who has tripped me in calculation or proved my figures wrong in a single instance in matters relating to theoretical computation."

But Smith would not be reassured. His expressions of fear and misgiving continued apace. By November it became clear to Ericsson that if the vessel was to be built on time, some arrangement would have to be made to free him of the necessity of answering Smith's queries, and at the same time afford some peace of mind to the anxious commodore.

Ericsson suggested that the Navy appoint an on-site representative who would look after the government's interest in the construction of the vessel. Smith readily assented, and they agreed on Alban C. Stimers, formerly chief engineer of the *Merrimack,* and an honest, competent technician. Armed with a copy of the contract along with specifications and plans, Stimers was charged by Smith to "be vigilant in the inspection of materials and work on this vessel to see that they are of the best quality of their kind, and certify to bills in triplicate for payments as they shall be earned according to the contract."

It was well that Smith and Ericsson arrived at their arrangement when they did. Shortly after Stimers assumed his post, Engineer-in-Chief Isherwood made a tour of several subcontractors and subsequently reported to Smith that the vessel would not be completed on time; that the specifications were not being met; that Ericsson and his partners stood to clear an immense profit of not less than one hundred thousand dollars; and that, in any case, the vessel would prove an abysmal failure. Among Isherwood's charges was the allegation that the turret was only six inches thick instead of the stipulated eight.

Stimers took a ladder and a pair of calipers and climbed up on the turret. After a number of measurements he found that it was indeed the required eight inches uniformly throughout, and so he was able to partially allay the fears of the rattled commodore, who continued to express his anxiety in a stream of correspondence. His letters now, however, were for the most part directed to Stimers.

As the deadline for completion approached, Ericsson drove himself even harder. It was apparent that they were locked in a race with the *Merrimack*. The stakes were incalculable. Ericsson expanded his working day. Now it began shortly after dawn with a stint at the drawing board. In the forenoon a waiting carriage sped him either to the Continental Iron Works in Greenpoint, Brooklyn, where the hull was being constructed and the whole vessel assembled, or to Delamater's on the Hudson River at 14th Street, where the engines and all machinery were being built. At Continental a ship house was constructed over the ways so that work could proceed at night and in all weather.

Ericsson's practice was to superintend the work at one of the sites until late afternoon, at which time he returned to Franklin Street, where he resumed at the drawing board, working far into the night, every night. At the edge of exhaustion and ever mindful of the stakes in the race, he had little patience with inefficiency or deviation from his design.

At Delamater's one afternoon he noticed an engineer with a measuring rod poking about in the bowels of the engine. Standing over the man on a runway, the captain roared down, "What are you doing there, sir?"

"Checking the length of the piston rod, Captain."

"Is it not on the drawing, sir?"

"Yes, sir."

"Then why do you come here with sticks, sir? Go and get the length from the drawing, sir. I do not want you to bring sticks when the drawing gives the size."

His approach to nonprofessionals was equally direct. At Continental one November morning, preoccupied with the battery's ventilation system, he tripped over an iron bar lying on the floor of the construction shed. Turning to two workmen who were standing by, he said, "Please remove that thing so that it isn't underfoot."

The two men exchanged quick glances, and one replied, "It's too heavy, Captain."

Without a word, Ericsson stooped, jerked the bar up, carried it across the shop, and flung it onto the scrap heap. At noon the two men, enlisting the aid of two others, weighed the bar. It tipped the scale at just over five hundred pounds. The date being November 13, 1861, Ericsson was four months past his fifty-eighth birthday.

That same November morning a little-known ceremony transpired at the county jail in Montgomery, Alabama. Seven months to the day after Worden's arrest, a young Confederate officer presented himself at the lieutenant's cell. Although it was ten o'clock, Worden was still on his cot, huddled under a thin cotton blanket over which was spread his service tunic. The morning air was mild and the Alabama sun shone, but it was apparent to the young officer, a newly made first lieutenant resplendent in his immaculate butternut gray uniform, that Worden was chilled and shivering under his covers. Disconcerted, he addressed Worden softly through the bars of the cell: "Sir."

There was no response. After several more tries, each louder and more peremptory, Worden replied. "Aye, sir." Hoarse and faint, it sounded as though he had just surfaced after a deep dive into arctic waters.

"I bear instructions from the secretary of war. You are to report without delay to the adjutant general in Richmond, Virginia. There you shall be paroled if first you swear on your honor as an officer and a gentleman not to disclose, to the detriment of the Confederate States of America, anything you may hear or see on your way to release."

Worden did not ask why the Confederate government was willing to accept his word when presumably they jailed him in the first instance for violating it. The irony, however, did not escape him. But he was battling to remain conscious, praying for the strength to get off the cot and begin the journey to Richmond.

With exquisite deliberation, Worden rolled back his covers. Then, with an apparently monumental effort he lifted his legs a few inches off the cot and let them drop to the floor. Bracing his hands on the iron frame, he prepared to get to his feet. That was the hardest part. When he stood he knew his head would swim and he would become faint and nauseous. Now, O Lord God, give me the strength. He struggled to his feet, it seemed to the young lieutenant, in sections.

Upright at last, he whispered hoarsely, "I do so swear." Through the bars the lieutenant handed him written orders. With a crisp salute and a smart about-face he left Worden, who was too weak or too stunned to move, standing in his long underwear.

The prospect of freedom lent Worden the strength to make the journey. He arrived in Richmond three days later on Saturday evening, November 16. There he was furnished with a letter from the secretary of war to General Huger, directing the general to carry out the arrangement agreed upon between himself and Commodore Goldsborough.

Early Monday morning, November 18, the mist still rising from the waters of Hampton Roads, a dory got underway from the Virginia shore at Sewall's Point. Four pairs of oars lifted and dropped with one motion; the white flag of truce stood rippling in the breeze. Aboard were five men, four rebel sailors pulling lustily, and a barely visible Worden huddled in a huge billowing cape, collar up, cap jammed low on his head against the autumn breeze. He bore a communication from General Huger to Commodore Goldsborough.

In about twenty minutes the boat was alongside the USS *Minnesota,* whose fabric of rope and spars loomed up in the dull haze like a monster cobweb. The oars were laid in and a sailor at the bow fastened the boat hook to the ringbolt next to the *Minnesota*'s ladder.

After being helped up the well-scrubbed steps—Worden couldn't negotiate them on his own—he saluted the ensign astern and, weaving unsteadily along the spotless white spar deck, escorted by a midshipman, he made his way to the quarterdeck. One of the sailors, who was washing the sleep from his eyes with saltwater from a bucket, watched the proceeding and later wrote his wife that the lieutenant could barely stand on his feet. His uniform was far too large and his color was that of a frog's belly.

Reporting to Goldsborough on the quarterdeck, the lieutenant managed a salute and delivered Huger's message, which advised that, in accordance with their agreement, Worden was being sent on parole, and as soon as Lt. William Sharpe of the Confederate Navy was returned to Norfolk, Worden's parole would be ended. Sharpe was at once dispatched in the waiting dory.

Thus was ended the seven-month captivity of Lt. John Lorimer Worden. He went directly home to Quaker Hill. En route he wrote Welles that, although he realized he should be reporting to the department, he was indisposed and felt it "most prudent to proceed at once to my home that I may receive the necessary medical treatment under the care of my family."

Welles quite understood. The lieutenant richly deserved a long period of convalescence at home.

*   *   *

In the fall of 1861, new word of the fearsome capabilities of the *Merrimack* was spreading waves of apprehension through Washington and the coastal cities of the North.

The November 9 issue of the *Scientific American,* a respected weekly, carried a disturbing combination of two articles. The first, on an inside page headed "Steam Battering Rams," reported on the destruction, near New Orleans, of the *Vincennes,* a sixteen-gun Union sloop that had been split open and sent to the bottom by the Confederate's *Turtle.* The *Turtle* was an old tugboat whose hull had been reinforced with iron and fitted up as a battering ram.

On the back cover of the issue was the second article, accompanied by a page-wide engraving of the new, transformed *Merrimack.* The engraving had been made from a sketch furnished by a mechanic who had worked on the ship. Before she was scuttled and torched, said the article, the *Merrimack* was "one of the finest frigates in the Navy, 3,200 tuns [sic] burthen, carrying 40 large guns, built at Charlestown, Mass. in 1855." The mechanic said that her hull had been cut down to a few inches above the waterline, and an iron bombproof house built on her gun deck, also bombproof. The house had been pierced for ten guns. No masts, only a pilothouse and a smokestack showed above the deck. Her most formidable feature, however, was the projecting angle of iron— a ram—for the purpose of piercing a vessel. The engraving, black and menacing, pictured a brutal, iron-shelled war machine thrusting a pointed, upswept, vicious prow.

The implications, even for the uninitiate in matters of naval warfare, were obvious. If an old tug fitted out as a ram could sink a sixteen-gun man-o'-war, what havoc could not be wrought by a modern ironclad steam ram of the size and armament of the *Merrimack?*

CHAPTER
XVII

On an evening in late November when the first chill blasts of winter were sweeping down from the Appalachians into the capital city, the president, accompanied by Secretary of State Seward and young John Hay, crossed Pennsylvania Avenue to 15th and H Streets, where stood the handsome house of General-in-Chief George B. McClellan.

After being advised by a servant that the general was attending a wedding, the president decided to wait in the hope that McClellan would soon return. About an hour later the general came in and, without acknowledging the porter who advised that the president was waiting, went upstairs, passing the door of the room where the three men were seated. They waited another half hour and sent a servant to tell the general they were still there. The answer came that the general had retired for the evening.

Walking back to the White House, the usually even-tempered and debonair Hay was speechless with anger. When Seward, who had become a confidant of McClellan, left to go home, and the president and Hay were alone in the executive chamber, Hay ventured to express his feelings. He considered the general's behavior inexcusable. Aside from being rude, insolent, and a clear instance of lèse majesté, it was an ominous sign of military contempt for civil authority.

The president, standing at the tall window, gazing into the dark

November night, heard his secretary through without interruption. Then, turning and nodding acknowledgment rather than approval of his sentiments, said, "Mr. Hay, I think we are well advised at this time not to be thin-skinned or to be making points about etiquette and personal dignity. I'll hold McClellan's horse if he will only bring us success."

Northern arms were in disarray. The defeat at Bull Run in July had gone unanswered. The old year was waning and the new looming with little reason for cheer. There was no prospect of a Union victory in sight. Only bad news and the gloom of winter seemed certain. Military leadership or the absence thereof was the president's gravest concern.

As far as prosecuting the war, Secretary of War Simon Cameron had proved more of a liability than an asset. His function was increasingly usurped by Seward, who saw in Cameron's negligence an opportunity to extend his own tireless thrust for domination of the government.

At a meeting in Scott's office a few days before the old general resigned, the subject of the defense of Washington arose. Lincoln turned to his secretary of war to ask how many troops were stationed in and around the capital. "Can't say," replied Cameron. "Don't rightly know."

The president next looked to McClellan, chief of the Army of the Potomac, responsible for the defense of Washington. The general could not or would not supply the information. General-in-Chief Scott, his gouty leg resting in a sling suspended from the ceiling, said that no reports on the subject had been made to him.

After a moment of silence during which the president canvased the room with his eyes, Seward said he thought he might be able to supply the information. The secretary of state, reading from a slip of paper that he took from his pocket, then gave a comprehensive answer that included a recitation of the number of regiments, their identity, and their commanders. When he finished his report, Seward looked to McClellan for confirmation. The general said he thought Seward's figures approximately correct.

Scott flushed a deeper shade of red. Summoning all the dignity an army officer can muster with one leg horizontal, he cleared his throat and declared, "This is indeed, Mr. President, a remarkable state of affairs. I am in command of the armies of the United States but have been wholly unable to get any reports, any statement of the actual forces. But here is the secretary of state, a civilian for whom I have great respect, who is neither a military man nor conversant with military affairs—though his abilities are obviously formidable—possessed of facts that are withheld from me."

Seward explained that he came by the facts through vigilance and observation, recording the arrival and departure of the various regiments.

"Obviously, sir, your labors have been arduous," said Scott with a withering glance in McClellan's direction. "I suspect that I am not aware of the whole of them."

Secretary of War Cameron broke in. "It is no secret that Mr. Seward busies himself with the affairs of all departments in matters that are of no concern to him. But since nothing or nobody can discourage him, I think we had best conclude this meeting and return to our duties."

The meeting seemed to be over. Welles was shocked by Cameron's denigrating allusion to the president's apparent inability to rein in Seward. And to add insult to injury, Cameron had also usurped the president's prerogative by calling the meeting to a close on his own initiative. However, despite the affront to Mr. Lincoln and to his own sensibilities, Welles was relieved that the unpleasant meeting was apparently over and done with. But it was not quite.

With a disturbed president looking on, General Scott addressed McClellan as he was walking out of the office: "General McClellan, you were called here by my advice. The times require vigilance and activity. I am not active and never shall be again. When I proposed that you should come here to aid, not supersede me, you had my friendship and my confidence." Scott paused. Turning away from McClellan, he concluded in measured and deliberate tones, "You still have my confidence."

The old man resigned a few days later. At four o'clock of a pitch-black November morning, in a pouring rain squall, his successor, General McClellan, and his staff, attended by a squad of cavalry in ponchos, saw the old general off at the Washington depot. He was on his way to New York, where he planned to embark on a tour of Europe before settling down to retirement.

If Seward was determined to dominate the government, Cameron seemed equally intent on selling it. The secretary of war, otherwise known as "The Czar of Pennsylvania," was engaged in paying off old political debts and building his political organization in his native state through the expedient of granting favors in the business of military procurement.

The highly respected editor of the New York *Evening Post,* William Cullen Bryant, noted that a man who wants to make a contract with the government for the sale of three hundred mules, provided he is a Pennsylvanian, had no difficulty obtaining access to the secretary of war. A citizen of any other region could be certain of denial. "Mr. Lincoln must know," he wrote, "that Cameron is worse than nothing in the cabinet."

That winter the House of Representatives learned through its Committee on Government Contracts that, curiously, the only horses worth procuring for the Army seemed inexplicably to come from Pennsylvania. A cavalry regiment being staged in Louisville, Kentucky, proverbial for its fine horses, saw four hundred eighty-five of the thousand horses imported from Pennsylvania condemned by a board of army officers. The horses were blind, spavined, ringboned, and suffering from the heaves, the glanders, indeed every disease horseflesh can contract. It had cost the government more than fifty-eight thousand dollars for the four hundred eighty-five animals in addition to ten thousand dollars for transporting them from Pennsylvania.

Under another contract, this one let by express order of the secretary of war, one thousand horses were to be delivered to the government at Huntingdon, Pennsylvania. An army inspector, apparently honest as he was innocent, began by rejecting three out of five. He was quickly replaced by other inspectors less meticulous. They accepted the remaining horses, many with running sores. The regiment to which the horses were consigned subsequently rejected more than five hundred as unfit for duty.

Dead and starving horses purchased but rejected by the Army were to be seen scattered all over the North. A walk around Washington revealed hundreds of horse carcasses tied to trees and posts, where they had pined away, living on bark and limbs until they starved to death. That winter the stench of decaying horseflesh succeeded the summer reek of open privies, with grave implications for the health of the city's inhabitants.

It was with the railroads, however, that Cameron and his friends profited most handsomely. His assistant secretary of war, Thomas A. Scott, a Cameron appointee, appearing before the house committee, testified that, yes, he had retained his position as vice president of the

Pennsylvania Central Railroad; and although, yes, it was true that the government was buying transportation from said railroad, and that he, Scott, was the buyer who set the rates, he saw no necessary conflict of interest.

The Northern Central Railroad, of which Cameron was a major stockholder, also fared very well as a consequence of the rates set by the assistant secretary. Scott fixed a rate of two cents per mile per soldier regardless of whether he traveled in a passenger car or a boxcar, with his regiment or alone. Immigrants traveled at half that rate, and they were given an eighty-pound free baggage allowance—a privilege not accorded the government. So enormous were the profits that railroad companies were paying up to twenty-five hundred dollars to any regiment that would give them the privilege of transporting them.

Scholarly and precise Lyman Trumbull, Republican senator from Illinois and member of the Joint Committee on the Conduct of the War, rose to recount to his peers the saga of Hall's carbines, a too-typical example of the government's procurement procedures. The carbines were originally sold by the government as useless and condemned property at $2.00 apiece. Subsequently the government repurchased 790 of them at $15.00 per. Two months later the government sold them at $3.50. After another two months the guns, presumably having been altered and repaired, were purchased by a government agent at $12.50. The agent subsequently turned them over to the government for $22.00 apiece.

Another agent, unrelated to the first except by a nose for profit, purchased for the government at a cost of one hundred thousand dollars a ship the Navy had previously condemned as unseaworthy. The vessel sank on her maiden voyage as a gunboat.

Charles H. Van Wyck, Republican member of the House Committee on Government Contracts, uncovered case after case of fraud and peculation in everything from army and navy procurement to treasury contracts. When it was brought to his attention that the presumably repaired Hall's carbines were so defective they would shoot the thumbs off the soldiers using them, the eloquent and normally genial congressman was moved to characterize the prevailing mood for his colleagues in the House: "The whole sky has been wrapped in gloom, and men go about the streets wondering where this thing will end. The mania for stealing seems to have run through all the relations of government—almost from the general to the drummer boy. Nearly every man who deals with the government seems to feel or desire that it would not long survive, and each had a common right to plunder while it lived."

Setting the tone and presiding at the top of the stinking mess like a king vulture on a mountain of excrement sat the secretary of war himself, controlling a twenty-two million dollar budget for firearms alone. Even the president, notoriously slow to indict character or besmirch reputation, was moved to muse aloud to John Nicolay that Cameron was utterly ignorant, heedless of the course of events, and obnoxious to the country.

But to a delegation of New York and Boston bankers who called on Lincoln and urged the removal of Cameron, the president replied, "Gentlemen, if you want General Cameron removed, you have only to bring me one proved case of dishonesty, and I promise you his head."

The taint of corruption in government contracts reached even to Gideon Welles. He had appointed his merchant-banker brother-in-law, Governor Edwin D. Morgan of New York, an agent in the procurement of ships for the Navy at a commission of two and a half percent. The going rate in Boston was one percent. Mr. Morgan turned a profit of ninety thousand dollars.

At a congressional hearing Representative Van Wyck conceded that Welles, honest himself, would not take a farthing from the treasury, and that Morgan as a buyer of ships had done very well by his country, buying sound stock at reasonable prices. "But," said Van Wyck, "if the men owning vessels have been compelled or induced to sell them at small prices, what right has the secretary to allow his brother-in-law to put his hands in the pocket of each seller and realize the immense sum of ninety thousand dollars in a few months? That money really belongs to the government."

When the subject of Van Wyck's remarks rose at a cabinet meeting, Welles nodded resignedly, "I knew that was a chicken that would come home to roost; but when I made the deal, time was of the essence. We needed the ships quickly. I knew my banker brother-in-law was making a handsome commission, but I also knew he would bring us reliable vessels without delay. I think it is well to bear in mind that he supplied us with some four hundred steamers—everything from ferryboats to private yachts—in a matter of weeks."

Lincoln understood. He was willing to let the matter drop without further comment, for it was at his direction, in those first frantic days of the war, that agents had been commissioned to spend vast sums with the emphasis on dispatch in an effort to mobilize men and materiel as quickly as possible. And now the administration was paying for its less-than-meticulous methods of war procurement. An inflamed press and public were demanding a cabinet reshuffle.

It was suggested many times to the president that he could relieve the pressure by sacrificing one or two lambs to the wolves. But Lincoln, though privately devastated by the obvious corruption pervading the government, stood fast. He refused to consider asking for the resignation of any cabinet member except on the presentation of irrefutable evidence of dishonesty.

Before the year came to an end, the administration would have to face yet another scandal of a financial nature. Though not so grand in scope as some of Cameron's, it was the unkindest to the president.

When Mary Todd Lincoln came to Washington in 1861, it was for the second time. Her first trip to the capital had been in 1847, when she arrived from Springfield as the wife of a freshman congressman. At the time she found the capital decidedly not to her liking. The city was crude and boisterous. The licentious behavior of congressmen away from home genuinely shocked her. After three months, despite Lincoln's efforts to do everything he could to make her comfortable, she packed up Robert and Eddie and went home.

When she returned as First Lady fourteen years later, it was as a virtual newcomer, eager to be accepted and somewhat anxious on that score, but at the same time mindful of who she was. Mary Todd was proud of her Southern antecedents. The Todds of Lexington were an established and distinguished family. She was proud too of her husband's accomplishments, in which she felt she had played no small part. And she was proud of her three sons, Robert, Willie, and Tad.

Washington society, however, the core of which was Southern, was unimpressed. Indeed, they had nothing but contempt for this renegade woman of the South who wore low-cut dresses with long trains, and who had formed a liaison with that vulgar oaf who was threatening to destroy their way of life.

After the better part of a year in Washington, Mary Todd found that her closest companion and confidante was her dressmaker and maid, Elizabeth Keckley. A former slave, Elizabeth was a handsome mulatto, a woman of vigor and spirit who had bought her and her son's freedom. To Elizabeth, Mary confided her plans and her dreams. Piqued by rejection, she was determined to show Washington society the error of its ways. In refurbishing the White House she would demonstrate to the world that the First Lady of the United States was a woman of exquisite taste and refinement, a happy union of Southern sensibility and cosmopolitan culture.

"Honey," warned Elizabeth, bent over her sewing, "if those Southern ladies don't like you when the White House is mean and shabby, they ain't going to like you any better when it's pretty and gussied up."

Mary Todd dismissed the counsel as well-intentioned but uninformed. She loved fashionable clothes and pretty things. She had always been a compulsive shopper. And now on her frequent buying tours in New York and Philadelphia, lashed by injured pride and spurred by a convenient sense of patriotism, her buying knew few restraints. The new elaborately carved rosewood furniture, plush brocatelle drapes and matching upholstery, velvet hassocks, sparkling crystal, gleaming silver, glittering vases, gorgeous carpets—all were ready and awaiting the scrutiny of guests invited for the fall season of holiday dinners and receptions.

Mary Todd, impeccably gowned, was happy as she surveyed the fruit of her labors. She had transformed the executive mansion from a dingy, tobacco-spattered jumble into a sleek and splendid manse, an abode worthy of America's chief executive.

But when the bills came pouring in, her pleasure turned to pain and then panic. She had overspent her $20,000 budget by more than a third, or $6,700. She didn't know how to tell the president. Wretched, she turned to Benjamin French, commissioner of Public Buildings, and asked him to intercede.

Mary Todd had correctly anticipated her husband's reaction. Lincoln was furious. Hay confided to Nicolay that he had never seen him so exercised with "Madame." To his wife the president raged that he would not ask the Congress for a deficiency appropriation. "It would stink in the nostrils of the American people to have it said that the president of the United States had approved a bill overrunning an appropriation of twenty thousand dollars for flubdubs for this damned old house when the soldiers cannot have blankets!"

When the storm receded and other, more pressing, events came to the fore, the problem was resolved in precisely the manner the president had decried. The Congress buried an extra appropriation for the executive mansion in the budget for the coming year.

But the damage was done. Thereafter, Mary Todd was the subject of vicious rumor and gossip by the very people she had sought to impress. For those of Southern sympathies she was ever the renegade; for pro-Unionists, the suspect parvenue. In both quarters it was meanly bruited about that on her shopping sprees she had, on more than one occasion, confused her personal account with that of the White House. A distressed president saw the episode as another reason for erosion of public confidence in his administration.

"The Tycoon," remarked Hay to Nicolay in the gloom of a December afternoon, "could stand some good news about now."

"Especially in the form of a military victory."

CHAPTER
XVIII

Dutchess County, a rolling, wooded enclave that stretches for ten miles along the east bank of the Hudson River, is about fifty miles north of New York City. Tucked in the county's southeastern corner, hard by the Connecticut line, is Quaker Hill, a picturesque eminence of small farms and sprawling estates.

At the top of the hill, in a low, rambling farmhouse where five generations of Toffey women had waited for their men, Olivia Toffey Worden, with a heart full of gratitude, awaited the arrival of her husband. Waiting with her were Johnny Jr., sixteen; Daniel T., fourteen; Grace, nine; and little Olivia, five. The excitement for the children, who had been excused from school, was almost too much to bear. They hadn't seen Papa in almost a year and now he was coming home for the holidays—for Thanksgiving, which was less than a week away, and for Christmas!

Shortly after breakfast, during the watch of Daniel and little Olivia, who were at their station near the front parlor window, a cry rang out from the two simultaneously, "Carriage, ho!"

The four children and Olivia rushed to the bottom of the path in time to see Worden's carriage pull up to the front of the house. Worden tried to get out and walk under his own power. But only by leaning heavily on the cabman and Johnny, who half carried him, was he able to make it into the house.

He embraced Olivia first. Wordlessly they clung, he unable to speak, she repeating endlessly to herself the Lord's Prayer by way of gratitude, holding his emaciated, trembling frame. There was nothing to her poor darling, just skin and bone. His features were honed to a fragility she had never known. She knew her task for the next few months.

Worden embraced each of his children. First, John Jr., the pride of his father, waiting impatiently for notice of his appointment to the military academy at West Point. He hoped the war wouldn't be over by the time he graduated. Then came Daniel Toffey, a manly little fellow who stood at attention when his father addressed him; then Grace, crippled from birth but fully comprehending the moment; and, finally, little Olivia, who so closely resembled her mother—dear, quietly beautiful, slim, erect Olivia.

Worden stumbled into bed, where he remained for ten days, dozing and waking to take the thick soups and porridges and cod liver oil that Olivia spooned into him. It was a bittersweet time, half lost in dreams and remembrances, by turns brilliant with the poignant light of November and dark with autumnal foreboding. He would awaken with the expectation of finding himself in the Montgomery jail cell, but there would be the sunshine filtering through the dimity curtains, and one of the little girls standing at the door, grave and wide-eyed, waiting to rush breathlessly to Mama and tell her that Papa was awake now.

Worden got out of bed briefly for Thanksgiving dinner, a meal graced by the best the local countryside had to offer. It had been a good year for the farms of the region. The barns were bulging with the fruits of a rich harvest.

The *New York Times* noted in its editorial columns that there was more to be thankful for this year than last. In addition to the bounteous harvest, there had been a sublime renovation of the moral life of the country. Although the nation had not been at war the previous Thanksgiving, it had been a peace full of wrongs and shames, horrible and hateful. The *Times* agreed with the governor of Massachusetts, who noted with sympathy the daughters bereft of fathers and brothers and wives bereft of husbands but felt nevertheless that we should "let our souls arise to God on the wings of praise and thanksgiving that He has again granted us the privilege of living unselfishly and dying nobly in a grand and righteous cause."

As the Worden family bowed heads and Worden asked the blessing, each, including little Olivia, said a private prayer of thanks because

Papa was home. After the blessing and while Worden was carving the turkey, Johnny said, "Papa, are you rarin' to get back at the rebs?"

Worden thought for a moment. "I'm not after revenge; I'm just grateful that I'll be able to do what I was trained for." Olivia, serving the yams, flashed a quizzical smile. "Well," he allowed, "it might feel good to get in a lick or two."

"Johnny," said his mother, "I think Papa may not want to talk about the war."

Directly after dinner Worden returned to bed. That night for the first time since his return, Olivia slipped into bed beside him. "I missed you and love you," she whispered into his ear. Worden turned to face her. She kissed him on the lips. He was fast asleep.

On the ninth day of his return, Worden's friend and family physician stopped by on one of his frequent visits. He pronounced the patient on the mend but warned that another two or three weeks of bed rest was essential. Worden wasn't to think of returning to duty for sixty days, "The merest chill, Jack, could set you back for months."

That night Olivia again slipped into his bed. This time she found him quite awake. They made love. With muffled sobs of joy they made love for the seven months they had been apart. They made love in gratitude. And with murmurs of delight they made love because they were in love. As Olivia prepared to return to another room so that he could rest undisturbed, she kissed him good night. He was fast asleep. "Poor darling," she whispered, "you have reason to be tired."

The following morning, at an early hour, Worden made his way down to the parlor. He was in uniform for the first time since his return. He surprised Olivia at her needlework. "Good morning," he said.

The slow, wide, tentative smile began to light her eyes, the smile that broke his heart the first time he saw it. But as the significance of the uniform became apparent, the smile faded. "Good morning, Jack." For a few moments they were silent, he letting the uniform speak, she comprehending the decision and slowly coming to terms with it.

"I don't believe I'll go to Washington," he said. "I think I'll report to the navy yard in Brooklyn. If they want me in Washington, they'll send for me." If she was going to recall the cautionary words of the doctor, he thought, now was the time. But she was his darling. She said, "You'll need all your warm things."

"Yes. I expect I'll be home for Christmas."

Worden reported to Commodore Paulding, commandant of the Brooklyn

Navy Yard, on December 3. Paulding, who was acquainted with Worden, took one look at him and remarked that he didn't look strong enough to stand up to a Caribbean breeze. He assigned him to recruiting duty at the rendezvous there.

By the end of the year Worden was chafing under the sedentary routine of his job. Although he was far from fully recovered, he felt he was on the mend. He was always cold and found that he chilled easily. He took to wearing socks to bed, and was rarely without a hot water bottle. He couldn't recall a more miserable winter. The icy north wind whipped off the East River, chilling the workers at the Brooklyn yard, where around-the-clock schedules called for nonstop work in the large, unheated, barnlike buildings. To Worden's further discomfort, the dizziness and lightheadedness that had afflicted him during the Alabama summer persisted when he rose from a prone or sitting position.

Nevertheless, he let it be known to Commodore Paulding and to the department in Washington that he was available for sea duty. His private expectation was that by the time the department took action, he would be completely recovered.

At the same time he wrote Olivia that he was humbly and profoundly grateful that a benevolent Providence had seen fit to heal him. There was now only one wish that remained. If only it were given him to serve his country in the manner in which he had trained for twenty-seven years, he would ask nothing more. In a philosophical aside, he admitted that, although he was not proud of the sentiment, he also harbored an inextinguishable desire to pay back the rebels in some measure for those seven months of unwarranted pain.

His stockinged feet crossed on the desk, the long spyglass resting between them, the president was engaged in what had become one of his favorite means of relaxation, surveying the blue-hazed hills across the Potomac, beyond Alexandria. Except for the few patches of evergreen, the horizon was laced with bare, delicate-limbed trees. An occasional sparrow hawk floated effortlessly, wings casually outstretched, across the tree line. The smoke of a few wood fires undulated lazily into the purpling autumn sky.

Hay knocked softly. "Mr. Sumner is here." The president leaned the glass against the window sill and rose to greet the senator from Massachusetts.

The man who at fifty was deemed by Washington society to be its most eligible bachelor, and the most handsome, most learned, most elegantly tailored member of Congress, loped across the room with his rapid and distinctive stride. As chairman of the Senate's Foreign Affairs Committee, he met regularly with the president. Lincoln noticed that he was favoring his left leg rather more than usual, although he barely depended on the gleaming ebony cane that swung jauntily from his left hand. It had been five years since that bizarre and tragic incident on the floor of the Senate when, after concluding an impassioned antislavery speech, the senator was struck repeatedly on the head with a walking stick wielded by South Carolina Congressman Preston Brooks. The congressman, proclaiming that the state of South Carolina had been libeled, struck blow after blow with all his strength until the stout gutta-percha stick shattered, damaging the senator's spine and disordering his central nervous system. Sumner struggled to rise and free his broad-shouldered six-foot-two frame, which was pinned by his desk. So powerful was he that he nearly wrenched loose the iron screws that held desk and chair to the floor. But he was battered to unconsciousness before he could defend himself.

After four years in a wheelchair recuperating, Sumner had not moderated his abolitionist position. If anything, he had grown more extreme.

After an exchange of warm but brief greetings, Sumner, in his direct (some said "humorless") fashion, came right to the point. "I think, Mr. President, that we need not today discuss our mutual antipathy to the 'peculiar institution.' Our sentiments on that score are well established." Lincoln nodded. Although, unlike Sumner, he was not an abolitionist, his loathing for slavery was profound and of long standing. Whenever the subject arose, the same image inevitably came to mind. Sailing down the Ohio on a river steamer twenty years before, he had the opportunity to observe a coffle of twelve slaves. Chained together "like so many fish on a trotline," they had been torn from their families in Kentucky and were being transported to the Deep South. The scene tormented him everafter and had the power to make him miserable.

"Mr. President, I believe the time has come for bold and forthright action. The war gives no promise of quick solution. It remains a full-fledged conflict with a desperate, rebellious, and wicked band of conspirators who threaten to destroy the United States.

"I believe emancipation is our single best weapon. And I believe that your year-end message to the Congress should incorporate an emancipation decree." With the aid of his cane, the senator shifted his weight in the chair. It pained him to sit in one position for more than a few minutes.

The president considered for a moment. This was to be no casual chat, no relaxed year's-end holiday greeting. But then that wasn't to be expected from Sumner. An earnest, serious man, driven by a mission, he was rarely casual. It was evident that he had come with a carefully prepared statement, one that called for an equally thoughtful response. That the senator was proposing an emancipation decree was hardly new. In every speech since his recovery, and in every public forum he attended, Sumner tirelessly promoted the cause of emancipation. But this was the first time he confronted the president directly.

Mr. Lincoln leaned back in his chair and, clasping his hands behind his head, gave himself a few moments to frame a reply. "Mr. Sumner, I appreciate and understand your sentiments, and am not necessarily opposed. I have been giving a great deal of thought to the subject of emancipation. But let's think for a moment on the consequences of such an edict: What would its impact be on the several regions of the country?

"What, for example, would be the probable effect on the border states—Delaware, Maryland, Kentucky, and Missouri? Now, I like to think that those states are irrevocably ranged on the side of the Union. But you and I know there are substantial insurrectionist elements in all of them, waiting for the opportunity to assert themselves. They are, after all, slave states. I cannot afford to alienate them. To lose the border would be to lose the war.

"To the best of my knowledge, the border and many in the North, perhaps a majority, are in this war not for the purpose of emancipation but to preserve the Union." Lincoln rummaged in a desk drawer and came out with a clip from the *Boston Advertiser,* which he handed to the senator.

"Here is one newspaper's reaction to your recent address before the Republican State Convention in Worcester. I don't hold that it's representative of all the Northern press, but I do believe it represents a fair amount of public opinion, perhaps the majority."

Sumner read the underlined portion: "We hold it for an incontestable truth that neither men nor money will be forthcoming for this war if once the people are impressed with the belief that the abolition of slavery and not the defence of the Union is its objective . . . ."

"Another thing to consider," said Lincoln, "is the constitutionality of an emancipation decree. Does the federal government have the right to deprive people in the several states of their property, and to interfere with the right of each state to order and control its domestic institutions? I think not.

"And even assuming I were to decide to abrogate the law and proclaim emancipation, how much validity would it have? Will some poor soul slaving in his master's field in Georgia or Mississippi be any more free because I proclaim it so?

"And, finally, please remember, Senator—and I am forced to think about this every day—what my mandate is. I am sworn to defend and uphold the Constitution. I am not sworn to abolish slavery."

Sumner took a moment before replying—a moment, it occurred to him, that he would not have needed before the injury. "Mr. President, I too understand and appreciate what you have said, but I must nevertheless insist that the best way for you to honor your oath of office is to proclaim emancipation.

"Although I do not agree that the majority of public opinion cares not about slavery and is concerned only with the preservation of the Union, I do admit that my own concern is leadership. I myself have never let the presumed authority of public opinion sway my purpose. As I have said more than once, 'I am in morals, not politics.' I well understand, however, that as a senator from a single state, my responsibilities are not comparable to yours. I enjoy a latitude that you do not."

Once again, with the aid of his cane, Sumner shifted his weight. "As to the legality of an emancipation proclamation, I submit that you do indeed have the authority. The precedent has been well established. War powers supersede any existing civil law or code. This principle was informally expressed as far back as the Peloponnesian War, when Greece suffered as we are now suffering. Thucydides tells us that slaves often passed over from one side to the other, sometimes carrying oxen and sheep and always practical knowledge of the country. And the Athenians were unwilling to punish them lest they desert—we have that from Aristophanes."

The Harvard-educated senator was fond of citing ancient history. It was widely known that he read the classics in the original Greek and Latin and was not loathe to use his learning to good advantage in debate. "In a later era we know that when Gaius Marius entered Rome he surrounded himself with a guard selected from the slaves who had repaired to his standard. Thus in other days have slaves played their part while slave masters dwelt in fear. A man is a difficult possession to hold. All this was clearly seen by the emperor of Russia three years ago when he called on his people to unite with him in emancipation of the serfs, which, he said, 'ought to begin from above, to the end that it may not come from below.'

"Closer to home, we have our own John Quincy Adams, who held unequivocally that the federal government possessed the authority to interfere with the institution of slavery in time of war.

"Mr. President, there are at this moment four million slaves toiling in rebel fields and digging in their camps. Calculation demonstrates that of this number more than one million are of an age for military service. Can we afford to reject this material alliance?" Lincoln evidently chose to interpret the question as rhetorical. He did not respond.

Sumner, his classic, clean-shaven features in earnest concentration, continued. "In my capacity as chairman of the Foreign Affairs Committee, I am obliged to advise—and I consider this to be one of the most compelling reasons for emancipation—that England would never intervene on the side of the Confederacy were she convinced that emancipation is a Union war objective.

"And finally, sir, it is my conviction that slavery is the root cause of the war. Uproot it, and the war will end. The pretended right of secession is born of slavery. Wherever slavery prevails, this pretended right is recognized. A pretended right to set aside the Constitution to the extent of breaking up the government is the natural companion of the pretended right to set aside human nature, making merchandise of men. They form a well-matched couple and travel well together.

"The institution of slavery in the South enables her to field a force much larger in proportion to her white population than the North. The slaves toil at home while their masters work at rebellion; thus by singular fatality is this doomed race engaged in feeding, supporting, succoring, and invigorating those battling for their enslavement." Fatigued by his argument, Sumner leaned back in his chair. From his breast pocket he withdrew an immaculate silk handkerchief with which he mopped his brow.

The president nodded in tacit but genuine appreciation of the senator's argument, a lawyer's acknowledgment of a brief well prepared. "Mr. Sumner, I have listened carefully to what you have said. And I know you know that I am in substantial agreement. I believe in emancipation and think it inevitable for the sake of the enslaved, and for the purpose of hastening the end of the war. But it would do no good to go ahead faster than the country would follow. One of the bits of Latin I know is *festina lente*." Sumner smiled. A singular accomplishment, thought Lincoln.

"While I do not believe," said the president, "in a federal edict at this time, I do believe in a state-sponsored program. I have already begun, with my friends in the Delaware state legislature, to promote a policy of gradual, compensated emancipation." Sumner noted a light of quiet excitement in the president's eye. Clearly, Lincoln was enthusiastic about the concept.

"This is the way it would work. The legislatures of the several border states would enact laws for the selling of their slaves to the federal government. The slave owners would be compensated. The federal government would buy and free the purchased slaves and then take steps to colonize them—Liberia and Haiti are possibilities. Emigration, however, would be voluntary. You see, such a plan would have the virtue of leaving to the states the freedom of arranging their domestic affairs.

"I have already drafted two bills for the Delaware legislature to consider. We have arrived at a price of four hundred dollars per slave. At that price the cost to the government for all the slaves in the border would be about one third of what we have spent thus far in prosecuting the war."

Sumner was pleased. "Money," he said, "should not be allowed to interfere with human freedom. Better an empty treasury than a single slave. Though I prefer a federal edict, and I think it will ultimately be necessary, I believe you should make the Congress a New Year's present of your plan."

Their talk turned briefly to the military situation, which was bleak, and to McClellan's apparent disinclination to move his Army of the Potomac. "The general," Lincoln allowed, "has a case of the slows."

They stood and shook hands, Sumner resplendent in fawn-colored frock coat with gaiters to match, a maroon vest, and a blue-violet necktie set off by a snowy white shirt. In his fashionable gaiters the senator was the same height as the president, who stood in stockinged feet and baggy black suit.

Returning for a moment to the subject of emancipation, Lincoln said, "Senator, just give us a little time and we'll fetch 'em. We didn't go into the war to put down slavery but to put the flag back. To act differently at this moment would, I have no doubt, not only weaken our cause but smack of bad faith. I never would have had the votes to send me here if the people had supposed I should try to use my power to upset slavery. Why, the first thing you would see would be a mutiny in the Army. No, we must wait until every other means has been exhausted. This thunderbolt will keep."

Before leaving, Sumner inquired after Mrs. Lincoln, who adored him. With her he played the gallant, occasionally escorting her to the opera or to the theater when the president was occupied. He then asked about the boys. Bob was attending Sumner's alma mater and doing well. Willie, eleven, a grave, delicate boy, his mother's favorite, had written his first bit of verse. And young Tad, eight, was doing his thing. Which was? "I reckon," said the president, "his hobby is raising the dickens." On that note Sumner left the executive office.

On a sudden whim he decided to stop at the telegraph office of the War Department before returning to the Capitol. He would be immensely cheered by any news suggesting that, contrary to expectation, McClellan had made an advance. The Army of the Potomac now numbered, by the general's own count, almost 170,000 troops and contained the best elements of the three-year militia. Nothing in the way of men and materiel had been denied him. McClellan's force was at once the key to Richmond and the defense of Washington. Sumner knew from intelligence reports that McClellan had three times the number of troops in his command as the rebels confronting him at Manassas. All through the late summer and fall, perfect weather for an advance to redeem Bull Run, the general had chosen to drill, maneuver, parade, review, and diddle and fiddle. But not a single belligerent gesture did he make toward the South. It was scandalous. And neither the president nor Cameron seemed to be able to light a fire under him.

At the entrance to the War Department, Sumner nearly collided with the stubby, bustling figure of Edwin Stanton, who was also entering the building. The two bid each other a brief good afternoon and went their separate ways. Sumner knew him casually as attorney general in the Buchanan administration. Stanton, who held no office in the current administration, continued to reside in Washington, where he was a well-known attorney retained by, among other notables, Simon Cameron and Gen. George B. McClellan.

Sumner had long since decided against seeking Stanton's company. Aside from having a reputation as a choleric little man, the former attorney general was known to voice violent and vulgar dislike of the president. Almost no one in government had not heard the story of Stanton's first meeting with Lincoln.

It was back in 1855 when Lincoln was involved in the celebrated McCormick reaper case as co-counsel with several Eastern lawyers, one of whom was Edwin Stanton. Referring to Lincoln as a Western hick and a low, cunning clown, Stanton and the other attorneys ignored him when he showed up at the courthouse in Cincinnati. They refused to dine with him or even consult the extensive brief he had prepared.

Thereafter, Stanton never tired of telling anyone who would listen how that "gorilla" came on the scene wearing a filthy linen duster for a coat on the back of which the perspiration had formed two wide stains that, spreading from the armpits, met at the center and resembled a dirty map of the Continent. "If that giraffe had appeared on the case," vouched Stanton to an amused McClellan, "I'd have thrown up my brief and left."

As a cabinet officer in the previous administration who had not been offered a post in the current one, Stanton relished the opportunity to attribute current setbacks and misfortunes to "the painful imbecility of Lincoln." After Bull Run he was widely quoted as saying that a better state of affairs was impossible in Washington until Jeff Davis turned out the whole concern.

On the morning of the day he encountered Sumner, a messenger had appeared at Stanton's Washington apartment with a request that he meet with Cameron at his office. Stanton was not surprised by the summons. He had been expecting it for some time. His beleaguered client was obviously in the way of needing some timely counsel. The Congress was pressing for information with respect to some of his more malodorous contracts. Its Joint Committee on the Conduct of the War and the House Committee on Government Contracts were, as Cameron put it, gunning for his hide.

Cameron, slender, gray-haired, with thin features and a shifty wariness, greeted his attorney in his customary distracted manner and nervously waved him to a chair. Stanton sat, his short legs barely reaching the floor. Regarding his client through small, wire-rimmed elliptical spectacles, he wore his usual expression of strained patience. "What can I do for you, Mr. Secretary?"

Moistening his lips, Cameron grinned as if to say, You know damn well what you can do for me. Aloud he said, "I expect you are aware of that posse in the Congress that's panting to get me." Stanton nodded. "Well, I believe I've found a way to keep them on a tight leash.

"Have you noticed that most of the barking dogs on that Conduct of the War Committee are also hellfire abolitionists and antislavers?" Again Stanton nodded. "Well, suppose we throw them a bone? What I mean is, you know they think the president is foot-dragging on the question of emancipation. But if I could show them that the War Department is ahead of the president in the matter of freeing the niggers, I just might get them off my back.

"Now, of course, as secretary of war I can't proclaim emancipation. That's fairly the president's business. But I might be able to get away with it as a military matter by recommending that our troops in enemy territory free and arm the niggers within our lines."

Stanton regarded his client with renewed interest. He had always held Cameron in substantial but limited regard as an adroit politician and as a poor boy who succeeded in amassing a fortune on his way to becoming "Czar of Pennsylvania." If he admired him at all it was because Cameron showed not a trace of hypocrisy. He never claimed to be anything but an "honest politician—one who, when he is bought, will stay bought." Of late when Stanton thought about Cameron he was inclined to feel that the secretary had reached the end of his political rope. Indeed, with two congressional committees breathing down his neck, an indictment on criminal charges was not unlikely. But Cameron was nothing if not resourceful. And it appeared now that he might have found a way out.

The secretary looked at Stanton quizzically, inviting him to respond. The lawyer thought long and carefully. For a moment all was silent except for the low, asthmatic wheeze of Stanton's breathing. "You say," the lawyer began, "that you would 'recommend' that Union troops free and arm slaves within our lines. Such a recommendation is properly put first to the president. When he receives it, obviously he'll over-rule."

"That," said Cameron, "is why I called you."

A hint of a smile flitted across Stanton's face. "I've never known you to espouse an abolitionist position before."

"Let's just say," replied Cameron, "that I got religion." The two got down to business.

Mr. Lincoln was preparing his year-end message to the Congress, which included the individual reports of all departments, when Nicolay brought it to his attention that the report of the secretary of war had already been printed and, without having been submitted to him or read by him, had been mailed to the postmasters of all major cities for release to the press as soon as the president's message was read to the Congress. Unusual, to say the least.

When the president secured a copy of Cameron's report, he found to his astonishment that it recommended that federal troops free slaves within Union lines and recruit them into a Negro army: "It is clearly a right of the Government to arm slaves when it may become necessary, as it is to use gunpowder taken from the enemy. Whether it is expedient to do so is purely a military question. If it shall be found that the men who have been held by the rebels are capable of bearing arms and performing efficient military service, it is the right, and may become the duty, of the Government to arm and equip them, and employ their services against the rebels."

Cameron had thus thrust himself forward as administration spokesman in this most delicate and explosive area. As Lincoln had indicated to Sumner, he was convinced that the loyal border would turn against the government were it to arm Negroes as soldiers. He was willing to let the Navy enlist free Negroes and fugitive slaves, because the Navy was not a presence on the border. But the Army was such a presence.

Urgent telegrams went forward at once to the postmasters. The Cameron report was recalled, but not before the newspapers got hold of it.

When the president's message to the Congress was released, the newspapers printed Cameron's original report side by side with the administration's revised version, which modestly raised the question of what was to be done with slaves abandoned by their masters to advancing federal troops: "They constitute a military resource and, being such, that they should not be turned over to the enemy is too plain to discuss." But there was not a word about freeing the slaves and certainly nothing about arming them.

Cameron was immediately acclaimed a hero in antislavery quarters.

He was seen as the perceptive officer of an administration that was timid and disorganized. The very congressmen who had been denouncing him and demanding his resignation were now loudly singing his praise. A few newspapers did carp that Cameron's conversion was remarkably sudden and that the crusader's mantle looked slightly comic on his shoulders. But the secretary of war had achieved his objective. Much of the congressional heat was turned off. Cameron, however, paid the price. Even a man of Lincoln's forbearance could not be expected to tolerate flagrant insubordination. Cameron's days as secretary of war were numbered.

The year 1861 ended without a significant Union military victory, without a response to Bull Run. Not only had the defeat gone unanswered, it had, some forty miles northwest of Washington, been compounded. There on a clear October day brilliant with autumn color, four federal regiments of McClellan's Army of the Potomac were ferried across the river from the Maryland shore to make a reconnaissance in force toward Leesburg. As elements of the vanguard debarked on the Virginia shore near a place called Ball's Bluff, their commander was cut down in a burst of rifle fire. The leaderless troops were driven back with a loss of more than half their number. A few were able to swim back to the Maryland shore. Many were shot in the water—"like fish in a barrel," said one wounded trooper.

The defeat was for the president dismaying beyond the numbers involved. A grandson of Paul Revere and a nephew of James Russell Lowell lay dead. Oliver Wendell Holmes, Jr., was gravely wounded. The commander shot dead was Col. Ned Baker, Lincoln's dear friend from Springfield days, the man whom he chose to introduce him at his inauguration, and the namesake of little Eddie Lincoln.

When the telegraph at McClellan's headquarters stuttered out the news, the president clutched his chest and nearly collapsed. Tears flowing down his furrowed cheeks, he stumbled out into the street, gasping for air. When would it all end, and why should the spirit of mortal be proud? Another funeral, another coffin, another memorial service.

The White House family, official and extended, was not unhappy to see the old year fade out.

CHAPTER

XIX

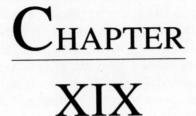

"Mr. President, I can't go back without definite word from you. And the only thing that committee wants to hear," declared the senator from Ohio, "is that you've thrown McClellan overboard. As general in chief, he'd make fine fish food. Here it is the new year; he's been in command of the Army of the Potomac since July, and he hasn't made so much as a threatening gesture toward Richmond."

Senator Benjamin Franklin Wade, the barrel-chested, square-jawed, tempestuous little chairman of the Committee on the Conduct of the War, was clearly outraged. That afternoon he had swept into the executive chamber almost before Nicolay could announce him.

"Whom do you propose I put in his place?"

"Anybody!"

"Wade," said Lincoln quietly, "anybody may do for you, but I must have somebody."

A few days before Wade's angry appearance at the White House, Senator Zach Chandler of Michigan, a member of Wade's committee, had come to see Lincoln to advise that they were planning to summon McClellan to a hearing at the Capitol. Chandler, a no-nonsense merchant millionaire who, with Wade and three congressmen, tried to stop the rout at Bull Run by confronting the fleeing Union troops with Maynard rifles and navy pistols, warned that the committee could be expected to demonstrate neither the patience nor the forbearance of the president with McClellan.

Lincoln said he could well appreciate the committee's impatience with the former Corps of Engineers officer. "McClellan," he said, "is a great engineer, but he has a special talent for the stationary engine."

As always, Lincoln preferred humor to confrontation, and temperance to temper; but the fact was he was anxious and depressed by events. The year 1862 was dawning on the same bleak note that had marked the old year. In no aspect of the government or the war could the president find reason for cheer. He was deeply concerned about the condition of the treasury. The war was costing more than a million dollars a day. Credit was exhausted with no relief in sight. Treasury Secretary Chase alternated between frenzy and despair. Because of the people's lack of faith in the government's ability to prosecute the war, bond issues could not be floated.

For the same reason, foreign relations were in a precarious state. Until the Union was able to demonstrate that it was capable of dominating the South, there was a real possibility of foreign intervention on the side of the rebels.

Press and political circles were demanding a cabinet reorganization. According to Attorney General Edward Bates, the cabinet did not represent the administration but was rather the "separate and disjointed action of seven independent officers, each one ignorant of what his colleagues are doing."

But of all the president's problems during the winter of 1861–62, the one that most vexed and perplexed him was why McClellan with his splendid Army of the Potomac did not move. The rift that John Hay had foreseen between the civil and military authorities as represented by the president and the Congress on one side, and General-in-Chief McClellan on the other, appeared to be widening.

When the president appointed George Brinton McClellan to replace Scott as general in chief, Mr. Lincoln said by way of encouraging McClellan to draw on him for help and cooperation: "In addition to your present Potomac command, the supreme command of the Army will entail a vast labor upon you."

"I can do it all," said McClellan quietly. At thirty-five, of trim, muscular build, with handsome, clean-cut features and a large, virile mustache, the general was the picture of confidence and control. He sat straight in the saddle, issued orders with an unmistakable ring of authority, published proclamations à la Napoleon, and thrust his right hand between the buttons of his tunic when he was photographed. His personal bravery had been proven in the Mexican War when two horses were shot from under him and his sword hilt shattered. His men adored him. Taking a disorganized mob after Bull Run, he shaped it into the most formidable fighting force on earth. His competence as engineer and tactician was unquestioned. Very much in question, however, were the general's regard for civil authority and his willingness to commit his beloved army to battle.

McClellan confided only in his attorney, Edwin Stanton, and in Ellen Mary, his handsome, young wife, whom he clearly adored and to whom he wrote faithfully and at great length. When he won command of the Army of the Potomac, he wrote Ellen Mary, who was the daughter of a regular army officer, "I find myself in a new and strange position here—President, cabinet, General Scott, and all deferring to me. By some strange operation of magic I seem to have become the power of the land."

But shortly thereafter the delusion that was to grow into obsession began to reveal itself: "I am here in a terrible place. The enemy have from three to four times my force." In fact, he outnumbered Gen. Joseph Johnston, whose army was ranged just north of Manassas, three to one. Johnston, who had turned the tide at Bull Run, knew the real strength of both armies. He was content to sit and neutralize the Army of the Potomac while being puzzled by McClellan's inaction.

Another aspect of McClellan's troubling behavior was that he couldn't tolerate the sending of troops to other departments no matter how urgent the need. He regarded any such move as betrayal of his Army of the Potomac; and the president continued to accede to his demands.

In a matter of weeks, McClellan's letters took on a bitter and contemptuous tone: "I was obliged to attend a meeting of the cabinet at eight P.M. and was bored and annoyed. There are some of the greatest geese in the cabinet I have ever seen—enough to tax the patience of Job." A few days later, feeling the president was too importunate in pressing for action, he wrote from the home of his lawyer: "I have not been at home for some three hours, but am concealed at Stanton's to dodge all enemies in the shape of 'browsing presidents.'" Lincoln was, in fact, finding it increasingly difficult to locate and consult with his general in chief.

The Joint Committee on the Conduct of the War, however, saw no reason to conceal its collective contempt for the general's behavior. They summoned him to a hearing.

McClellan was under no illusions about the nature of the hearing, but it was an invitation he dared not ignore. Just prior to his scheduled appearance he wrote Ellen Mary, "I have a set of men to deal with, unscrupulous and false. If possible, they will throw whatever blame there is on my shoulders, and I do not intend to be sacrificed by such people." After some preliminary sparring over the date, McClellan made his way, on a chill morning in the middle of January, to the windowless committee room situated in the basement of the Capitol.

The room, like the day, was bare and chill. It was minimally furnished with a long, light oak committee table and the flag of the United States, which stood in back of and slightly to the right of Chairman Wade. In addition to the four committee members, all strong-willed, assertive men, there were only a stenographer and a bailiff. There were no witnesses and no accusers, since the committee required none. There was no counsel, either for the committee or for the general. The Joint Committee on the Conduct of the War had, it was charged by those who had felt its lash, arrogated to itself the extraordinary powers of a star-chamber.

Those testifying were sworn, questions were asked, and recommendations were made, the committee acting as prosecution, judge, and jury. As a consequence of its findings, one general, Charles P. Stone, responsible for the humiliation at Ball's Bluff, was reposing in a jail cell on an island in New York harbor—an example to all who incurred the wrath of the joint committee.

McClellan, standing at the foot of the long table, cap under his arm, was sworn in by the bailiff. Wasting no time on polite introductions or formalities, Senator Zach Chandler put the question bluntly: Why didn't the general move out of his town house in Washington and go on the attack with his army?

McClellan replied that it was a question of bridges. There were only two across the Potomac to Washington. Sound strategy, he explained, required more safeguards against a possible retiring movement.

"General McClellan, if I understand you correctly," replied Chandler, "before you strike at the rebels you want to be sure of plenty of room so that you can run in case they strike back . . . "

"Or in case you get scared," added Chairman Ben Wade, who continued the questioning. "General, you have all the troops you have called for, and if you haven't enough you shall have more. They are well organized and equipped, and the loyal people of this country expect that you will make a short and decisive campaign. Is it really necessary for you to have more bridges over the Potomac before you move?"

"Not that," said McClellan, "not that exactly. But we must bear in mind the necessity of having everything ready in case of a defeat, and keep our lines of retreat open."

When McClellan left the committee room, an indignant Wade agreed with an angry Chandler that the general's testimony smacked of "infernal, unmitigated cowardice," and such was their report to the president.

A bruised and shaken McClellan repaired to his town house, there to lick his wounds. What did those doddering asses know about military affairs? Corrupt politicians. Their expertise was in getting elected. And how dare they question his courage.

It was then, brooding in his handsome book-lined study, that the germ of a wordless idea with tiny, persistent hooks stubbornly caught hold and lodged in his mind. Finding the environment warm and receptive, the idea began to germinate and grow, only to fade and wither . . . then to revive with relentless vitality.

He had written Ellen Mary, "I only wish to save my country, and find the incapables around me will not permit it." He had seen into the highest councils of government and found them wanting. He was surrounded by fools and knaves. His country hungered for a brave and resolute man who could take hold and drive out the corrupt and timid geese. A shining and certain trumpet was desperately needed.

What if the war were to drag on for another two years until '64—an election year—with no end in sight? The people would be fed up; clamoring for change; ready for bold, resolute action; hungering for one charismatic leader who would rise to the occasion and carry the nation to victory. Even now he could see thousands of adoring faces lifted up to him astride his prancing charger as he acknowledged them from the steps of the Capitol. No. Impossible dream. He was a military man in a nation of civil authority. But yet . . . but yet . . . the idea clung. Had not a grateful nation turned to General George Washington?

CHAPTER

XX

During the first two weeks of the new year, both the president and his secretary of the Navy arrived at separate personnel decisions that they both felt might affect the course of the war.

The president decided to replace Cameron. There was no point in letting him hang on. Although no word had passed between them on the subject of the secretary's unauthorized release to the press, both men realized at the time that his usefulness, such as it was, had come to an end.

For the president the difficult part was not so much letting Cameron go as finding a politically expeditious way to do it. In the second week of the new year an opportunity presented itself. A messenger was dispatched from the White House, carrying the following note across the park to the Department of War:

> Executive Mansion, Washington
> January 11, 1862

Hon. Simon Cameron, Secretary of War

My Dear Sir:

As you have more than once expressed a desire for a change of position, I can now gratify you consistently with my view of the public interest.

I therefore propose nominating you to the Senate next Monday as Minister to Russia.

Very sincerely, your friend,
A. Lincoln

Cassius M. Clay of Kentucky was resigning the post of minister to Russia so that he could come home to fight for the Union.

When the new appointment became known, many expressed the opinion that Cameron was getting off much better than he deserved. The president, however, took the view that while the secretary of war may have played fast and loose in some of his dealings with contractors, he was, like others, a victim of those early days of the war when dispatch seemed more important than observing the niceties of procurement procedure.

The Senate debated heatedly for four days over confirmation of the appointment. Among Cameron's supporters were the more outspoken antislavers. He was finally confirmed by a vote of twenty-eight to fourteen. Cameron, however, did not get off scot-free. By a vote of seventy-nine to forty-five the House censured him for negligence and for pursuing policies injurious to the public service. He was also the subject of unofficial censure on the part of several journals that commented editorially that the former secretary of war was at last being exiled to Siberia, where he belonged. Thaddeus Stevens, acidulous congressman from Pennsylvania, was heard to remark, "Send word to the Czar to bring his things in of nights."

Censure official and unofficial behind him, "The Czar of Pennsylvania" sailed off to meet the Czar of all the Russias at Peterhof Palace in St. Petersburg, in the opinion of most political observers, well ahead of the game.

If there was controversy over Cameron's appointment as minister to Russia, there was, by contrast, little or none over the appointment of his successor. The new secretary of war enjoyed almost unanimous approval. From the senate to the cabinet and McClellan, no voice was raised against him. The president's attitude toward his new appointee was characteristically pragmatic and charitable. When reminded by Nicolay and Hay of Edwin Stanton's reputation as a vilifier of Abraham Lincoln, he replied that he had neither the time nor the luxury to carry grudges. All he asked was that Stanton do the job at War.

Only Gideon Welles had misgivings. He despised the newest member of the cabinet for the same reason he despised Seward—their expressed contempt for the man they were presumed to serve. Coincidentally, Welles too was confronted by the need to make a critical appointment, one that he felt was as crucial to the course of the war as the appointment of the new secretary. He agonized over the choice for many days, grateful that his deliberations were subject to neither the approval of the Senate nor the glare of public notice.

During the past year, 373 officers of the United States Navy, about one fourth of the officer corps, had embraced the rebel cause and gone south. The ever-present question in Welles's mind was, how many officers of Southern sympathy still remained in Northern ranks awaiting only the moment most damaging to Union fortunes before they too fled south. Loyalty was a primary and constant concern in matters relating to detailing or personnel assignment.

The moment had come to appoint a commander for Ericsson's battery, which was scheduled for completion by January 14. At Welles's request, Commodore Smith reviewed the availability lists and subsequently came forward with the name of one officer. Welles was somewhat surprised by Smith's choice, a forty-four-year-old lieutenant with an undistinguished if satisfactory record of twenty-eight years in the service.

Welles had, of course, met him briefly that April night when war hung in the balance, with both Pickens and Sumter threatening to erupt. Worden impressed him favorably, else he wouldn't have entrusted to him a mission of such delicate nature. But the fact was, had it not been for Olivia Worden's barrage of letters concerning her husband, the lieutenant would, in all probability, have slipped from Welles's mind. As it was he retained only a vague memory of a tall, slender, quiet man with a gentlemanly manner.

In any event, there was no reason to doubt Worden's loyalty. He was born in the North; and if he had had any lingering sympathy for the Confederate cause, it should have been thoroughly erased during his difficult and unmerited stay in an Alabama jail. If his service record had a distinguishing aspect, it was that he always seemed to inspire the loyalty and respect of the men in his command—for Welles, the highest accolade. In his estimation there was no better indication of an officer's competence, the example of George McClellan notwithstanding.

But none of the foregoing considerations was the decisive factor in Welles's decision. Ultimately it was the romantic streak in the dour New Englander's character that moved him to approve Smith's choice.

There was a touch of poetic justice in giving Worden an opportunity to greet his former captors. Welles instructed Smith to advise the lieutenant that, health permitting, the command was his if he wanted it.

Smith wrote Worden, adding that the vessel was an experiment and that he believed Worden the right sort of officer to command her.

Worden wasted no time. The moment he received Smith's letter, he took a cab from the navy yard for the mile up the Brooklyn bank of the East River to Greenpoint and the Continental Iron Works. There he met Alban Stimers and twenty-two-year-old Samuel Dana Greene, a newly commissioned lieutenant who, having developed a consuming interest in the battery, was spending his leave time studying the exotic vessel.

Stimers took Worden on a tour of the nearly completed craft, which was still on the stocks and lacked only the last of her armor plate, the full turret assembly, and interior appointments.

Worden's reaction to the battery was mixed. He was favorably impressed with the idea of a revolving turret that could fire two powerful guns independent of the ship's heading. And he was well pleased with her low silhouette and thick armor, which seemed to render her all but invulnerable. He had some misgivings about her stability and about the provisions for ventilation, but he shared only his positive thoughts with Stimers. As they came topside after completing the inspection, they came face to face with John Ericsson. Stimers introduced Worden as the likely commander of the battery.

Ericsson, reared in the ancient Norse tradition where song and story celebrate sea captains as kings and figures of awe and veneration, assessed the lieutenant. Worden, still wan and emaciated, and visibly uncomfortable in the harbor's January chill, congratulated the captain on his vessel and expressed faith in her capabilities. Ericsson acknowledged the compliment. They exchanged a few words on the likely launching date and went their separate ways.

Ericsson was decidedly unimpressed with the putative commander of his battery. The captain felt his vessel required someone of greater vigor and stronger kidney. He had previously, in correspondence with Smith, expressed his preference for an officer with whom he was acquainted. But, according to Smith, the officer in question was unavailable.

Worden wrote Smith that he thought the battery might prove a success and that in any event he was prepared "to devote whatever capacity and energy I have to that object."

On January 13 the following went forward to Worden:

> Sir: You are hereby detailed from the rendezvous, New York, and will report to Commodore Paulding for command of the U.S. ironclad steamer building by Captain Ericsson. I am respectfully,
>
>   Gideon Welles
>   Secretary of the Navy

At the same time Welles noted to Fox that the vessel still lacked a name, and why didn't he invite Ericsson to give her one. Ericsson in a subsequent written reply to Fox said that his floating battery would serve to admonish the leaders of the Southern rebellion that the batteries on the banks of their rivers would no longer present a barrier to Union forces. He noted that others, such as the Lords of the Admiralty, would also be warned by this latest "Yankee notion." He proposed therefore to name the new battery *Monitor*.

On January 16, Ericsson received a letter from Smith advising that the deadline for completion of the battery had expired on January 12. Smith warned that he planned to demand heavy forfeiture for delay over the stipulated time of completion. A baffled and frustrated Ericsson explained to Fox and Smith for the third or fourth time that the reason for the delay was that he had been obliged to cancel all overtime work since he was unable to pay his subcontractors the premiums they justly demanded. The government was weeks behind in its payments to him.

As of January 4 he had received only $37,500. According to the contract he was to have received four installments, or $150,000, by that time. The Navy had been presenting the proper drafts on time, but the Treasury, teetering on the edge of bankruptcy, had not been honoring them. Ericsson and his associates had advanced almost $160,000 of their own funds in order to keep the project from foundering.

Griswold was angered to the point of threatening withdrawal from the project. "The sensible thing to do," he said to Ericsson during a trip to the city, "would be to abandon the thing now and cut our losses. The government has us precisely where they want us. They haven't paid for our out-of-pocket expenses or for our labor; and the terms of the contract do not oblige them to pay us unless the craft meets their own insane standard of performance." It was only because he had exploited his connection with a Troy bank that the "Battery Associates" were able to stay afloat. Angrily, Griswold insisted to Ericsson that they must be paid the full amount minus only the agreed twenty-five percent reservation before the vessel was released to the Navy.

Ericsson, interested only in completing the project, found himself in a delicate balancing act, placating partners on the one hand and subcontractors on the other. He assured Griswold that his wishes would be respected. When his subcontractors threatened to stop all work unless they were paid, he referred them to Griswold (happily almost two hundred miles north), assuring them that the Troy banker would furnish all the money Ericsson approved.

On the day Ericsson received the letter from Smith advising that he had violated the deadline for completion of the craft, Worden received authorization to select his crew from any ship of war in New York harbor. The lieutenant had long since decided on his course of action in that regard, having thought about his crew from the day he saw the craft for the first time.

On successive days he addressed the men on the receiving ship *North Carolina* and on the sailing frigate *Sabine,* to which Worden had borne his message to Captain Adams from Gideon Welles the previous April. Both ships were anchored off the navy yard. Speaking to the men in the January chill of an open deck, Worden was succinct and straightforward. He made no attempt to persuade or promote service on the ironclad; his manner was reserved and conversational: "Many of you are aware of Captain Ericsson's new ironclad battery called *Monitor.* She is berthed but a mile north of us.

"I must tell you, her design is novel; it is untried and, as such, must be regarded as an experiment. I believe in her; but I know that certain questions regarding her systems will not be resolved until she is at sea and, in some instances, until she is engaged."

Some sailors at the fringe of the group clustered round him complained that they couldn't hear him. Worden mounted an upturned water barrel and, with his back to the mainmast, continued: "I can assure you that *Monitor* is destined to perform important service. Because of the experimental nature of the craft and because of the dangers she is apt to encounter in a heavy sea, I have chosen to ask for volunteers rather than to detail a crew."

The sailors responded enthusiastically. Many more volunteered than were needed, a somewhat surprising development, both in view of

Worden's reserve and the scuttlebutt that was circulating throughout the harbor. Anyone worth his salt along the Brooklyn and Manhattan waterfronts was predicting that the Ericsson battery would sink like a stone as soon as she was launched.

In his crew selection Worden adopted a qualitative approach, choosing the best he could find and taking the least possible number required for operation. For executive officer he chose Lt. Samuel Dana Greene, the enthusiastic young Marylander who had spent his leave studying the vessel. Chief engineer was Alban Stimers, who, if he had not been directed by Welles to remain aboard after construction to report on the vessel's performance, would have volunteered. Of the others, five officers and twenty-one men were of the line or seaman branch; five officers and seventeen men belonged to the engineer branch; three officers and seven men were surgeon, paymaster, clerk, storekeepers, cooks, and stewards—a crew of fifty-eight in all.

In a letter to Olivia, Worden wrote from the battery:

> I am well pleased with the crew, and I am satisfied that every member aboard is here because he chooses to be.
>
> With any luck *Monitor* should be completed with time enough for us to become acquainted with her systems, and meet *Merrimack* before she has the opportunity to do damage to the fleet at Hampton Roads.

Upon meeting Worden for the first time, Paymaster William F. Keeler wrote home to his wife in Illinois:

> Captain Worden is in the regular service. He is tall, thin, and quite effeminate looking, notwithstanding a long beard hanging down his breast; he is white and delicate probably from a long confinement. But if I am not very much mistaken he will not hesitate to submit our iron sides to as severe a test as the most warlike could desire. He is a perfect gentleman in manner.

As Worden was assigning watch and stations to his crew, Mr. Lincoln in Washington was finding it increasingly difficult to account to the Congress for the inaction of the Army of the Potomac. It had become impossible to convince the country that a longer period of preparation was needed before this army could be led against one inferior in numbers and not superior in discipline or equipment. McClellan's latest excuse was illness. He (and little Willie Lincoln) had succumbed to the fever prevalent in Washington, the probable legacy of Simon Cameron's herd of horse carcasses rotting throughout the capital.

Although some officials were, during the general's illness, able to gain admission to his bedside in order to carry on the business of the Army, Lincoln was kept outside or denied polite entry. It was then, to the delight of young Hay, that the president decided to make no more calls on McClellan. Henceforth the general would be summoned to the executive chamber.

Amid the wintry gloom that enveloped the capital, one bright note did emerge. In the short time since the new secretary of war had taken office, he was proving a decided asset. Even Hay, who was not predisposed to regard Stanton with favor, admitted that he was a man of action, and of tremendous physical and mental energy. There was no question but that he brought executive talent and rigorous standards to the War Department. He would see no contractor, claims agent, lobbyist, or petitioner except in the open company of all such callers, in a crowded room, fifteen feet by twenty. If one wanted to proposition the secretary of war, he did it within earshot of twenty interested spectators.

So thorough and vigorous was Stanton with his new broom that inevitably he stepped on a few tender toes. When petitioners brought their bruised feelings to Lincoln, he considered for a moment and drawled, "We may have to treat the secretary of war as they are sometimes obliged to treat a Methodist minister I know of out West. He gets wrought up to so high a pitch in his prayers and exhortations that they are obliged to put bricks in his pockets to hold him down. We may be obliged to serve Stanton in the same way. But I guess we'll let him jump awhile first."

That a successful political appointment is not an unmixed blessing was further brought home to the president by a delegation of senators who called on him to urge additional reform of the cabinet. Concerned by what they perceived as the purposeless drift of the administration, and with the war going badly, they felt he would do well to reorganize the entire cabinet.

To the delegation Lincoln said: "Gentlemen, your request for a change of the whole cabinet, because I have made one change, reminds me of an Illinois farmer. The poor feller was pestered by skunks, and his wife was especially wrought up and continually after him to get rid of the varmints. One moonlit night he loaded his shotgun and went out while his wife waited in the house. She heard the shotgun blaze away. And soon her husband came in. 'What luck?' she asked. 'I hid myself behind the woodpile,' said the farmer, 'and before long there appeared not one skunk but seven. I took aim, fired, killed one, and he raised such a fearful stink I concluded it was best to let the other six go.'" The senators got no further on their mission that day.

But it was after that meeting that the president sat at his desk and, without consulting anyone, wrote out his General War Order Number One. The order fixed February 22, 1862, as the day for a general movement of the land and naval forces of the United States against the insurgent forces. To avoid any possible misunderstanding, a few days later he appended a special order directing that the Army of the Potomac, after providing for the defense of Washington, move on the aforementioned day to seize and occupy Manassas Junction.

The orders were read to the cabinet by John Nicolay, not for sanction but for information.

On January 29, Commodore Smith wrote Ericsson that the *Merrimack* was out of dock and ready for her trial trip. He needn't have bothered. The New York *Tribune* for that day reported that the rebel ironclad had been launched and that the people of Norfolk believed she could sink the entire federal fleet at Hampton Roads.

On the following morning, Thursday, January 30, at eight o'clock, in the midst of a chill drizzle, a large crowd gathered around the dock at Thomas F. Rowland's Continental Iron Works in Greenpoint. Although no public notice had been given, the word had spread that the *Monitor* was to be launched. As the crowd waited, hundreds of dollars were wagered on the outcome. Educated opinion held that the strange little craft with the shallow hull and the long, overhanging deck—much longer at the stern than at the bow—would "throw pitch pole," that is, her stern would immediately sink and she would turn a somersault. Rowland took the precaution, for the launch, of putting air tanks under the stern to prevent any such eventuality.

Shortly before ten, Ericsson strode through the crowd onto the battery, where he took a position at the extreme stern. A small boat stood by, ready to take him off in the event the battery began to sink. The braces were knocked away and the *Monitor* began moving, slowly at first, then gathering speed; flags at her bow and stern filling and fluttering in the breeze, she slid stern first into the East River with a quiet splash. "It was very evident," observed a reporter from the New York *World,* "even to the dullest observer that the battery hadn't the slightest intention of sinking." Cheers rose from the onlookers. Hats and handkerchiefs waved. Whistles and sirens throughout the harbor shrieked and wailed their welcome. Even some who lost their bets rejoiced.

Ericsson, whose feet didn't get wet, was delighted that the *Monitor* drew even less water than anticipated. Spectators and reporters thronged about the inventor. He told them that the *Monitor* could sink the *Merrimack* in a few minutes. He hoped they would meet, and if the *Merrimack* didn't venture forth, the *Monitor* would seek her out at Norfolk. He concluded his short speech with an invitation to all to go aboard and inspect the vessel.

The *Monitor* was lashed to the dock and work was immediately begun to complete her turret and interior.

CHAPTER
XXI

Aboard his flagship, USS *Minnesota,* in Hampton Roads, Commodore Louis Goldsborough was in the middle of a difficult decision. The Union command was mounting an expeditionary force for landings off the coast of North Carolina, the first target being Roanoke Island. The operation was to be a joint army-navy effort, with Goldsborough in charge of the navy contingent.

Goldsborough's dilemma was that he couldn't be in both places at once, the North Carolina coast and Hampton Roads. His personal preference was to join the expeditionary force. It promised to be interesting, the kind of aggressive operation he relished. With McClellan languishing in his Washington town house and showing no sign of budging, the North Carolina operation presented an opportunity, at long last, to pay back the rebels for Bull Run.

In truth, the restless commodore was getting a bit weary of sitting in the Roads and waiting for the *Merrimack* to make her long-heralded appearance. Of course, if he knew for sure that she would be making a move in the next month or two, he would, without question, elect to remain with the fleet. Any threat to the Atlantic Blockading Squadron had first priority.

Shortly before the *Monitor* was launched, he had received reports that the rebels were removing the obstructions in the Elizabeth River, north of the Norfolk Navy Yard, to clear the channel for the *Merrimack*. But there were so many conflicting rumors, one didn't know which to credit. He had also heard that the rebel ironclad just might be an empty threat.

Goldsborough summoned Captain Van Brunt, commander of the *Minnesota,* and asked his opinion as to the imminence of the *Merrimack*'s appearance. "Sir," replied Van Brunt, "she can't come too soon for me. I have heard that they have miscalculated her buoyancy, and that she floats with her roofing under water. Her battery is therefore useless. I also have it on good authority that she's exceeding crank, and if she does manage to get across the tide, more than likely she'll turn turtle."

Goldsborough had heard the same reports. Concluding that the threat posed by the *Merrimack* was not imminent, he decided to take personal command of the navy contingent off the Carolina coast, and several days later sailed for Roanoke Island with a small force.

Coincidentally, the flag passed to the forty-gun frigate *Roanoke,* whose commander, Capt. John Marston, being senior officer in the Roads, now became commander of the North Atlantic Blockading Squadron.

The day after Goldsborough sailed, a mechanic who claimed to have worked aboard the *Merrimack* was brought to Van Brunt on the *Minnesota.* When he warned that the rebel ship was a most formidable weapon, capable, he thought, of blowing any wooden ship out of the water, Van Brunt angrily dismissed him as an imposter. The captain was sick of tall stories about the phantom ironclad.

A surgeon aboard the frigate *Congress,* lying off Newport News Point about two and a half miles west of the *Minnesota,* confided to his diary that he thought the *Merrimack* a myth. He was weary of waiting for her and devoutly wished for a change of scene. Blockade duty was dull dull dull.

The Northern press joined in the speculation about the *Merrimack,* generally taking the view that although she might prove a tough customer, she was nothing the U.S. Navy couldn't handle. What harm could a single Confederate warship, ironclad though she might be, do to powerful vessels such as the *Roanoke, Cumberland, Congress,* and *Minnesota*? And if the *Merrimack* tried to squeeze past Fortress Monroe or the Rip Raps at the mouth of the Roads in an effort to escape to the Atlantic, she would take a large hole in her side for her pains.

In a well-planned and discreet program of disinformation, elements of the Southern press encouraged the view that the *Merrimack* posed little or no danger. Virginia papers let it be known that she was indeed a failure. An error had been made calculating her displacement. A long period of repair and alteration was in the offing. One paper said in an editorial that it had always anticipated trouble with her because of her vast proportions and prodigious length. Another hoped that the ironclad could at least be salvaged for use as a floating battery for harbor defense.

The editor of the Wilmington, North Carolina, *Journal,* quite innocent of the conspiracy and sincerely alarmed by Virginia press reports, complained in his paper that good money was being "bungled away on the *Merrimack.* . . . Fantastical Merrimackal experiments should be abandoned," he advised.

But in Washington, Welles, Smith, and Fox refused to lend credence to reports in the Southern press. They remained apprehensive about the prowess of the rebel ironclad and began a barrage of anxious letters to Ericsson requesting a definite completion date.

Ericsson fielded their queries with sanguine responses, pointing to the latest step in the progress of construction. To one he wrote that the guns were being installed. To another he reported that the guns were now mounted and they were indeed a formidable pair. To the third he wrote that the vessel's machinery had been put in motion and the ventilation system tested. A few days later he telegraphed that the turret was completed and its rapidity of motion exceeded his expectations.

On February 19, the battery underwent its long-awaited trial run, after which it was to be turned over to the Navy. At one o'clock of a frigid Wednesday afternoon, with Thomas Rowland, owner of the Continental Iron Works, and Worden already aboard, Captain Ericsson strode down the dock. As he stepped onto the vessel he called to Rowland, "What are the smoke pipes up for? Why don't you take them down, sir!" Ericsson preferred the lean look of the *Monitor* when she was stripped for combat, with only the turret and the pilothouse showing.

"We must have them up in order to carry fifty pounds of steam," said Rowland.

"Take them down, sir!"

Rowland ordered the pipes stowed. For the sake of dispatch they were left on the dock instead of being stored below.

The lines were cast off, and the battery moved downriver at her rated speed of six knots, a tug following in the event of emergency. The sea was quite calm, although a brisk headwind of about nine miles an hour was blowing from the southwest. Ericsson and Rowland stood together at the bow; Worden alone, a few feet aft. The lieutenant, still not fully recovered, was enervated and distressed. Blue lipped and, despite his efforts at control, shivering, he stood, resolved not to go below as long as Ericsson and Rowland remained topside. The headwind and the forward motion of the vessel combined to whip the frigid midwinter cold off the water and through Worden's navy greatcoat as if it were tissue paper, chilling him to the marrow of his wretched bones.

After some forty-five minutes, the *Monitor* having cleared Governor's Island, the engine room reported that her boilers were delivering less than twenty pounds of steam and no more could be coaxed from them. "Who, sir," asked Rowland of Ericsson, "is responsible for the safety of this vessel during this trial?"

"You, sir."

"Very well, then up go the smoke pipes." Rowland hailed the tug and ordered her captain to return to the Continental dock to retrieve the pipes. And then, as though in afterthought, he asked the tug's captain to take Worden aboard and set him ashore at Whitehall Street.

For a brief moment the lieutenant debated with himself. After concluding that continued exposure to the elements meant inviting serious illness, he deferred to Rowland's well-intentioned if peremptory invitation to go ashore. Ericsson remained silent and stonyfaced, his expression eloquently reflecting his sentiments regarding the navy's choice of commander for his battery.

Worden was not present when the *Monitor* was officially delivered to the Navy late that night.

At five o'clock the following afternoon, Thursday, February 20, the president, disbelief etched in his haggard eyes, with trembling hand lifted the bed sheet from the face of his child. He gazed at it for a long moment, then murmured, "It is hard, hard to have him die." Willie Lincoln, eleven, was dead. Thoughtful, affectionate, poetry-loving little Willie, who his mother said would be the hope and comfort of her old age, had slipped away despite weeks of day and night nursing by his mother, his father, and Elizabeth Keckley. Despite the assurances of the attending physician who held to the last that he would recover, the child succumbed to the fever that was plaguing the capital.

Elizabeth closed the fever-worn eyelids for the last time, washed and dressed him, and prepared him for the funeral. His mother moaned and shook with grief. Lincoln, walking back to his office, came upon Nicolay. "Well, Nicolay, my boy is gone—he is actually gone."

Willie was buried on a storm-lashed Monday morning, with most of official Washington in attendance. Pallbearers and a group of children from the boy's Sunday school class carried the little coffin into the keening gale and placed it in a hearse. Mary Todd, too stricken to attend, remained in her room amid rumors and whispers that the First Lady was losing her mind.

Welles, noting that he had never seen the president more worn, or the lines in his face more deeply etched with grief, wept dry-eyed and prayed for his friend and for the soul of his little boy. Abe Lincoln and Mary Todd had lost two children; he and Mary Jane, three. No wound cut more deeply. O Lord, asked Welles, how much more is this good man to be tested?

February 22, the date the president had set for a general advance of the armed forces, came and went between Willie's death and the funeral. A McClellan aide came to the White House to advise that the Army of the Potomac could not advance.

"Why not?" asked the president.

"The pontoon trains are not ready."

A ravaged and heartsore Lincoln swore, "Why in hell and damnation ain't they ready!"

As Willie Lincoln was being laid to rest in Washington, Secretary of the Navy Stephen Mallory in Richmond came to a personnel decision that he, like Welles, had pondered long and seriously. He had waited until the last possible moment before appointing Capt. Franklin Buchanan to command of the Naval Defenses, James River.

It was, Mallory felt, his most important appointment to date, and probably destined to be his most critical of the war. The James River reached north up through the heart of Virginia to Richmond. At its southern end it drained into Hampton Roads, headquarters of the Union's North Atlantic Blockading Squadron.

Buchanan's flagship was the repository of the Confederacy's fondest hopes; it was the vessel to which the South looked for deliverance from the hated blockade; it was the means for bringing England and France to her side as allies; it was the key to ultimate victory. And Mallory shared the dream. He envisioned the *Merrimack* smashing the federal fleet in the Roads. He saw her steaming to New York, and shelling and burning the city and the shipping. "Such an event," he declared to Buchanan, who was not unsympathetic to the plan, "would eclipse all of the glories of all the combats of the sea, would place every man in it preeminently high, and would strike a blow from which the enemy would never recover."

The pudgy little man's voice rising with excitement, he continued, "Bankers would withdraw their capital from the city, the Brooklyn Navy Yard and its magazines and all the lower part of the city would be destroyed. Peace would inevitably follow. Such an event by a single ship would do more to achieve an immediate independence than would the results of many campaigns."

The reason that Mallory procrastinated in appointing Buchanan had nothing to do with questions concerning the captain's commitment or his qualifications. Buchanan's animus against the U.S. Navy Department in the person of Gideon Welles was well known. He despised the outspoken secretary as a rude and insensitive vulgarian. During the antigovernment riots in Baltimore, Buchanan resigned his commission as captain in the U.S. Navy on the ground that he could not bear arms against his native state. But weeks later, when it became evident that Maryland was not going to secede, he applied to the department for reinstatement. His petition was summarily dismissed by Welles, who by that time had had a belly full of disloyal officers. Buchanan, a proud man, never forgave and never forgot.

Certainly there was no question as to his competence. With forty-six years of naval service, Buchanan was the most experienced and distinguished officer in the Confederate Navy. When the war began he was commander of the navy yard in Washington. Prior to that he had fought with distinction in the Mexican War, had served as the first superintendent of the Naval Academy at Annapolis, and had accompanied Commodore Perry on his historic trip to Japan.

It was nevertheless with a great sadness and many misgivings that Mallory made the appointment. The captain's brother, McKean Buchanan, was an officer aboard the Union frigate *Congress* on blockade duty in Hampton Roads, and a certain target of the *Merrimack*. Mallory knew that Franklin Buchanan would not stay his hand, would do what had to be done in the cause of victory. The question that gave the ebullient

Mallory pause, and caused him to agonize, was did he (an orphaned boy, sisterless, brotherless) have the right to ask?

In his letter of appointment Mallory gave no orders as to the method of attack Buchanan should employ, since the *Merrimack* was a novelty in construction. He could not, however, resist offering a suggestion: "Her powers as a ram are regarded as very formidable, and it is hoped you will be able to test them. Like the bayonet charge of infantry, this mode of attack, while the most distinctive, will commend itself to you in the present scarcity of ammunition. It is one also that may be rendered destructive at night against the enemy at anchor. Even without guns the ship would be formidable as a ram. Could you pass Old Point and make a dashing cruise on the Potomac as far as Washington, its effects upon the public mind would be important to the cause."

At the navy yard in Norfolk, Lt. Catesby ap Rogers Jones, a tough and seasoned sailor and the *Merrimack*'s designated executive officer, was responsible for outfitting the ship, organizing and training her crew, and molding ship and men into a supremely effective fighting unit. In his charge were 1,500 shipwrights, mechanics, ironworkers, and carpenters in addition to a pool of 350 mariners from which he was to draw his crew of 150 officers and men. In a relentless day and night all-out effort, driving his men to a controlled frenzy, alternately lashing and lecturing, Jones made certain there was not one who didn't realize that the survival of the Confederacy depended on smashing the federal blockade; nor was anyone unaware that the Union was constructing not one but three ironclads to counter the *Merrimack*.

Despite the scarcity of ammunition, Jones drilled his gunners twice a day with live rounds. Mallory made certain that every pound of gunpowder that could be searched out and bought or commandeered was sent to Norfolk for the *Merrimack*. Jones himself conducted extensive tests of various combinations of shot and powder to ensure peak performance of his artillery.

At the beginning of the last week in February, in a rare moment of reflection, Jones confided to a deck officer that whoever was finally chosen to command the *Merrimack* would have at hand "the most destructive force afloat."

Three hundred miles north at the Brooklyn Navy Yard, where the *Monitor* now in the charge of the United States Navy was moored, it was Ericsson's turn to chafe with impatience and concern. On February 24 he wrote Fox:

> We fully expected the vessel would have been put in commission today but Captain Worden, whose health and energy are not equal to the occasion, does not think his arrangements sufficiently advanced.
>
> Mr. Blunt, whom Captain Worden employs to regulate the compass, appears to me altogether too slow. Commodore Paulding has given peremptory orders to hasten everything, yet the nice system of doing work in the yard is not calculated to forward matters.

Ericsson on that occasion did not mention another source of concern, one that dismayed him as much as the Worden appointment— the *Monitor*'s guns. At the outset Ericsson had proposed that guns of fifteen-inch caliber be employed. But the Bureau of Ordnance under the command of Captain Dahlgren was opposed on the ground that such guns were too large for use in an enclosed turret.

Ericsson had then proposed his twelve-inch gun, the Oregon, which in 1841 he had mounted aboard the *Princeton*. But, again, the shadow of disaster looming large, his proposal was rejected.

The Navy ordered that two eleven-inch Dahlgren smoothbore cannon be taken from the USS *Dacotah* for use aboard the *Monitor*. "My object and my pride is fixed upon these eleven-inch guns," confided Smith to Stimers.

To fill Ericsson's cup of wrath, on the eve of the battery's commissioning, an order came down from the Bureau of Ordnance directing that no more than fifteen-pound, or half charges of powder be used. The reason advanced for the limitation was the possibility of concussion in the close confines of the turret. Ericsson knew from experience as an artillery officer firing cannon from small, concealed huts in Swedish forests that the full charge would present no problem. But the Navy was adamant. "That Princeton millstone," said Ericsson to Fox, "shall not, I promise you, carry me to the bottom. But it may very well sink the U.S. Navy."

While Fox in New York was commiserating with Ericsson over the ways of bureaucracy, Welles in Washington heard a commotion outside his office. He opened the door to find a guard trying to reason with a large, determined Negress who was insisting on a private interview with the secretary. Welles motioned the guard to admit her.

"My name," she said, "is Mary Louvestre, and I come from Nor-folk." She reached into her generous bosom and produced a crumpled piece of paper, which she handed to Welles. It was a note from a pro-Union workman on the *Merrimack*, warning that the ironclad was ready.

By Thursday, February 27, having taken aboard powder, shot, grape and canister, tobacco, soap, candles, thread, buttons, needles, provisions, and the thousand-and-one things necessary for crew and craft, the *Monitor* was ready to sail for Hampton Roads. In what seemed to be an inauspicious omen, dawn brought a howling, wind-driven snowstorm.

The boat ran first to the Manhattan side of the river, then back to Brooklyn, back and forth several times, careering like the proverbial drunken sailor, until it brought up against the gasworks near the Fulton Street Ferry with a shock that nearly threw all aboard off their feet. The vessel was not answering to her rudder. Looking more like a drowned waif than a man-o'-war, she was towed back to the navy yard.

One of New York's newspapers made the unhappy maiden voyage the subject of a scathing editorial on Ericsson—"that incapable schemer, wasting the resources of the country."

The Navy decided to dry-dock the boat and install a new rudder. On learning of the Navy's intention, and mindful that the vessel had not yet been paid for, Ericsson, roaring a Swedish oath, thundered, "The *Monitor* is mine, and I say it shall not be done! Put in a new rudder! They would waste a month. I'll make her steer in three days." He changed the gearing ratio, multiplying the power of the wheel on the rudder. The job was done in a day. The vessel was now able to turn in three times her length within five minutes. If it had not been for the storm, the likelihood is that she would have sailed for Hampton Roads with faulty steering gear.

On March 3, the *Monitor* was given another trial, this time with a three-man navy commission aboard at Worden's insistence. At the start of the journey, the compass did not work. Compass placement on ironclads presented new and special problems. But Alban Stimers was able to reposition it until it functioned accurately.

Off Sandy Hook, blank charges of fifteen pounds were fired to determine the effect of concussion in the turret. There was no ill effect. The battery's average speed was clocked at five and a half knots; maximum, six and a quarter. The commission pronounced the trial satisfactory.

One minor mishap did occur, which had to do with living in a submerged environment. Waste matter was ejected below the waterline by releasing it into a duct closed at the lower end. The upper end was then closed and a pump activated, forcing the water in the duct out with its contents. Surgeon Logue, attending to a call of nature, neglected an essential part of the ritual. He found himself propelled into the air at the end of a column of water rushing up from the depths of the ocean and pouring into the cabin.

The *Monitor* was, at last, ready for sea duty, awaiting only calm weather. On the day after the successful trial, Worden hosted a farewell dinner for some officers from the navy yard, including Commodore Paulding. Unhappily, in honor of the occasion, Steward Daniel Moone got blind drunk. Dinner was a disaster, the dishes being served in the wrong order. Moone was clapped into chains. Upon being released, filled with remorse at having betrayed his shipmates, he got drunk again, this time from the wardroom stores to which he had the key. He was ironed and locked up in the chain locker.

Thursday, March 6, dawned chill but clear. The sea was calm. At five, when the bosun's whistle shrilled its clean, three-note summons, it seemed to sound more purposeful. When the mate ran through the berth deck, shouting, "All hands rise and roll out . . . up all hammocks," one could detect a new note of urgency.

At half past nine, Worden gave the order to beat to quarters. Before the drum had sounded its last shuddering note, every man was at his station. For young Lieutenant Greene and the eighteen men in the turret, it was a moment of epiphany. Face to face with the engines of war— sixteen tons of sleek, black, iron cannon enclosed in the twenty-foot turret—it was clear as it had never been before that the ship was built for the guns.

There was a final dockside inspection. At eleven o'clock, the *Monitor,* with orders to sail for Hampton Roads, slipped her moorings and moved smoothly into the channel, joining the gunboats *Sachem* and *Currituck.* At Governor's Island the steam tug *Seth Low* came alongside and took her in tow, the purpose being to speed the journey and to serve as added protection for a crew that was taking an ironclad to sea for the first time.

Proceeding south through the Upper Bay and the Narrows to the Lower Bay, she was opposite Sandy Hook when Commodore Paulding at the navy yard received an urgent order from the department changing the *Monitor*'s orders. Instead of sailing for Hampton Roads, she was now to proceed directly to Washington to defend the capital.

Paulding dispatched a tug in hot pursuit. But it was too late. And since the *Monitor* had already cleared the lighthouses off the Atlantic Highlands, there was no way to reach her by telegraph.

The light wind from the west and the smooth sea favored the journey. At two in the afternoon, the crew enjoyed a fine celebratory dinner of soup, fish, meats, puddings, fruits, and nuts, topped by cups of strong coffee. In the wardroom Worden entertained the officers with stories of his experiences as a midshipman. After dinner some took a cigar and a stroll on deck.

Worden, touring the boat, was pleased to hear the sounds of a settled crew. Someone was strumming a banjo:

> O needles and pins, needles and pins,
> When a man marries his trouble begins.

From the berth deck he heard a sailor shout, "I'll pay a dollar, who'll write a letter for me?"

"What do you want me to write?"

"I dunno . . . just tell the little gal to keep her eyes peeled for me when my time's out."

On Friday morning at six, when Lieutenant Greene turned out, he noted that the good weather was holding. But about noon the wind freshened and the sea turned rough. By afternoon the sea was breaking over the deck in huge waves and coming in the hawse pipe forward. Paymaster Keeler noticed that their escorts were heeling so violently that their gun muzzles were dipping into the water.

Most of the *Monitor* crew, including their captain, were green with seasickness. This iron tub had a motion they were unused to. They could not seek relief on deck, and to remain below, where bilge and body and galley odors mingled, was to get sicker.

It quickly became apparent that the hatch to the berth deck was not watertight. But that proved only a minor inconvenience. It was next discovered that sheets of water were cascading down between the base of the turret and the deck. Stimers assumed that the bottom of the turret had not been properly backed. On investigation he found that someone at the navy yard had decided to improve on Ericsson's design, which specified: "A flat, broad ring of bronze is let into the deck, its upper face being very smooth in order to form a watertight joint with the base of the turret without the employment of any elastic packing." Before the craft left Brooklyn, a well-meaning workman had inserted a plaited hemp rope between the base of the turret and the bronze ring for the purpose of making the joint watertight. Rough and uneven, the rope did not form a seal, and thus permitted the water to flow through freely.

It was not until the storm broke that Stimers noted too that, although everything on deck was to have been caulked, the vessel had sailed without a particle of oakum.

By four in the afternoon, water was pouring down the six-foot-high smoke pipes and the four-foot air intake ducts. The former were for dissipating the stack gases, the latter for ventilation and furnace draft. The water coming through the intake ducts caused the belts on the furnace blowers to slip, stretch, and break. When the engineers tried to mend one belt, another broke. Now there were heavy fires in the furnace but no draft. The water coming down the smoke pipes caused the fire to back up through the coals and the ash pan doors into the fireroom, filling the place with hydrogen and carbonic acid gas. The mixture if breathed is fatal to animal life within minutes.

When the second belt broke and the engines stopped for lack of steam, Stimers, who was off duty and asleep, was summoned. He rushed to the engine room, where he found men around him dropping senseless to the deck. He got them all topside and remained working until he became lightheaded and weak in the knees. Struggling up to the top of the turret for fresh air, he noted three engineers and several firemen laid out, unconscious.

Stimers set up relays of engineers and firemen, who took turns going down to the engine room and working for short, fixed periods. As long as the engines could be kept working, there was no problem pumping out the water the vessel was shipping. But as soon as the engines stopped, the water began rising to dangerous levels.

At about seven in the evening, Greene reported to Worden, "Ship's making water fast, sir. Won't be able to float much longer."

Worden, wet, chilled, and seasick, replied, "Man the hand pump." He betrayed no evidence of his misery. That evening he confided to his private journal that he had no fear of the *Merrimack*. Nothing she was preparing for them, he was convinced, could be more devastating than the chills and nausea he was suffering. He thanked a benevolent Providence that he was able to conceal his condition from the crew.

Greene ordered the hand pump to be rigged on the berth deck. But because the hose had to stretch up through the turret and then overboard, manual operation was not able to generate enough power. Now the only alternative was to bail. But, again, this meant passing buckets up through the turret, an operation that consumed so much time as to make the effort futile.

Fortunately, the storm subsided enough that they were able to restore communications with the tug. Worden directed it to take them closer to the shore, where the sea was not as rough, the wind being offshore. By eight in the evening, after four hours of nonstop heroic effort, Stimers and his men succeeded in getting the engines working again.

The seas remained heavy all that night. When Stimers, exhausted, turned in shortly after midnight, the blowers were working, but barely, since the sea was still breaking over the deck and down the ducts. He was awakened again at one in the morning, when the tiller ropes jumped off the wheel and jammed.

Stimers made the repair, returned to bed at two, and was up at six. By then the sea had moderated considerably. He observed to Worden that if Ericsson had made the blower pipes as high as he, Stimers, had wanted, about fifteen feet instead of four, and if the deck had been properly caulked, they would have laughed at the storm. He had never seen a vessel more buoyant or less shocked in a heavy sea. The movement aboard was not sufficient to upset a glass of wine standing on a table.

CHAPTER

XXII

The storm that nearly foundered the *Monitor* as she made her way down the Atlantic coast had also been buffeting the navy yard at Norfolk. Captain Buchanan was in a frenzy of impatience. He had taken command on March 4 with the intention of moving out immediately. But here it was the evening of the seventh and the *Merrimack* was still tied to her dock.

Buchanan had information no one else had. The *Monitor* was steaming for the Roads, possibly for Norfolk, to shell and destroy the *Merrimack* while she was still berthed. For that reason, and because he desperately wanted to engage the Union fleet while it consisted solely of wooden vessels, his stomach churned with anxiety, and his anxiety doubled with each passing day.

Furiously pacing the ship's topmost deck, which was actually a grating that covered the gun deck, he waited for the weather to clear, for the last iron plate to be bolted into place, and for the last pound of powder to be stored.

At sixty-two, with weathered, sharp—almost harsh—features and clear, piercing blue eyes, Buchanan was known as a strong-willed commander who demanded exemplary performance from his men and from himself.

Saturday, March 8, dawned with the promise of a calm, sunny day.

The ship was still crawling with workmen hurrying to complete the final touches. But Buchanan had had enough. His patience was at an end. He ordered everyone ashore except the 150-man crew and gave orders to prepare for immediate departure.

The commandant of the yard protested that some of the armor plate for the vessel's sides below the waterline had not yet arrived and that not all the gunport shutters had been attached. "I mean to try her against the enemy, sir!" replied Buchanan. "There'll be time enough to complete the shutters and armor after we have proved her in action."

He summoned his chief engineer, Maj. H. Ashton Ramsay, who had been an assistant engineer aboard the preconversion *Merrimack*. Continuing to pace with long, furious strides, hands clasped behind, Buchanan fired questions and instructions at the major, who, though much younger, had difficulty keeping up with the captain. "Ramsay, what would happen to your engines and boilers if there should be a collision?"

"They are braced tight, sir. Though the boilers stand fourteen feet high, they are so securely fastened that no collision could budge them."

"I'm going to ram the *Cumberland*. She has the new rifled guns— I'm told they can penetrate more than four inches of armor—the only ones in their fleet we have cause to fear. The moment we're in the Roads, I'm going to make right for her.

"Now how about your engines? I understand they were in poor shape in the old ship. Can we rely on them? Should they be tested by a trial trip?"

"She will have to travel some ten miles downriver before we get to the Roads," said Ramsay. "If any trouble develops, I'll report it. I think that will be sufficient trial, sir."

Frustrated by the tides, which would not permit him to clear the bar at the mouth of the Elizabeth River until midday, Buchanan waited until almost nine before giving the order to fire up the boilers. At about eleven, Confederate stars and bars fluttering in the sparkle of a sunlit, storm-washed sky, the *Merrimack* cast off her lines and slipped into the channel of the river. As she turned downstream she was joined by two small gunboats of one gun each, the *Raleigh* and the *Beaufort,* whose principal duty was to ward off any ramming attempts on the *Merrimack,* especially those aimed at her vulnerable rudder and propeller.

Her funnel belching black smoke, the ironclad made her way north.

As she passed Portsmouth and Norfolk her crew was treated to wild and thunderous ovations by thousands of cheering, waving well-wishers who lined the banks all the way to Craney Island.

As the *Merrimack* approached Sewell's Point, Buchanan summoned the crew to the gun deck. "Sailors," he said in a clear, ringing voice, "in a few minutes you will have the long-looked-for opportunity of showing your devotion to our cause. You are now to face the enemy. Remember that you strike for your country and your home. The Confederacy expects every man to do his duty. You may be sure I intend to do mine." (No one was unaware that the captain's brother was aboard the *Congress*.) "Beat to quarters!"

The mess caterer touched Ramsay's elbow and whispered, "Better get your lunch now; it will be your last chance. The galley fires must be put out when the magazines are opened."

Passing along the gun deck to the wardroom, Ramsay noted the gun crews standing stiffly at their guns, ramrods and sponges in hand. They were young and, like the ship, for the most part untried. They looked pale and determined. They knew the odds: ten guns against three hundred; one hundred fifty men against three thousand—plus the Union shore batteries at Newport News, where fifty guns were manned by four thousand Union Army troops. Brave men . . . brave boys, reflected Ramsay.

In the wardroom he found a number of officers picking at cold tongue and biscuit. At the end of one table, in a cleared space, he noted the ship's surgeon examining a case of surgical instruments. Lint and bandages were lying about. The sight numbed his appetite. He turned away and descended the ladder to the engine room. Satisfied that the sixteen furnaces, fourteen-foot-high boilers, and two engines were working as expected, he climbed to the pilothouse, where he asked the ship's speed. "Eight or nine knots," he was told. Ramsay was delighted. True, they were going downstream, but the *Merrimack* was faster now than she had been with her top hamper of masts and sails.

The two pilots, who were civilians recruited for the mission, did not share the major's enthusiasm. The ship steered badly, she drew twenty-three feet of water, and she could not be turned in less than half an hour.

Ramsay reported to Buchanan that everything was in order. The *Merrimack* steamed steadily north, down the channel toward Sewell's Point, one of the teeth in the lower jaw, or southern shore, of Hampton Roads.

Five miles across the gently choppy, glinting expanse, lying off Newport News Point, a tooth in the upper jaw of the Roads, were the Union ships—*Congress,* a twenty-year-old frigate carrying fifty guns, and *Cumberland,* a twenty-four-gun sloop of war, also twenty years old. Both were sailing ships, tall and stately, every line and spar proudly defined against the blue March sky. Despite their white-winged grandeur, however, they had both been on the verge of being decommissioned as unseaworthy when Beauregard fired on Sumter. In combination with the federal shore batteries at Newport News, the two ships effectively blocked the channel of the James River, which stretched northwest from the western, or closed, end of the Roads.

As the *Merrimack* was approaching Sewell's Point, the crews of both Union ships were finishing their noon meal. Routine watch was in force. Saturday being wash day, the rigging of the *Cumberland* was gay with the red, white, and blue of sailors' clothes hung out to dry.

Strung out to the east for about eight miles along the upper jaw of the Roads, which terminates in Chesapeake Bay, lay the rest of the blockading squadron, a varied assortment of eighteen ships that included everything from a one-gun tug to the mighty steamships *Minnesota* and *Roanoke,* sister ships of the *Merrimack,* six years old and mounting forty guns each. The *Roanoke,* however, with a main shaft that had been broken for six months, was wholly dependent on sail— a circumstance that did not cause undue concern to her command given the widespread bias against steam. Also scattered throughout the Roads were a number of commercial vessels, some flying the flags of foreign nations keenly interested in the events that were shaping up that lovely Saturday afternoon.

Aboard the *Congress,* acting commander Joe Smith was in a good mood as was all the crew. Notice had been received that in a day or two the ship was to be relieved of blockade duty—welcome news— for a more active assignment. For several months they had been lying at anchor with little to do but watch and wait. That morning Smith had gone ashore with some fellow officers to bid friends farewell. There had been wine and fresh oysters, and the bantering exchanges that have attended military farewells since the time of Caesar's legions. Smith, a handsome young officer, with a full though close-cropped beard, was a man of generous inclination and good cheer, an immensely popular and competent officer.

At one o'clock, dinner hour on the *Congress* was over. The meal pendant was hauled down and the crew turned to the business of preparing the ship for departure. It promised to be an afternoon like many that had gone before—peaceful, the James flowing by into the sunlit Roads, the work proceeding at an unhurried pace in keeping with a mild, springlike day.

But at about half past one there was a stir on the poop, a pointing of glasses, a sudden, quiet urgency in the tones of the officers who had been taking their afternoon airing. Messenger boys darted down the hatches, while more officers came topside.

The object of attention was a group of three steam vessels, one of which was a huge, glistening black mass, moving in a channel where for months nothing larger than a small tug had been seen. As the large vessel cleared Sewell's Point and encountered the crosscurrents of the Roads, her speed slowed perceptibly, to something under four knots. All at once it struck the officers of the *Congress* that the large vessel was the rebel ironclad, *Merrimack*.

At first they assumed she was making her way east toward the *Minnesota* and the other Union ships strung out toward Fortress Monroe. But the ironclad's bow turned to port, toward Newport News. It became evident that she was bent on attacking the *Congress* and the *Cumberland* in a move to clear the channel of the James River.

Joe Smith turned to the officers on the poop deck with his cheery smile and said quietly, "Gentlemen, we shall go to quarters. . . . Beat to quarters!" The officer who transmitted the order rubbed his hands briskly as if in anticipation of something to do, at long last. As the drummer rapped out the call, the *Cumberland*'s drum was heard in answering echo.

Signal flags began their rapid ascent and descent on the masts of the federal fleet, advising commanders of the *Merrimack*'s intentions. The clotheslines of the *Cumberland* vanished as she lowered boats astern. The *Congress* shook out her topsails. Smoke began to pour from the funnels of the *Minnesota*. Gleaming black guns aboard all ships were uncovered and run out.

As the Union commanders cleared for action, one thought was common to all: Despite daily warnings and alerts from Washington, the *Merrimack* had taken them quite by surprise.

Three key commanders were not at their posts. Commodore

Goldsborough was in the Carolinas. Captain William Radford, commander of the *Cumberland,* was attending a board of inquiry aboard the *Roanoke,* which was without the use of her engines. The commander of the *Congress* had been detached the previous day, leaving the executive officer, Joseph Smith, in command. The *Congress* itself was grossly undermanned, the enlistment time of her crew having expired. So short were her numbers that elements of the 99th Infantry, New York, had been taken aboard for temporary duty. Before departing, Goldsborough had left orders that the *Congress* and the *Cumberland* should never be left without tugs to manage them should the *Merrimack* come out. But not a tug was to be seen in the vicinity of either ship. The *Merrimack* advanced to within three quarters of a mile of the *Cumberland* before the sloop was cleared for action.

The disposition of the Union fleet was an invitation to disaster. Strung out in shoal water, ungrouped, with no concerted firepower and with limited room for maneuver, it was, from Buchanan's perspective, a naval commander's dream. He was able to single out his targets and pluck them one at a time.

The initial response of the fleet was catastrophic. The *Minnesota, Roanoke,* and *St. Lawrence,* a fifty-gun sailing frigate, in attempting to go to the assistance of the *Congress* and the *Cumberland,* all ran aground as they tried to get underway without the assistance of tugs. Aboard the *Congress,* Smith gave the order to spring ship, a turning maneuver designed to bring her broadside on the approaching enemy in order to exert maximum firepower. But perhaps because a good part of the crew was experienced with land operations rather than maritime maneuvers, tug though the infantrymen would, the ship did not respond. "Never mind! Avast hauling! Back to your guns!"

For a half hour, the men of the *Congress* stood by the side of their shotted guns in dead silence, rams and sponges at the ready, magazines open, as the behemoth, with agonizing deliberation, bore down on them. Now she was in full view, and for the first time the U.S. Navy got a good look at her.

The *Merrimack*'s masts and rigging had been removed and her sides cut down to the level of the gun deck, which barely cleared the water. Over the greater part of the deck had been constructed a casemate of oak and pitch pine two feet thick, seven feet high, and one hundred seventy feet in length. The structure's sides slanted out at an angle of thirty-five degrees from the roof to a point two feet below the waterline;

the fore and aft ends of the casemate were circular and slanting like a mansard roof. The whole casemate was sheathed in two layers of bar iron, each bar two inches thick and eight inches wide, the first layer applied horizontally, the second vertically, for a total thickness throughout of four inches. The armor had been flushed with tallow and wax to help deflect shot and shell. The unarmored portions of the deck that projected from under the casemate fore and aft had been cut down still further so that they were completely submerged.

The casemate was pierced for ten guns: two deadly seven-inch pivot rifles at bow and stern, six nine-inch smoothbore Dahlgrens, and two thirty-two-pounder rifles. All guns were fixed except for the rifles at bow and stern. Projecting from her stem at the waterline was her eighteen-inch cast-iron ram, a weapon that dated from the wars of Rome and Carthage.

To some aboard the *Congress* and the *Cumberland* she resembled a house submerged to the eaves; to others, a crocodile. Her grease-smeared black armor glistened monstrously in the noonday sun.

In a coordinated movement three rebel steamships that had been converted to men-o'-war—*Patrick Henry,* a side-wheeler with twelve guns; *Jamestown,* a sister ship with two guns; and *Teaser,* a river tug mounting one gun—began steaming down the James to join the *Merrimack* and her two consorts. To achieve their objective of breaking out into the Roads, the three ships had to sail under the guns of the *Congress,* the *Cumberland,* and the Union batteries at Newport News.

When the *Merrimack* was within three hundred yards of the *Congress,* Smith gave the command, "Commence firing!" The *Congress*'s two stern guns bucked and boomed. The thirty-two-pound solid shot slammed into the *Merrimack*'s sloping iron sides, glanced harmlessly upward, and fell hissing into the sea.

A shutter in the rebel ironclad's forward battery swung open. A stand of grape came rattling into the stern ports of the *Congress,* sounding like giant hailstones on a roof. Six men were cut down. While the dead and wounded were passed below, a whisper made the rounds, "Never mind. Just wait til we get her under our broadside."

Steaming past the *Congress,* the *Merrimack* was in a few minutes exposed to her broadside. The *Congress* reeled as the twenty-three guns of her port batteries roared in unison. All were on target. To the dismay of all aboard the Union ships and the thousands of blue-clad soldiers lining the northern shore, the *Merrimack* continued on course, shaking off the barrage of shot and shell as a rhinoceros might shed insects. The rebel ironclad had taken the best the *Congress* had to offer.

A return of shellfire from three of *Merrimack*'s rifles swept the gun and spar decks of the *Congress*. A sparkling stretch of white, holystoned timber lined with gleaming cannon, shining racks of arms, and stalwart sailors became in a flash of gunpowder a streaming red-splashed abattoir. Lopped-off limbs and blackened bodies sprawled in unlikely attitudes over guns and in the rigging. Blood and brains dripped from the upper deck. One sailor, chest impaled by an oak splinter thick as his wrist, tried to crawl below. The quartermaster, whose alert had first discovered the *Merrimack,* was carried below, cheering feebly and exhorting the men to stand to their guns. Both his legs had been sheared off.

The crew of the *Congress* was stunned to disbelief by the effects of the *Merrimack*'s heavy, rifled shellfire. Solid shot, even shellfire from smoothbore cannon, was one thing; but shellfire from heavy, rifled artillery was another—something of which they had been happily innocent.

The accuracy of the guns and the devastation caused by the exploding shell fragments were such that one shot took out all seventeen men of a midship gun crew. Comparatively few were wounded. The fragments were for the most part lethal.

The *Merrimack*'s ordnance in combination with her apparently invulnerable armor caused many a Union sailor that Saturday afternoon to feel a sense of betrayal. It was as though the rules of the game had suddenly and arbitrarily been changed.

The ironclad continued to steam past the *Congress*. The frigate's decimated crew, thinking the rebels had unaccountably had enough, began a feeble cheer, until it became evident that the rebel ship was simply disdaining the *Congress*. Without pausing to assess the damage she had wrought on the frigate, the ironclad continued to steam straight for the sloop *Cumberland,* lying immediately ahead. When the sloop was within hailing distance, Buchanan roared through a bosun's trumpet, "Do you surrender?"

"Never!" came the reply of the acting commander, George Morris. "I'll sink first!" The ironclad steamed steadily on course. In her engine room two gongs sounded the signal to stop, quickly followed by three gongs for reverse. The collision was not violent. The ram nevertheless pierced the *Cumberland*'s aged timber just below the starboard forechains, like a knife cutting through ripe cheese. At the same instant, the *Merrimack*'s bow rifle fired point-blank, opening a hole large enough for a horse and carriage.

The *Cumberland,* also armed with rifled artillery, responded with her bow and starboard batteries. Shot rained on the *Merrimack*'s starboard shutters, followed by an ear-splitting roar that shook the entire ship as a shell exploded in her stack. Locked in violent embrace, the two men-o'-war were momentarily lost in a pall of smoke billowing from their guns, from the ironclad's smokestack, and from the grease frying on her sides.

Merrimack's prow, with her ram still engaged, bearing the full weight of the *Cumberland,* began to sink. A horrible thought crossed the mind of the *Merrimack*'s executive officer, Catesby Jones. The *Cumberland*'s sheet anchor was hanging off the forward deck. If someone had the presence of mind to release it, both ships would go down together.

Desperately, *Merrimack* tried to back off and withdraw her ram. But the tide caught her and skewed her about so that she was parallel to her adversary. Her iron beak twisted off and remained in the hull of the Union sloop.

At muzzle point, gunwales almost touching, the vessels poured volley after murderous volley into each other. The *Merrimack*'s two life-boats were shot to pieces in their davits, and the muzzles of two guns were shattered in a barrage of solid shot, the fragments killing one man and mortally wounding another. Each time the two truncated guns fired, they ignited their ports.

"Keep loading and firing," screamed Jones. "Do the best you can! Keep away from the ports! Don't lean against the shield!" Some of the men didn't heed the warning and were stunned by the concussion. They collapsed, bleeding from the ears.

The *Merrimack* began to ship water through the hole where the ram had been twisted off. What was left of her stack was riddled. Her flag, shot down several times, was secured to a jagged hole. But despite the punishing barrage, her casemate remained intact.

The deck of the *Cumberland* was red and slippery with blood. The gun crews kicked off their shoes for better traction. They worked only as men can work when death is in hot pursuit. Stripped to the waist, heads tied with black neckerchiefs, they trained and sighted the guns, jumping to the screamed litany: "Sponge! . . . Load! . . . Fire!" Between rounds they dragged their dead and wounded amidships. A gun captain who had lost both legs at the knee and one arm at the shoulder wound the lock string around his remaining hand, and while sprawled on the deck continued to pull the string on command until his blood ran dry.

The sloop's after pivot gun broke loose, slid down the deck, and caught young Quartermaster Murphy. He was struck down, and the gun bounding on his back like a maddened animal broke his spine and knocked him overboard. He rose to the surface with a look of perplexed anguish, then disappeared.

In the sick bay some of the men had their wounds partially dressed when the *Merrimack* sent a rifled percussion shell through the spar deck hatch. It burst, killing four. A hopelessly wounded marine was lying propped against a bulkhead, a blood-soaked bandage around his chest, when his "chummy" came in to have his hand dressed. He was about to return to his station when the marine said, "Tom, are you going to leave me?"

"No, I will not." Tom sat on the deck and, taking his friend's head in his lap, remained with him.

The *Cumberland* began to settle at the bow. From the quarterdeck the order came, "All save who can!" As the ship listed to starboard, the crew took to the water or to the boats that had been lowered before the action commenced. A fat drummer boy escaped by throwing his drum overboard, clinging to it until he was rescued. The ship continued to settle. Her gunners maintained their fire until the water rose to the muzzles. The high-pitched wail of a powder boy pierced the din: "Oh, Mr. Marmaduke, you're going to die. Give me back my money." The cries of the wounded begging to be shot rather than left to drown were heard by the troops ashore.

At 3:35 P.M., fifteen minutes after being rammed, the *Cumberland* sank in fifty feet of water. She created a vortex that sucked five flailing sailors down with her. Of her 376-man crew, 121 were dead.

Buchanan now steamed toward the James in a wide turning maneuver, leaving the *Cumberland* with only her topgallant masts showing above water, her ensign still flying. The three rebel steamers that had been locked in the James River steamed to join the *Merrimack* . The twelve-gun *Patrick Henry* took a shell from the shore batteries to her boiler, which exploded, filling her engine and firerooms with steam that scalded four firemen to death. Their screams were heard aboard the *Merrimack.*

The six ships of the rebel squadron made straight for the hapless *Congress,* which, realizing their intent, slipped her chains, set her topsails and jib, and with the help of a tug ran up on the mudflats off Newport News. Thus heeled over, most of her fixed guns were useless. But now she had the support of the shore batteries.

The *Merrimack* and her consorts took a position off her quarter, and for half an hour raked her fore and aft with shot and shell. A shell from the ironclad's bow pivot rifle tore through the *Congress*'s berth deck, cut down a line of powder passers like a row of dominoes, and fired the powder buckets in a staccato of blinding explosions that left a trail of blood and mutilated bodies. From stem to stern the ship ran red and was festooned with isolated limbs and hunks of bleeding flesh.

The ship's purser, McKean Buchanan, dashed up to Smith and volunteered for duty on one of the upper decks. He was given command of the berth deck, where the officer in charge had been killed.

Aboard the rebel gunboat *Beaufort,* which carried a largely foreign crew, an English sailor was mortally wounded by fire from ashore. The commanding officer asked what he could do to make him comfortable. "A cup of tea and a pair of clean socks would be lovely," said the sailor. They complied with his request. After finishing the tea, he died peacefully.

On the quarterdeck of the *Congress* where he was directing the action, young Joe Smith's head was separated from his shoulders by a shell fragment, which also dismounted the last gun that could be brought to bear. It was 4:20 in the afternoon.

Lieutenant Austin Pendergrast, next in command, surveyed the situation for a few minutes, deemed it hopeless, and ordered the colors struck. At 4:30 the white flag was run up. Buchanan gave the cease-fire order then ordered the *Beaufort* and the *Raleigh* to go alongside the *Congress* and take off her wounded before firing the ship. Pendergrast surrendered his sword to the commander of the *Beaufort*.

Despite the *Congress*'s white flag of surrender, a regiment at Newport News Point opened fire on the rebel ships. Buchanan, raging at this breach of the military code, screamed for a rifle. Standing topside, he was handed rifle after loaded rifle which he pumped at the troops until he was struck in the groin by a bullet. His femoral artery was severed. Bright red blood spurted through a hole torn in his trouser leg. As he was handed below he instructed Catesby Jones in furious but explicit tones, "Plug hot shot into her and don't leave her until she's afire. They must look after their own wounded now."

Jones gave the order for incendiary action. Two furnaces aboard the *Merrimack* had been reserved for heating shot, which was rolled from a grating above the fire into iron buckets. These were hoisted to the gun deck and rolled into the muzzles of guns that had been prepared with wads of wet hemp. The guns were quickly touched off. Of the *Congress*'s 434-man crew, 240 were dead; among the survivors, McKean Buchanan.

When Jones was satisfied that the *Congress* was burning freely, he directed his squadron to the *Minnesota,* still hard aground two miles east. The *Merrimack,* having the same draft as her sister ship, was able to approach to about two thousand yards, which was the edge of her effective range. She and her consorts fired a few broadsides, some of which found the mark. The *Minnesota*'s return fire had no effect on the *Merrimack* but did drive off the smaller rebel vessels. With daylight fading fast, both the *Merrimack*'s civilian pilots insisted on drawing off into deeper water. Jones decided to call it quits. He ordered the return to Sewell's Point, their anchorage for the night. The *Minnesota* and the *Roanoke* would be there tomorrow morning, when the tide would be more favorable.

It wasn't until eight in the evening that the *Merrimack* dropped anchor, and it was half past eleven before her cooks and stewards started their fires and got stores together for a meal. After supper Jones and some fellow officers took a stroll topside to relax and watch the *Congress* burn. Below, in his cabin, Captain Buchanan argued with the ship's surgeons. They wanted him to go ashore for treatment. Though wracked by waves of nausea and spasms of breath-robbing pain, he insisted on remaining aboard. The physicians prevailed. As he was carried off the ship on a litter, he ordered, "Mr. Jones, fight the ship to the last. Tell the men I am not mortally wounded and hope to be with them very soon."

Forward, at the waterline, engineers and shipwrights from ashore were frantically working by the light of torches to repair the hole where the ram had been attached.

Jones, leaning on a rail, absorbed by the scene across the Roads where the *Congress* was now a flaming pyre, reflected on the day's events. The *Merrimack* had left the Norfolk yard shortly after eleven. By five she had rammed and sunk the twenty-four-gun *Cumberland,* set fire to the fifty-gun *Congress,* crippled the forty-eight-gun *Minnesota,* driven the forty-gun *Roanoke* and the fifty-gun *St. Lawrence* aground, and frightened off the rest of the federal fleet like a flock of small birds. While sustaining two killed and five wounded, the *Merrimack* had taken thirty prisoners, killed or wounded four hundred enemy officers and men, and caused considerable damage ashore in casualties and destruction of Union arms. Not a bad afternoon's work. And tomorrow promised to be even better. Jones had learned a great deal about the handling and operation of his ironclad.

A lesson had also been learned by every foreign power with a fleet of warships: Only iron can compete with iron. The events of Saturday, March 8, 1862, in Hampton Roads had, inter alia, scuttled the wooden navies of the world.

CHAPTER

XXIII

It wasn't until late Saturday afternoon as the *Monitor* was passing Cape Henry that her crew gained an inkling of the action in the Roads. Heavy cannon fire was audible from the engagement some twenty miles distant. Worden assumed that the *Merrimack* was involved and that she was attempting to break out of the Roads.

He at once ordered his vessel stripped of her sea rig. The turret was keyed up off the bronze ring so that it could be rotated freely. The drummer beat to quarters for a gun handling drill.

As they neared Fortress Monroe they took a pilot aboard who told them that the *Cumberland* was sunk and the *Congress* burning. He was not entirely believed. But at dusk as they entered the Roads, *Congress*'s flaming hull became visible. Worden anchored alongside the *Roanoke* and reported to Captain Marston, commander of the North Atlantic Blockading Squadron in the absence of Commodore Goldsborough.

Forty-eight hours before Worden boarded the *Roanoke,* Marston had received unequivocal orders telegraphed from the secretary of the Navy:

> For Captain John Marston: Direct Lieutenant Commanding John L. Worden,
> of the *Monitor,* to proceed directly to Washington with his vessel.
> Gideon Welles, Secretary of the Navy

Sixty-six-year-old John Marston had fashioned a checkered career in the Navy. Having entered as a midshipman in 1813, his service spanned forty-nine years. But of those years, a total of eighteen had been spent either on leave of absence, on furlough, or "waiting orders." During the years of the war with Mexico he was listed as "waiting orders." His periods of active service were singularly free of citation, positive or negative. It can, however, be safely assumed that he did not rise from midshipman to captain by disobeying direct orders of the secretary of the Navy.

Nevertheless, Marston agonized. Clearly, Welles's order had been issued prior to, and therefore in ignorance of, that day's events. Welles could have had no knowledge that *Merrimack* was under sail, and certainly he could not have known of the devastation she had wrought when he issued the order directing Worden to Washington. Still, how could he, Marston, on his own authority send the *Monitor* into the Roads and commit her to an engagement with the *Merrimack* in direct contradiction of Secretary Welles's order? The *Monitor* was now the last hope and the most valuable vessel in the Navy. She was all that stood between the *Merrimack* and the rest of the fleet—and, for that matter, the capital of the United States. It was a whimsical fate that decreed at that moment that he, Capt. John Marston, should occupy the most critical command position in the United States Navy.

But there was something else on Marston's mind. Would the day's events have turned out differently if the *Congress* and the *Cumberland* had been attended by tugs, in accordance with Commodore Goldsborough's orders? Who was to blame for the omission and for the tragedy? The facts were not comforting. He was the senior officer in command. The devastation and the humiliation wrought by the *Merrimack* would not be redeemed by directing the *Monitor* up the Potomac to Washington. Nor would sending Worden and his vessel to Washington help maintain the integrity of the blockade.

Marston made the decision of his career. In direct contradiction of Welles's telegram, he ordered Worden to proceed immediately to Newport News, where he was to report to Van Brunt aboard the *Minnesota*. "I believe that *Merrimack* will attack her at first light," said Marston, "and that's where your vessel is needed." Worden was in complete agreement. He felt that to avoid the *Merrimack* was unthinkable. From the moment he stepped aboard Ericsson's battery that January day in Greenpoint, he knew that the confrontation was fated.

Reboarding the *Monitor,* Worden dictated a telegram for relay from Fortress Monroe to Secretary Welles:

> Hampton Roads, 3/8/62: Sir, I have the honor to report that I arrived at this anchorage at nine o'clock this evening and am ordered to proceed immediately to the assistance of the Minnesota aground near Newport News.
>
> > Very respectfully, your obedient servant,
> > J. L. Worden
> > Lt. Commdg.

Before weighing anchor he penned a short note to Olivia for posting ashore:

> March 8th, ten PM, Hampton Roads. My Darling Wife, I arrived here an hour since and am going immediately to the assistance of the *Minnesota* near Newport News. She is aground. The *Merrimack* has caused sad work among our vessels. She cannot hurt us. God bless you and the little ones. Yours ever and devotedly, Worden.

Skillfully steered through the treacherous waters of the Roads by a volunteer pilot, the path along the northern shore illuminated by the blazing *Congress,* the *Monitor* dropped anchor alongside the *Minnesota* around midnight. A shaken Van Brunt (he who had dismissed the *Merrimack* as a phantom ship) received Worden with less than enthusiasm. The *Monitor,* dimly perceived in the midnight blackness, did not inspire confidence.

Worden was struck by the atmosphere aboard the *Minnesota* in contrast to that of the *Roanoke.* The former had been briefly but badly mauled by the rebel squadron. Ugly, smoldering gashes disfigured her hull. Huge splinters, great shafts of wood several feet in length and half a foot across, had been gouged out of her deck, masts, and sides, killing or maiming those in the vicinity. The splinters were as lethal as shell fragments and accounted for more casualties than the shot or shell itself. Despite the obvious attempt to scrub them clean, the white decks were stained with huge, irregular splotches of blood that had been absorbed by the timber.

The crew, in their haste to lighten the ship by off-loading every-thing movable—provisions, ammunition, even guns—to small boats, had inadvertently dropped crates into the sea, where they were to be seen ringing the ship like floating coffins.

The men were stiff with fear and tension. They had seen their shipmates killed and mutilated by the *Merrimack*'s rifles while their own heavy guns had no effect. Only the rebel ironclad's deep draft had saved them from the fate of the *Cumberland* and the *Congress*.

Worden briefly recapitulated for Van Brunt his conversation with Marston, and asked the captain's intentions.

"If I cannot lighten my ship and float her," replied Van Brunt, "I shall destroy her." Their conversation was momentarily interrupted by a loud report from the *Congress*, two miles west. The fire had reached one of her guns and touched off a shot that went screaming through the night in a mad, random course.

"I will stand by you to the last," said Worden as he prepared to return to his vessel. Van Brunt accompanied him to the ladder.

"No, sir, you cannot help me," said the captain, peering down through the gloom at the diminutive *Monitor*, which was as a spaniel to a horse.

Worden had no sooner reached his ship when the fire aboard the *Congress* reached her magazine. With a series of raging roars, huge columns of fire shot toward the stars like monstrous, vying Roman candles. The old ship's hull burst like a bomb, scattering bits of the vessel in a shower of flaming splinters. Then all was quiet and dark as the broken hull settled into the black waters of the Roads.

At half past five Sunday morning, after a few hours of fitful sleep, the crew of the *Monitor* was awakened by the usual, "All hands rise and roll out . . . up all hammocks," followed by the order to clear sea rig and make battle ready.

When dawn broke and the haze lifted, signaling another fair day, the lookouts reported the *Merrimack* and her two consorts, *Jamestown* and *Patrick Henry*, off Sewell's Point. Judging the confrontation to be a couple of hours off, and aware that the crew had not had a de-cent meal since Friday morning, Worden ordered all hands on deck for a hot breakfast. As he issued the order it occurred to him that he was instinctively fulfilling at least part of the officers' credo: "You must care for your men's welfare; you must show physical courage." The first part was reflexive; had always come quite naturally to him. He wondered about the second part.

When the men were assembled on the open iron deck, ranged in a semicircle between turret and short, rectangular pilothouse, Worden addressed them. "We have shipped together long enough for you to know that I am not given to lengthy speeches. And I believe you also know that I mean what I say."

Speaking in a quiet, almost conversational tone, he continued: "From what we saw here last night, it is clear that today will be a time for serious work. *Merrimack* means nothing less than the complete destruction of the fleet. We are the only vessel equipped to thwart her.

"For the sake of all aboard I want no one on this vessel who is not absolutely certain that he wishes to be here. You are, with only a few exceptions, volunteers. If there are any among you who wish to change your mind about serving, I shall arrange for your transport to shore, and I shall do so without prejudice. Now, those of you who wish to be put ashore, please signify."

There was a moment of breathless silence. The only sounds to be heard were those of the water quietly slapping the gently rocking hull of the ship. Above them ranged the huge, scarred black hull of the *Minnesota*. For a few seconds no one stirred. Then the entire crew leaped to their feet as one and gave three mighty cheers that echoed off the water and carried to the troops ashore. They turned to their breakfast of fruit, porridge, flapjacks, bacon, and steaming mugs of coffee or tea.

Breakfast was quiet if not somber. The men ate in silence, mindful of those who had gone down in the *Congress* and the *Cumberland,* whose colors were still visible a few feet above the glinting surface of the sea. Their captain had served aboard her during a Mediterranean tour in happier days.

At half past seven, thick black smoke pouring from her funnel, the *Merrimack* and her consorts began steaming on a northeast course toward the Rip Raps at the mouth of the Roads. Short of the Rip Raps she turned to port, evidently planning to approach the *Minnesota* through the north channel; Jones judged that by taking this indirect route that he could bring his ship closer to the hapless *Minnesota,* still aground. Van Brunt had apparently undergone a change of heart during the night. Despite his avowal to destroy the *Minnesota* if he was unable to float her, dawn revealed her exactly as Jones had left her the previous evening.

At about eight o'clock, when the rebel squadron was two miles from the *Minnesota,* some of the crew aboard the *Patrick Henry* made out a strange little craft lying in the shadow of the *Minnesota*'s stern. Some thought it was a tank bringing water to the Union frigate. Others believed it was a floating magazine for replenishing ammunition. It looked to them like a large cheesebox on a raft. They dubbed it "The Yankee Cheesebox." But when Catesby Jones surveyed her through his glass, he knew instantly that it was Ericsson's battery and so informed his executive officer.

"What are you going to do?"

"Fight her, of course," said Jones, who rarely walked away from a fight. "She has many advantages over us, if she sees them. Our knuckle [where the armored superstructure met the wooden hull] is our great weakness. If she concentrates her fire on that, she will make short work of us. She has nothing to do but fire at the waterline."

Aboard the *Monitor* all hands were at battle stations with the exception of Paymaster Keeler and Surgeon Logue, who had no assigned stations. Everyone was as still as a statue. The rule of silence was in force so that no order would be lost or misunderstood. Except for two spotters in the turret, and captain, quartermaster, and pilot, whose heads and shoulders filled the pilothouse, no one could see out. The atmosphere was dim and claustrophobic as they awaited the *Merrimack.* All were aware that if the *Monitor* came to grief, there was no escape. Once the hatches were closed over them, their fate was sealed with the vessel.

In Washington, Secretary Welles was hurrying from Navy to the executive mansion, picking his way around the puddles and the late winter mud in the President's Park. He had been summoned to an urgent meeting of the cabinet.

Instead of going to church that morning with Mary Jane and the children, he had gone to the department to read the latest dispatches. Waiting for him was the news of Saturday's debacle, of which he had had no prior knowledge. Waiting too was Worden's wire advising that he had arrived in the Roads and was going to the assistance of the *Minnesota.* Doubtless the president had read the same telegrams—and Stanton too, that repulsive little man.

More bad news for Mr. Lincoln, and this time it was the Navy that was clearly responsible. How could the *Merrimack* have prevailed against the whole blasted North Atlantic Blockading Squadron? Had they all been napping? Or was the rebel ironclad that formidable? And

Goldsborough—the commodore. A fine time he picked to be in the Carolinas. Thank God, the *Monitor* is there. It could have been a lot worse. Suppose Worden had followed the orders issued over his name. The *Monitor* would be on its way to Washington now. He'd issued that order against his will. No choice. It was a cabinet decision, made hastily under pressure of the moment. All because of that damnable little Stanton. The secretary of war was behaving as though his cabinet precedence gave him the right to treat the Navy as his private fleet. Acting as McClellan's mouthpiece, Stanton had succeeded in persuading president and cabinet that the *Monitor* was best used to defend Washington and to cover McClellan's flanks on the long-awaited advance—an advance Welles would have to see to believe.

A somber discussion was in progress when Welles arrived at the executive office. There was a momentary pause as the assembled looked to him, in their eyes the guarded hope that perhaps he had some later, better news, knew something they didn't. But he merely nodded briefly to the president and slipped silently into his seat at the long table. As they turned to resume, he thought he detected a look of confirmed contempt in Stanton's expression as though he was saying, No use looking to the secretary of the Navy for help. How he loathed that man.

Stanton had the floor: " . . . She will change the whole character of the war, destroy seriatim every Union vessel in the service." His asthmatic wheeze was more pronounced when he was agitated. "She will lay all the cities on the seaboard under contribution—destroy New York and Boston." Welles's eyes flitted around the table. Seward, usually ebullient, looked worn and discouraged. A frown of disbelief clouded Chase's patrician features. McClellan and Quartermaster General Meigs, a confidant of the president, sat, jaws set, their expressions somehow suggesting that they knew it was just a question of time before a naval catastrophe occurred. There were no naval officers present. Welles wished Fox were there, but he had left for the Roads.

"What do you suppose," asked Chase of no one in particular, "her next move will be?"

"I have no doubt," declared Stanton, "the monster is at this minute on her way to Washington." Jumping to his feet he strode to the tall window and gestured toward the Potomac, "Not unlikely we shall have a shell or a cannonball from one of her guns in the White House before we leave the room."

"It's certain," said Welles drily, "that the *Merrimack,* despite her evident prowess, cannot be in Washington and New York and Boston at the same time."

"What have you to stop her?"

"Two things. There is the *Monitor*—Ericsson's battery—and there is the *Merrimack* herself. I am told she draws twenty-three feet of water. That means she cannot clear the Kettle Bottom Shoals, about fifty miles downriver from Washington."

Seward brightened. "That's the first hopeful thing I've heard all morning."

"Are you certain of your facts, Mr. Welles?" asked the president.

"To the best of my knowledge, sir, the shoals will not pass the *Merrimack,* assuming our information that she draws twenty-three feet is correct."

"About this *Monitor,*" demanded Stanton. "Beyond the fact that she's an ironclad, I know nothing of her. What can you tell us?"

Somewhat taken aback by this unaccustomed confession of ignorance, Welles replied slowly, carefully choosing his words. "She is something of an experiment. She arrived in Hampton Roads last night. I am fairly confident that if she does not overcome the *Merrimack,* she will at least give a good account of herself. It was our original intention, if she had been completed on time, to send her to Norfolk to destroy the *Merrimack* before she came out of dry dock. But the contractors disappointed us."

"How many guns has she?"

Welles paused. He didn't appreciate Stanton's prosecutorial manner. He glanced at the president, hoping that perhaps he would be moved to recall that he had been favorably impressed by a model of the battery. But the president, clearly bemused, said nothing.

"Two."

"Two!" exploded Stanton.

"His mingled look of incredulity and contempt," wrote Welles in his diary that evening, "cannot be described." It was only then, as he wrote, that he realized the little son of a bitch had known all along that she mounted only two guns.

"Two!" stormed Stanton. Striding furiously back and forth before the window (ugly little brute . . . small wonder he's rumored to suffer blood to the brain and blinding headaches), the diminutive secretary declared in tones ringed with sarcasm, "We are asked to rely for the defense of the capital and the government on an 'experiment' that has two guns to the *Merrimack*'s ten." His alarm was compounding the anxiety of the others. Seward shook his head in despair. Chase frowned in anger and frustration.

The president, expressing guarded confidence in the *Monitor,* tried to calm Stanton: "She may well be our David to their Goliath."

But Stanton was not to be reassured. Shouting now, he declared, "I shall notify the governors and municipal authorities to take instant measures to protect their harbors! I shall direct Dahlgren and Meigs to fill canal boats with stone and gravel and have them sunk at the river approaches to the capital."

Welles demurred, addressing the president: "Sir! For the past six months the Navy and War departments have labored to keep the channel open for, among other things, support of McClellan's anticipated advance. I am absolutely opposed to any move that would block the channel. It is unnecessary and it is destructive." The two adversaries glared at each other. Welles hated this kind of confrontation. It invariably made for more heat than light. Animosities were deepened and sharpened. It was the kind of situation on which Stanton seemed to thrive. But he couldn't let that officious bully undo months of work and give McClellan another excuse for not advancing.

The president stepped in. "The boats may be loaded," he said, "but they are not to be sunk until it is certain the *Merrimack* is approaching." Lincoln then declared his intention to consult Captain Dahlgren at the navy yard. He ordered his carriage and directed that the meeting be resumed at noon.

Shortly after the president left the room, Welles followed. He walked out the north side of the White House to Lafayette Park and St. John's Episcopal Church, where the Sunday service was in progress. In the vestibule he asked the sexton to call Commodore Smith.

Smith was generally aware of the havoc the *Merrimack* was causing in the Roads, but he knew none of the details. When Welles told him the *Congress* had surrendered, the old man nodded in the manner of one receiving news he had been anticipating. He said quietly, "Then my Joe is dead."

Welles tried to comfort him, pointing out that reports indicated there were survivors. Smith shook his head. "You don't know Joe as I do. He would never surrender his ship."

The *Minnesota* fired first. Her stern guns, towering over the *Monitor,* shattered the Sabbath peace of the springlike Sunday morning with a booming roar that signaled the start of hostilities. Her shot crashed into the casemate of the *Merrimack* and, like dozens of shots fired the previous day, glanced off her greased ironsides and fell hissing into the sea. Van Brunt signaled the *Monitor* to attack, expecting her to fire from the protection of the *Minnesota*. To his astonishment she moved out and stood directly for the rebel ironclad.

There was a puff of smoke from the *Merrimack*'s bow rifle. A shell screamed over the *Monitor* and slammed into the *Minnesota*, leaving a smoking gash in her side. On the deck of the *Monitor,* Worden turned to Dr. Logue and Paymaster Keeler, "Gentlemen, it is time to go below." The three men ascended the tower and went down the hatch. As they passed through the turret, the gunners were lifting 175-pound shot into the breeches of the guns. "Send them that with our compliments, my lads," said Worden.

In the pilothouse Worden discovered that the speaking tube to the turret was not working. He detailed Keeler and Clerk Toffey to relay messages from himself to Greene, who was in charge of the turret.

Keeler was no sooner at his station under the hatch leading to the turret when Greene's first order came, "Paymaster, ask the captain if I may fire." Keeler sprinted the fifty-five feet to the base of the ladder leading to the pilothouse. "Tell Mr. Greene not to fire till I give the word, to be cool and deliberate, to take sure aim and not to waste a shot."

While the *Minnesota* and the *Merrimack* were exchanging fire, Worden worked his ship to within a half mile of the rebel vessel and gave the command, "Commence firing!" Greene ordered a gunport shutter up, a gun was run out; he sighted, waited until the turret swung the gun into line, and pulled the lock string. The sixteen-thousand-pound bottle-shaped Dahlgren roared its first shot in anger. Though the blast was music to the ears of all aboard, the shot was wide of the mark. But Greene's second shot rattled the sides of the *Merrimack*.

Lieutenant Jones immediately asked for a damage report. "Nothing serious, sir. The bars are parted a bit." Jones decided to turn his attention to the Yankee ironclad. The *Merrimack*'s wooden consorts, *Patrick Henry* and *Jamestown,* withdrew, leaving the field to the two ironclads. If the *Merrimack* prevailed, the *Patrick Henry* would steam to England and France and announce the welcome news that the Yankee blockade had been broken and that full trade could be resumed.

Jones's first response to the *Monitor* was a round of grape and canister, which rattled on the iron deck like a flurry of hailstones. A *Monitor* gunner stuck his red head out the turret, "Well, them egg-sucking rebs are firing canister at us." He grinned broadly and ducked back in.

The *Merrimack*'s subsequent broadsides, however, were of exploding shell that found the *Monitor*'s turret, sides, and deck. Most of the crew, enclosed and blind to the action, could only stand breathless, away from the bulkheads, and pray that the iron sides of the *Monitor* would withstand the pounding. The vessel shuddered and rocked under the bombardment, but there was no other ill effect. The crew heaved a collective sigh of relief. Two major questions had been resolved: A heavy shot to the turret would not derange the geared rotating mechanism, and shells striking iron bolts in the turret would not make lethal flying missiles of them.

Worden was also concerned about the pilothouse. Standing four-square it would not deflect shot and shell as did the cylindrical turret. He anticipated trouble.

Like two boxers of grossly unequal size—the rebel ironclad was a good hundred feet longer than the *Monitor,* towered over her, and was more than three times her tonnage—the two ships, tentative at first, circled at long range. Then Worden, exploiting his craft's ability to turn in a sixth of the time it took the *Merrimack,* brought his ship in close at an angle blind to the *Merrimack*'s fixed guns. The nine-foot-high turret swung around, a port flew open, and the eleven-inch muzzle thrust out, firing in a cloud of flame and smoke. Before the 175-pound solid shot slammed into the Confederate vessel, the turret was turning away to leave a blank iron wall for the frustrated rebel gunners.

The gun crews of the *Merrimack* were practiced as a team. They had had weeks in which to perfect their routines. Jones had brought them to the peak of coordinated efficiency. Their ordnance presented no challenge, being conventional and identical to that in current use by both navies. But their major advantage, of incalculable value, lay in that one prodigious day of combat—a day that gave them that quality of confidence and esprit that can be acquired only by a unit that has been under fire. They were relatively well rested after a triumphant Saturday afternoon, and had retired that night anticipating an equally glorious Sunday.

The men of the *Monitor* were in a different situation. Their battery was novel and relatively complex in operation. Although there had been a few test firings, the crew had never worked as a unit under battle conditions. All hands had had virtually no sleep for the previous forty-eight hours, a period following a difficult, dangerous voyage that saw the vessel twice on the verge of foundering.

The sensation for the nineteen men in the *Monitor*'s turret when it was struck by enemy shell was like being in a cauldron belabored by two powerful men with sledgehammers. The impact of enemy fire combined with the blast of the Dahlgrens—the largest guns in use— left the fatigued gunners slightly stunned and disoriented.

Although the crew had been warned against coming into contact with the armor, Master Stodder, who was responsible for rotating the turret, and two of the gunners leaned against the wall in an unguarded moment. The impact of an enemy shot flipped them over the guns for almost twenty feet to the opposite wall. They were carried below unconscious. Alban Stimers replaced Stodder, slipping into the seat at the control wheel.

Lieutenant Greene, who had not slept for the previous fifty-one hours, made several crucial decisions early in the engagement. Because of the hazard presented by the pilothouse—it was in the direct line of fire when *Merrimack* was bow on—he decided to aim and fire every shot himself.

Perched between the breeches of the two guns, which stood side by side, it was awkward if not impossible for him to use the inch-high sighting slits that circled the wall of the turret. He chose instead to view through the gunports, which limited his visibility to the few inches between the muzzle of the gun and the sides and top of the port. And because the port shutters were so heavy and cumbersome as to require nine men to open and close one, Greene elected to keep the ports open throughout the battle. His major defensive concern then became that of preventing an enemy shell from entering the turret through an open port. As it was, sharpshooters aboard the *Merrimack,* quickly realizing that the shutters were not being closed, took to firing rifles and handguns at the open ports. From time to time leaden slugs hummed around the circular iron walls like huge, maddened bees. As a defensive measure against shell and small arms fire, Greene decided to keep the turret rotating continuously and was therefore obliged to fire on the fly. This expedient meant sacrificing accurate aiming, concentrated fire, and any real attempt to strike at the *Merrimack*'s vulnerable waterline and machinery.

Each time he fired, Greene had to send to the pilothouse to ask the effect. He was also continually compelled to inquire of Worden, "How does *Merrimack* bear?" The answer would come, "On the starboard beam," or "On the port quarter." But Greene and his men were constantly losing their bearings in the circular turret, the hastily drawn markings on the deck denoting port and starboard, and fore and aft, having been quickly erased by smoking powder and scuffling shoes.

If the beleaguered Greene had a moment during the battle to reflect, it was when he pulled the lock string and wondered if that shot was the one that would find his dear friend and former roommate at Annapolis, Walter Butt. Lieutenant Butt was aboard the *Merrimack* in command of a gun firing at the *Monitor*.

The gun crews of both ships worked for an hour without respite in precise, choreographed routines, powder-blackened figures leaping to commands screamed above the din: "Sponge! . . . Load! . . . Fire! . . . Don't lean against the shield!"

Although the range was close, sometimes a brutal few yards, there was no appreciable damage to either vessel. Every crewman aboard the *Monitor* who saw her shot find the mark, only to be shaken off, damned the Bureau of Ordnance to the hottest regions of hell for imposing a fifteen-pound limit on the powder charge.

Aboard the *Merrimack,* Catesby Jones came down from the pilot-house to the gun deck and, observing Lieutenant Engleston's division standing at ease, said, "Why are you not firing, sir?"

"Because our powder is precious, sir, and I find I can do the *Monitor* as much damage by snapping my fingers at her every five minutes."

At about half past nine, the supply of shot in the *Monitor*'s turret having been exhausted, Worden hauled off for about fifteen minutes to replenish. The hoisting of shot was a tedious business, requiring that the turret be motionless so that the two scuttles, one in the deck, the other in the floor of the turret, be lined up.

Worden took advantage of the lull to climb out through a port and walk to the edge of the deck. A shell had struck the vessel's plank-sheer, where the iron deck met the wooden hull at right angles, her most vulnerable point. Lying on his chest amid a hail of rebel small arms fire, he examined the area and found the hull undamaged except for a few splinters. Crawling back through the port, miraculously untouched by a bullet, he announced to the crew that the *Merrimack* could not sink them if she pounded for a month. The men cheered. Worden was pleased. He had fulfilled the second part of the officers' credo.

Catesby Jones had long since arrived at Worden's conclusion—nothing the *Merrimack* could throw at the *Monitor* would be able to sink her. He ordered his pilot to make for the *Minnesota* once again. When they were within two miles of the Yankee frigate, the *Merrimack* ran aground. The *Monitor,* with half her draft, freely circled and poured shot after shot into the immobilized *Merrimack,* rattling her iron plates and denting her timbers.

Two days of coal consumption plus expended ammunition had lightened the rebel ironclad so that her unarmored sides, normally under water, were now above the surface. She was dangerously exposed and vulnerable. If the *Monitor* were to lower her gunsights she would crush the wooden hull like an eggshell.

From the gun deck Major Ramsay charged down the ladder to the engine room to work with his men in an effort to build more steam for the power to push off the shoal. Sixteen furnaces belched fire and smoke as firemen, stripped to the waist, curiously clean and free of coal dust because of the streaming perspiration, their torsos reflecting the orange wells of flame, worked like madmen at the shovels, slice bars, and grappling hooks.

Ramsay ordered the safety valves lashed. Quick-burning combustibles were heaved into the raging fires—anything that could be torn or hammered loose—wooden furniture, rope, oiled cotton waste—anything that would burn faster than coal. It seemed impossible for the boilers to stand another ounce of pressure. No one checked the gauges. All were aware of the consequences if the boilers burst.

The propeller, screaming with the effort, churned mountains of mud and water. After fifteen heart-clutching minutes, the groaning thirty-two-hundred-ton ironclad, shuddering and swaying, lurched off the shoal.

"Now or never," vowed Jones. He ordered the pilot to stand for the *Monitor* in a ramming attitude. He also raised the black flag, signaling no quarter given or asked. The *Merrimack* maneuvered for position. "Hard aport! . . . Stop! . . . Astern! . . . Stop! . . . Ahead!" But she was taking water in her engine room and was even less responsive than she had been before she went aground. Her abbreviated stack, truncated by a shell from the *Cumberland,* was not delivering sufficient draft to her boiler fires.

"This blasted tub," swore Jones, "is as clumsy as Noah's blasted ark!" A ramming opportunity offered. "Ahead full!" But before the

Merrimack could gather headway, the *Monitor* turned and took a harmless, glancing blow from the beakless prow. The Union ironclad circled and came up on the *Merrimack*'s quarter, her bow touching. The twin Dahlgrens bucked and roared simultaneously. The shots struck halfway up the *Merrimack*'s shield, abreast of the after pivot gun. The impact forced the side in about three inches. The crews of the after guns were knocked down and they bled from the nose and ears.

"Boarders, stand by!" roared Jones. He was determined to strangle the turret, lash *Monitor* to *Merrimack,* and lead her to Norfolk like a prize bull. Twenty men were dispatched to man the hawsers and chain cables. The boarding crew armed themselves with sledgehammers, wedges, crowbars, and bits of heavy chain and spikes, with which to derange and immobilize the turret. Others took flasks of turpentine, balls of oakum, matches, and torches. If they could get combustibles through the recessed grating that covered the top of the turret, they could suffocate the gun crew.

Worden, sensing Jones's intention, called down, "Mr. Keeler, pass the word for the grenade detail to stand by." If the rebels succeeded in boarding, they would receive a warm welcome. Keeler noted with satisfaction that Worden issued orders clearly, in even tones, and without haste.

Gunwales now inches apart, a bosun's pipe shrilled and Jones bellowed, "Boarders away!" But at the last moment the *Monitor* sheered off for shoal water, where she was quite safe. "Give me that vessel," said Jones to a subordinate, "and I would sink this one in twenty minutes."

Aboard the *Monitor,* Worden ordered Keeler to break open the spirit room and, in lieu of lunch, deal out half a gill of whiskey to all hands.

For the third time that morning, Jones turned to attack the *Minnesota.* The *Monitor* cut him off as Worden circled full speed for the *Merrimack*'s stern, planning to ram her unprotected propeller. He missed by a few feet. Lieutenant Wood of the *Merrimack* trained his stern pivot rifle on the Yankee vessel, which was not ten yards from the muzzle. The pointed shell struck the flat forward surface of the pilothouse directly on the sighting slit. For a split second the pilothouse, jammed with the heads and shoulders of captain, quartermaster, and pilot, was fixed in a lightning glare. Then a clap of thunder rocked the ship and the three men were momentarily obscured in a cloud of smoke.

Worden, who was standing to the right, directly behind the vertical slit, staggered and put both hands to his eyes. Keeler rushed up the ladder. "Are you hurt, sir?"

"My eyes, I am blind!" Keeler shouted for Dr. Logue. Quartermaster Peter Williams at the helm sheered off to starboard. "Tell Mr. Greene that I am seriously wounded and to take command at once!"

With the surgeon's assistance, Keeler got Worden out of the pilothouse and onto a sofa in his cabin. He then called Greene from the turret. Blood was streaming from Worden's powder-blackened face and eyes as his officers collected around him. "Gentlemen," he said, "I leave it to you. Do what you think best . . . save the *Minnesota* if you can."

Logue did what he could to repair Worden's wound, removing bits of unburned powder and iron splinters that had been driven into both eyes and surrounding tissue. At the same time he applied cold compresses to ease the pain. His patient drifted in and out of consciousness.

Greene's first act was to examine the damage to the pilothouse. He found that the twelve-inch-thick iron log adjacent to the sight hole had been fractured and bent in for about an inch and a half. The iron hatch overhead had been partially blown off but it was easily repositioned.

The *Monitor* was at that point caught in a crossfire between the *Minnesota* and the *Merrimack,* having been struck several times by the Union ship. To Jones it appeared that the *Monitor* was withdrawing from the fight, since, in the absence of orders, Quartermaster Williams was simply taking evasive action and making certain the vessel did not go aground. Jones gave the order to withdraw, explaining to Ramsay, "The pilots will not place us nearer the *Minnesota* because we cannot risk running aground again." The *Merrimack* headed for Sewell's Point.

Now Greene was faced with a command decision—whether or not to pursue the *Merrimack.* The *Monitor* was at that moment the most valuable vessel in the federal fleet. Greene declared to Stimers that if she took another shot to the pilothouse, he feared the steering would be disabled and thus leave them at the mercy of the batteries at Sewell's Point and of the *Merrimack,* which, he was aware, had raised the black flag.

Stimers examined the pilothouse and concluded that the damage was not sufficient cause to withdraw. The crew was hot to finish the fight. But Greene, who declared he was acting in accordance with Worden's last words, which were to defend the *Minnesota,* hauled off to stand by the Union frigate. When Greene's decision became apparent to the men, there were angry words against him. Some bitterly accused him of cowardice. But the *Monitor* steamed for the side of the *Minnesota.*

Fortunately for Worden, his good friend and former classmate Lt. Henry Wise had witnessed the battle from Fortress Monroe. As soon as the *Monitor* was alongside the *Minnesota,* Wise, joined by Fox, came aboard. Wise embraced his friend. "Jack! Jack! You have just fought the most glorious battle in naval history!"

"Have we saved the *Minnesota*?"

"Yes, and whipped the *Merrimack* to boot!"

"Then I can die happy." He sank back, unconscious.

Wise and Fox agreed that Worden should be put aboard a Washington-bound steamer immediately. Wise decided that Worden's best chance for recovery lay in being nursed at Wise's home. He wired his wife to expect them. She, in turn, alerted Olivia.

As they prepared to transfer Worden to a tug, the *Monitor* crew assembled on deck in spontaneous tribute. When he was handed over the side, they raised their hands in salute. William Durst, a coal heaver, wept openly, "There'll never be another like him."

The *Monitor* had been struck twenty-two times (including several hits by the *Minnesota*), taking two shots to the pilothouse, nine to the turret, three on her deck, and eight on her sides. The only one that did appreciable damage was the last to the pilothouse.

With her two guns the *Monitor* had fired a total of forty-one shots in a period of something under five hours, twenty of them striking the *Merrimack* but doing little more than cracking a few plates on her shield. The nearest hit to the waterline was more than four feet above it. The rebel ironclad was, however, in far from battle-worthy condition, largely as a consequence of her encounter with the *Cumberland.* Her ram had been twisted off; she was taking water in her engine room; her engines were barely operating because of deficient draft; two guns were disabled; and her boat davits, railings, and lightwork of every description had been shot away.

In New York, when a disappointed Ericsson learned the details of the battle, he was, as always, outspoken and unequivocal. "The *Monitor,*" he told Fox, "ought to have sunk her in fifteen minutes. The *Merrimack* is not rusting on the bottom of Hampton Roads only because you had a miserable executive officer who, in place of jumping into the pilothouse when Worden was blinded, ran away with his impregnable vessel." He also had a few words for "Dahlgren and Company" on the score of the limited powder charges. "Timidity," he declared, "is not a becoming characteristic for a naval bureau of ordnance."

But Ericsson did not minimize the *Monitor*'s achievement. Some years later he wrote his brother Nils:

> Ask those acquainted with the matter why England and France did not take part with the Southern states on April 1, 1862, as was intended, and they will answer you: Because the *Monitor* saved the American Navy from destruction the 9th of March. It was the cannon in the rotary turret at Hampton Roads that tore the fetters from millions of slaves, and afterward made the French abandon Napoleon's project in Mexico.

A few weeks after the battle at Hampton Roads, a letter made its way to Franklin Street from London, England.

> I duly received the illustrated paper announcing the most surprising intelligence of the result of your genius, which I think has startled all Europe. You are now on an eminence from which you can survey with scorn those in Europe who never gave you a fair field for your talents.
>
> My gratification at your triumph makes my nights sleepless with excitement, and though in reality I am not tangibly identified with it, I am in heart and soul made happy.
>
> My prayer for your success has been granted by Providence for this proud climax of your reputation, and I feel sure soon in the midst of the tumultuous roar of praise and idolatry, a stray thought of yours will waft its way to my home.
>
> Amelia

CHAPTER
XXIV

On Monday afternoon, the day after the battle, eleven-year-old Charlotte Wise was looking out the window of her white frame house on tree-lined H Street, anxiously awaiting her papa, when a carriage drew up. She watched her father and two other men help a naval officer, his head wrapped in blood-stained bandages, out of the carriage and up the steps. Charlotte rushed to the vestibule to greet them and recognized the wounded man as her father's friend Jack Worden. Quickly they got him upstairs and laid him on the first available bed, which happened to be in the nursery.

At that moment, a few blocks east in the executive mansion, Mr. Lincoln was presiding over a jubilant cabinet meeting, where the subject of discussion was the previous day's events at Hampton Roads. Despite the terrible loss in lives and ships, the cabinet saw the day as an unqualified victory for Union arms. The rebel threat in the brutal form of the *Merrimack* had been turned. The blockade was intact. The chances of European intervention had suddenly, miraculously, become remote. It was just a question of time before the South, squeezed dry by total blockade, would be forced to surrender her ill-conceived and sense-less notion of secession.

The cabinet, unaccustomed to celebrating military victory, was making the most of it. Each member congratulated Welles. Seward said that if indeed the secretary of the Navy in his zeal for building the *Monitor* had been inspired by Noah's ark, then we were all obliged to return to the Old Testament.

Stanton, who chose to be last, was gracious and generous. He admitted that he had not been "sanguine" at the prospect of two guns opposing ten. The secretary of the Navy was to be congratulated for seeing merit in the battery and for literally sticking to his guns.

Welles was modest. The true heroes were the men of the *Congress* and the *Cumberland* and the others who had given their lives. Ericsson and Worden and the crew of the *Monitor* came in for high praise. And the president himself, who early on saw the battery's possibilities, was to be congratulated.

Lincoln then began reading to the cabinet the text of a telegram he was about to send to Cornelius Bushnell ("We will pay for your vessel. Build six more like her."), when John Hay came in to whisper a few words in the president's ear. Lincoln stood and announced the meeting adjourned. He was going to pay a call on the commander of the *Monitor*.

Mrs. Wise, awaiting her husband and the president at the top of the stairs, anxiously cautioned her tall visitor not to bump his head against the low ceiling. Thanking her he said, "Yes, Mrs. Wise, it's just like our own little house in Springfield."

Wise dashed ahead to the nursery. "Jack, the president is here! He's come to see you!" Worden, his eyes completely covered, made a gallant effort to get to his feet. But the president was at his bedside, grasping both his hands.

"Don't move, please don't move. I have come to thank you for saving the country. I shall send your name in for promotion at once and for the thanks of the Congress."

"You do me great honor, sir."

"The honor is mine."

Six weeks after Mr. Lincoln's visit, a letter dated April 24, 1862, Hampton Roads, came for Worden, who was now in his own home in Pawling. Olivia read it to him.

To our Dear and Honered Captain

Dear Sir These few lines is from your own Crew of the Monitor with the kindest Love to you there Honered Captain Hoping to God that they will have the pleasure of Welcoming you Back to us again soon for we are all ready able and willing to meet death or anything else only give us back our own Captain again dear Captain we have got your Pilot

House fixed and all ready for you when you get well again and we all sincerely hope that soon we will have the pleasure of welcoming you Back to it again (for since you left us we have had no pleasure on Board the Monitor we once was happy on Board of our little Monitor But since we lost you we have lost our all that was dear to us Still) we are Waiting Patiently to engage our Antagonist if we could only get a chance to do so the last time she came out we all thought we would have the Pleasure of Sinking her But we all got disappointed for we did not fire one Shot and the Norfolk papers says we are coward in the Monitor and all we want is a chance to Shew them where it lies with you for our Captain we can teach them who is cowards But there is a great deal that we would like to write you But we think you will soon be with us again yourself But we all join in with our Kindest Love to you hoping that God will Restore you to us again and hoping that your Sufferings is at an end now and we are all so glad to hear that your eye sight will be Spared to you again, we would wish to write more to you if we have your Permission to do so But at Present we all conclude By tendering to you our Kindest Love and affection to our dear and Honered Captain.

We remain untill death your Affectionate Crew
The Monitor Boys

EPILOGUE

On May 10, 1862, to avoid capture by Union forces, the *Merrimack*'s command destroyed her by ramming her full speed into Craney Island at the mouth of the Elizabeth River. They then put her to the torch.

Near midnight on December 29, 1862, the *Monitor* foundered in a gale off Cape Hatteras. Four officers and twelve men were drowned; among the forty-nine survivors, Lt. Samuel Dana Greene, executive officer.

Despite the permanent loss of sight in his left eye, and blackened tissue over half his face, John L. Worden went on to win further distinction in the service of the U.S. Navy. Before retiring as an admiral in 1886, he served as superintendent at the Naval Academy, and as commander of the European Squadron.

Samuel Dana Greene committed suicide on December 11, 1884.

John Ericsson went on to win perfect vindication of his name as an honored inventor and designer. He died in New York on March 8, 1889, exactly twenty-seven years after the battle in Hampton Roads. He was never rejoined by his wife, Amelia, who predeceased him in 1867.

Ericsson's body was returned with honors to his native land at the request of the Swedish government.

Abraham Lincoln won reelection in November 1864 by a landslide vote over his opponent, Gen. George B. McClellan.

In his box at Ford's Theater on the evening of April 14, 1865, the president was shot in the head by an assassin. He died the following morning.

BIBLIOGRAPHIC NOTE

One of the more pleasurable aspects of writing *Ironclad* lay in the research. The sources, for the most part, were rich and plentiful. Often I had the luxury of reading an official or government version of an event, a newspaper account, a personal view as expressed in a diary or correspondence, and, finally, one or more historical treatments.

While this comparative reading served to reinforce the definition of history as myth agreed upon, I was most impressed by the fact that each correspondent—historian included—necessarily takes a parochial or specialized approach. Who, after all, especially in a contemporary account, can see any event in all its ramifications?

Here then, it seems to me, lies the justification for fictive treatment of history. An imaginative and responsible author can fill in the interstices in such a way as to enhance the historical reality.

Some of my most frequently consulted sources:

Books:

Baxter, James Phinney. *The Introduction of the Ironclad Warship*. Cambridge: Harvard University Press, 1933.
Church, William C. *The Life of John Ericsson*. New York: C. Scribner's Sons, 1890.

Lee, Richard M. *Mr. Lincoln's City: An Illustrated Guide to the Civil War Sites of Washington*. McLean, Virginia: EPM Publications, Inc., 1981.

Nicolay, John G. and John Hay. *Abraham Lincoln, A History*. New York: Century, 1904. Ten volumes.

Oates, Stephen B. *With Malice Toward None*. New York: Harper & Row Publishers, Inc., 1977.

Sandburg, Carl. *Abraham Lincoln, The War Years*. New York: Harcourt, Brace & World, Inc., 1939. Four volumes.

Seward, Frederick William. *William Henry Seward*. New York: D. Appleton and Company, 1877.

Trexler, Harrison A. *The Confederate Ironclad "Virginia" (Merrimac)* Chicago: The University of Chicago Press, 1938.

Welles, Gideon. *Diary of Gideon Welles*. Boston and New York: Houghton Mifflin Company, 1911.

West, Richard S. Jr. *Gideon Welles, Lincoln's Navy Department*. Indianapolis and New York: The Bobbs-Merrill Company, 1943.

Other Sources:

Alabama Review, Alabama Historical Association. Vol. 21, April 1968.

Civil War Times Illustrated. Gettysburg, Pa.: Historical Times, Inc.

Lincoln Museum. Ford's Theatre, Washington, D.C. (Restored by National Park Service.)

Monitor Collection. Rare Book Room, New York Public Library.

Naval Letters Series. Annapolis, Md.: U.S. Naval Institute, 1964.

The New York Times. New York, NY.

U.S. Navy Department. Official records of the Union and Confederate navies.

U.S. War Department. The War of the Rebellion: a compilation of the official records of the Union and Confederate armies. 1880-1901, 70 volumes.